RELIGIOUS TOURISM

By
Charlie Sampson

DISCOVERY PUBLISHING HOUSE PVT. LTD.
NEW DELHI-110 002

Published by:
Namit Wasan

DISCOVERY PUBLISHING HOUSE PVT. LTD.
4383/4B, Ansari Road, Darya Ganj
New Delhi-110 002 (India)
Phone : +91-11-23279245; 23253475; 43596065
E-mail : discoverybooksindia@gmail.com
discoverypublishinghouse@gmail.com
namitwasan9@gmail.com
web : www.discoverypublishinggroup.com

Reprinted: **2020**

First Edition: **2011**

ISBN: 978-81-8356-945-3

Religious Tourism

Printed at:
Infinity Imaging Systems
Delhi

PREFACE

Religion is historically associated with tourism. Some of our most popular tourist destinations are founded on ancient places of worship: the Temple of Hathor - the Pharaonic Mother Goddess at Dendera in Upper Egypt; Dodona, location of the oracle devoted to Zeus, in pre-historic Greece, Bodhgaya and other sacred places in India associated with the life and teachings of the Buddha. Jerusalem, Amritsar, Mount Fuji: pilgrims travelling to these holy places were effectively the world's first tourists. Religious tourism has a big future in India. India is richly endowed with ancient temples and religious festivals. Religions originating in India, be it Hinduism, Sikhism, Jainism or Buddhism, have a vibrant culture and spiritual philosophy. Together, they present a viable, alternative way of life as compared to the materialism and confrontation prevalent in the West.

A tourist attraction is a place of interest where tourists visit, typically for its inherent or exhibited cultural value, historical significance, natural or built beauty, or amusement opportunities. Some examples include historical places, monuments, zoos, aquaria, museums and art galleries, botanical gardens, buildings and structures (e.g., castles, libraries, former prisons, skyscrapers, bridges), national parks and forests, theme parks and carnivals, living history museums, ethnic enclave communities, historic trains and cultural events. Many tourist attractions are also landmarks.

There are many beautiful Gurdwaras around the world. The Harmandir Sahib in Amritsar, India - also known as the Golden Temple - is the most visited Gurdwara in the world. There are no idols, statues, or religious pictures in a gurdwara, but the essential feature of a gurdwara is the presiding presence of the holy book, the Guru Granth Sahib. The Sikhs hold high respect for the commandments laid down in the Guru Granth Sahib.

A gurdwara has a darbar (main) hall, a free community kitchen langar, and other facilities. A gurdwara is identified from a far away place by nishan sahib. Many of the gurdwaras in Punjab have a pool (sarovar) for bathing in. The Sikh marriage, called Anand Karaj is performed inside gurdwara. The first gurdwara was built in Kartarpur, Pakistan Kartarpur in the year 1521 by the first Sikh guru, Guru Nanak Dev.

Our country boasts of innumerable religious places in all corners. Religious tourism (also called faith travel) is the fastest growth sector in the holiday industry. Many of today's most popular tourist destinations are related to ancient places of worship or to the site of apparent miracles. Places as unique and diverse as Bodhgaya, Lourdes and the Victoria Falls. According to the World Tourism Organization, an estimated 300 to 330 million pilgrims visit the world's key religious sites every year. Americans traveling overseas for "religious or pilgrimage" purposes has increased from 491,000 travelers in 2002 to 633,000 travelers in 2005 (30% increase). This book features sacred destinations and places of pilgrimage. Simple and flawless language is the hallmark of this book.

—Author

CONTENTS

1 Religious Tourism : Introduction

Religious tourism, also commonly referred to as faith tourism, is a form of tourism, whereby people of faith travel individually or in groups for pilgrimage, missionary, or leisure (fellowship) purposes. The world's largest form of mass religious tourism takes place at the annual Hajj pilgrimage in Mecca, Saudi Arabia. North American religious tourists comprise an estimated $10 billion of this industry. Faith Travel or religious tourism is the fastest growth area in the holiday industry. Many of today's most popular tourist destinations are related to ancient places of worship or to the site of apparent miracles. Places as unique and diverse as Bodhgaya, Lourdes and the Victoria Falls. This website features sacred destinations and places of pilgrimage associated with the mainstream faiths: Christianity, Islam, Hinduism, Buddhism, Judaism and Sikhism. Many photographs feature monuments on the World Heritage List. All are irreplaceable sources of life and inspiration in this turbulent period of history.

Religion is historically associated with tourism. Some of our most popular tourist destinations are founded on ancient places of worship: the Temple of Hathor - the Pharaonic Mother Goddess at Dendera in Upper Egypt; Dodona, location of the oracle devoted to Zeus, in pre-historic Greece, Bodhgaya and other sacred places in India associated with the life and teachings of the Buddha. Jerusalem, Amritsar, Mount Fuji: pilgrims travelling to these holy places were effectively the world's first tourists. In fact pilgrim hospices in Europe were the forerunners of modern hotels. And pilgrims are on the move as never before. The collapse of Communism in the former Soviet republics sees people now able to worship legally in churches and at historic shrines. Countries such as Italy, Spain and the Slavic states are experiencing an explosive interest in the old pilgrim routes subsequent to the..2000th anniversary of the birth of Christ. More than 10 million Christians are expected to visit Lourdes in 2008 for the 150th anniversary of the apparition of the Virgin Mary. Muslims performing the annual *hajj* pilgrimage to Mecca number three million while the *Kumbh Mela* held every 12 years in Allahabad northern India attracted 75 million Hindus on the last occasion in 2001. Joining the colourful melting-pot at Allahabad are tourists staying in luxuriously equipped tents to view but not to participate in the devotional when river water is elevated to.the status of "Divine"

Cultural tourism frequently overlaps places of worship considered to have special artistic merit. Tour groups visiting Chartres Cathedral in France or the Hassan II Mosque in Casablanca are notable examples. And somehow, despite the dangers posed by religious extremism, moderate believers are finding new confidence to practise their chosen faith resulting in an emergent interest in undertaking sacred journeys. Accompanying them are more and more of the 'uncommitted'; persons who for various reasons - the death of a loved one, the loss of a job or other emotional setback are seeking somewhere, usually ancient and well trod, offering solace, enlightenment or at least a temporary escape from the stresses of modern life. Delegates to ICORET the first ever international conference on religious tourism hosted by the Cyprus Tourism Organisation in 2006 emphasised that spiritual travel is set to become a *tour de force* across all age-groups in the 21st century. Cyprus with its rich Christian history and numerous Byzantine churches was an ideal starting point for religious discourse. A World Religious Tourism Association has since been formed to facilitate the exchange of dialogue between faith groups and travel agents while a charter airline launched by the Vatican is forecast to carry some 18 million religious tourists visiting sacred Christian sites.

The purpose of religious tourism is encouraging incoming tourism for holy places visits Jewish Christian, or Islamic. Alexandria has a numerous holy places

1. Jewish holy places : The Synague is located in the city center in Naby Danielle Street where some Jewish delegations come to visit.

2. Christian holy places

- Protestant churches "Swiss church"
- Orthodox churches "Roman Orthodox parish- Marcos church- Greek church "
- Catholic churches "Saint Catherine church – catholic cathedral Jesus priests church- Armenian catholic church- sacred heart church"
- Anglican churches : "St.Mark church – the Anglican church"

3. Islamic Holy Places :

Include several mosques and burial places

El Morsi Abou El Abbas mosque- El Bosery mosque – Sidi Yakout mosque – El Shatby mosque – Sidi Gaber mosque- Sidi Bishr mosque – El Qabari mosque

History of Tourism

The **Grand Tour** was the traditional travel of Europe undertaken by mainly upper-class European young men of means. The custom flourished from about 1660 until the advent of large-scale rail transit in the 1840s, and was associated with a standard itinerary. It served as an educational rite of passage. Though primarily associated with the British nobility and wealthy landed gentry, similar trips were made by wealthy young men of Protestant Northern European nations on the Continent, and from the second half of the 18th century some American and other overseas youth joined in. The tradition was extended to include more of the middle class after rail and steamship travel made the journey less of a burden, and Thomas Cook made the "Cook's Tour" a byword.

Recently *The New York Times* described the Grand Tour in this way: The primary value of the Grand Tour, it was believed, lay in the exposure both to the cultural legacy of classical antiquity and the Renaissance, and to the aristocratic and fashionably polite society of the European continent. In addition, it provided the only opportunity to view specific works of art, and possibly the only chance to hear certain music. A grand tour could last from several months to several years. It was commonly undertaken in the company of a Cicerone, a knowledgeable guide or tutor. The Grand Tour had more than superficial cultural importance; as E.P. Thompson opined, "ruling-class control in the 18th century was located primarily in a cultural hegemony, and only secondarily in an expression of economic or physical (military) power."

In essence the Grand Tour was neither a scholar's pilgrimage nor a religious one, though a pleasurable stay in Venice and a cautious residence in Rome were essential. Catholic Grand Tourists followed the same routes as Protestant Whigs. Since the 17th century a tour to such places was also considered essential for budding young artists to understand proper painting and sculpture techniques, though the trappings of the Grand Tour— valets and coachmen, perhaps a cook, certainly a "bear-leader" or scholarly guide— were beyond their reach. The advent of popular guides, such as the Richardsons', did much to popularize such trips, and following the artists themselves, the elite considered travel to such centres as necessary rites of passage. For gentlemen, some works of art were essential to demonstrate the breadth and polish they had received from their tour: in Rome antiquaries like Thomas Jenkins provided access to private collections of antiquities, among which enough proved to be for sale that the English market raised the price of such things, as well as for coins and medals, which formed more portable souvenirs and a respected gentleman's guide to ancient history. Pompeo Batoni made a career of painting English *milordi* posed with graceful ease among Roman antiquities. Many continued on to Naples, where they viewed Herculaneum and Pompeii, but few ventured far into southern Italy and fewer still to Greece, still under Turkish rule.

In Britain, Thomas Coryat's travel book *Coryat's Crudities* (1611), published during the Twelve Years' Truce, was an early influence on the Grand Tour but it was the far more extensive tour through Italy as far as Naples undertaken by the 'Collector' Earl of Arundel, together with his wife and children in 1613-14 that established the most significant precedent. This is partly because he asked Inigo Jones, not yet established as an architect but already known as a 'great traveller' and masque designer, to act as his cicerone (guide). Larger numbers of tourists began their tours after the Peace of Münster in 1648. According to the *Oxford English Dictionary*, the first recorded use of the term (perhaps its introduction to English) was by Richard Lassels (c. 1603–1668), an expatriate Roman Catholic priest, in his book *The Voyage of Italy*, which was published posthumously in Paris in 1670 and then in London. Lassels's introduction listed four areas in which travel furnished "an accomplished, consummate Traveller": the intellectual, the social, the ethical (by the opportunity of drawing moral instruction from all the traveller saw), and the political.

The idea of traveling for the sake of curiosity and learning was a developing idea in the 17th century. With John Locke's *Essay Concerning Human Understanding* (1690) it was argued, and widely accepted, that knowledge comes entirely from the external senses, that what one knows comes from the physical stimuli to which one has been exposed, thus, one could "use up" the environment, taking from it all it offers, requiring a change of place. Travel, therefore, was necessary for one to develop the mind and expand knowledge of the world. As a young man at the outset of his account of a repeat Grand Tour the historian Edward Gibbon remarked that "According to the law of custom, and perhaps of reason, foreign travel completes the education of an English gentleman." Consciously adapted for intellectual self-improvement, Gibbon was "revisiting the Continent on a larger and more liberal plan"; most Grand Tourists did not pause more than briefly in libraries. On the eve of the Romantic era he played a significant part in introducing, William Beckford wrote a vivid account of his Grand Tour that made Gibbon's unadventurous Italian tour look distinctly conventional.

The typical 18th century sentiment was that of the studious observer traveling through foreign lands reporting his findings on human nature for those unfortunate enough to have stayed home. Recounting one's observations to society at large to increase its welfare was considered an obligation; the Grand Tour flourished in this mindset.

The Grand Tour not only provided a liberal education but allowed those who could afford it the opportunity to buy things otherwise unavailable at home, and it thus increased participants' prestige and standing. Grand Tourists would return with crates of art, books, pictures, sculpture, and items of culture, which would be displayed in libraries, cabinets, gardens, and drawing rooms, as well as the galleries built purposely for their display; The Grand Tour became a symbol of wealth and freedom. Artists who especially thrived on Grand Tourists included Carlo Maratti, who was first patronized by John Evelyn as early as 1645, Pompeo Batoni the portraitist, and the vedutisti such as Canaletto, Pannini and Guardi. The less well-off could return with an album of Piranesi etchings.

The "perhaps" in Gibbon's opening remark cast an ironic shadow over his resounding statement. Critics of the Grand Tour derided its lack of adventure. "The tour of Europe is a paltry thing", said one 18th century critic, "a tame, uniform, unvaried prospect". The Grand Tour was said to reinforce the old preconceptions and prejudices about national characteristics, as Jean Gailhard's *Compleat Gentleman* (1678) observes:

"French courteous. Spanish lordly. Italian amorous. German clownish." The deep suspicion with which Tour was viewed at home in England, where it was feared that the very experiences that completed the British gentleman might well undo him, were epitomised in the sarcastic nativist view of the ostentatiously "well-travelled" maccaroni of the 1760s and 1770s.

After the arrival of steam-powered transportation, around 1825, the Grand Tour custom continued, but it was of a qualitative difference — cheaper to undertake, safer, easier, open to anyone. During much of the 19th century, most educated young men of privilege undertook the Grand Tour. Germany and Switzerland came to be included in a more broadly defined circuit. Later, it became fashionable for young women as well; a trip to Italy, with a spinster aunt as chaperon, was part of the upper-class woman's education, as in E.M. Forster's novel *A Room with a View*. At least into the late 1960s organized bus tours staffed by teachers took American high school graduates on eight week trips across Europe. These roughly followed the traditional route, but flying the longer segments expanded the area covered to include parts of Scandinavia.

The most common itinerary of the Grand Tour shifted across generations in the cities it embraced, but the British tourist usually began in Dover, England and crossed the English Channel to Ostend, in the Spanish Netherlands/Belgium, or Calais, or Le Havre in France. From there the tourist, usually accompanied by a tutor (known colloquially as a "bear-leader") and if wealthy enough a league of servants, could rent or acquire a coach (which could be resold in any city or disassembled and packed across the Alps, as in Giacomo Casanova's travels, who resold it on completion), or opt to make the trip by boat as far as the alps, either traveling up the Seine to Paris, or up the Rhine to Basel.

Upon hiring a French-speaking guide (French served as the language of the elite in Europe during the 17th and 18th centuries from the Netherlands to Italy) the tourist and his entourage would travel to Paris. There the traveler might undertake lessons in French, dancing, fencing, and riding. The appeal of Paris lay in the sophisticated language and manners of French high society, including courtly behavior and fashion. Ostensibly this served the purpose of preparing the young man for a leadership position at home, often in government or diplomacy.

From Paris he would typically go to urban Switzerland for a while, often to Geneva (the cradle of the Protestant Reformation) or Lausanne.

("Alpinism" or mountaineering developed in the 19th century.) Sometimes he would go to Spain, to visit Barcelona, and in rare occasions, the itinerary would include Madrid and Seville. From there the traveler would endure a difficult crossing over the Alps into northern Italy (such as at the St. Bernard Pass), which included dismantling the carriage and luggage. If wealthy enough, he might be carried over the hard terrain by servants.

Once in Italy the tourist would visit Turin (and, less often, Milan), then might spend a few months in Florence, where there was a considerable Anglo-Italian society accessible to traveling Englishmen "of quality" and where the *Tribuna* of the Uffizi gallery brought together in one space the monuments of High Renaissance paintings and Roman sculptures that would inspire picture galleries adorned with antiquities at home, with side trips to Pisa, then move on to Padua, Bologna, and Venice. The British idea of Venice as the "locus of decadent Italianate allure" made it an epitome and cultural setpiece of the Grand Tour.

From Venice the traveler went to Rome to study the ruins of ancient Rome. Some travelers also visited Naples to study music, and (after the mid-18th century) to appreciate the recently-discovered archaeological sites of Herculaneum and Pompeii, and perhaps for the adventurous thrilling ascent of Mount Vesuvius. Later in the period the more adventurous, especially if provided with a yacht, might attempt Sicily (the site of Greek ruins) or even Greece itself. But Naples - or later Paestum further south - was the usual terminus.

From here the traveler traversed the Alps heading north through to the German-speaking parts of Europe. The traveler might stop first in Innsbruck before visiting Vienna, Dresden, Berlin and Potsdam, with perhaps some study time at the universities in Munich or Heidelberg. From there travelers visited Holland and Flanders (with more gallery-going and art appreciation) before returning across the Channel to England.

Published (and often polished) accounts of personal experiences on the Grand Tour provide illuminating detail and a first-hand perspective of the experience. Of some accounts offered in their own lifetimes, Jeremy Black detects the element of literary artifice in these and cautions that they should be approached as travel literature rather than unvarnished accounts. He lists as examples Joseph Addison, John Andrews, William Thomas Beckford, whose *Dreams, Waking Thoughts, and Incidents* was a published account of his letters back home in 1780, embellished with stream-of-consciousness associations, William Coxe, Elizabeth Craven,

John Moore, tutor to successive dukes of Hamilton, Samuel Jackson Pratt, Tobias Smollett, Philip Thicknesse, and Arthur Young.

In 2009, the Grand Tour featured prominently in a PBS miniseries based on the novel *Little Dorrit* by Charles Dickens. Produced with masterful attention to detail, and in sumptuous settings, mainly Venice, it faithfully portrayed the Grand Tour as an essential ritual for entry to English high society.

Kevin McCloud presented *Kevin McCloud's Grand Tour* on Channel 4 during the late summer and early autumn of 2009. The four part series saw Kevin retrace the popular tour by British architects through the last four centuries.

In 2005, British art historian Brian Sewell followed in the footsteps of the Grand Tourist for a 10 part television series *Brian Sewell's Grand Tour*. Produced by UK's Channel Five, Sewell travelled across Italy by car stopping off in Rome, Florence, Vesuvius, Naples, Pompeii, Turin, Milan, Cremona, Siena, Bologna, Vicenza, Paestum, Urbino, Tivoli. His journey concluded in Venice at a masked ball.

In 1998, the BBC produced an art history series *Sister Wendy's Grand Tour* presented by Carmelite nun Sister Wendy. Ostensibly an art history series, the journey takes her from Madrid to St. Petersburg with stop offs to see the great masterpieces.

Advantages

Tourism is one of the very important factors which promote a country's economy. It is considered to be the most powerful tool to promote national integration and unify people from all over the country. All in the states of the USA promote all kinds of tourism, especially the state of Ohio. Ohio offers tourists various historical places and also scenic beauty, which is a pleasure for any tourist. Cincinnati is famous for its tourism and one of the comforts this city offers is its Apartments. It offers quality peaceful living to all its residents. Since 2002, the crime rate in Cincinnati has fallen to a great extent, therefore tourists prefer living in rental apartments as that increases their pleasures during their vacation and gives them the required comfort.

Education provides the true advantages of tourism. Knowledge of a place can best be acquired if that region is properly seen and understood. Students eagerly look forward for such opportunities when they are taken out of the four walls of classrooms to distant places. Englishmen consider their schooling complete only after a tour of the continent. Tourism is one of those experiences which a student cherishes all his life.

Geography can also become interesting if students are taken out of their books to see the scenes depicted in pictures with their own eyes. When students actually visit and witness the wonders of the world, they tend to learn more and remember for a longer time. History can be made very interesting as well if students are allowed to visit historical monuments, architectural structures, battle fields and all similar historical cities. Thanks to tourism, education actually becomes enjoyable.

We can learn a lot more when we actually come in contact and witness all the sights of the world. Sitting at home will give us a very narrow vision. Our outlook towards life becomes blurred. By staying in our own cities, we will fail to understand the positive and negative effect of environment on the life of human beings. Just reading about the place won't give you much information about it. You must know the habits, manners, cultures and way of living of people in other places. Traveling takes people to the sphere of practical knowledge. While traveling, you will learn to adjust to the changed conditions of living and the environment also. In addition, you will get experience of the world and discover that the differences between you and others are trivial and can be overcome.

The learning of a foreign language is a very important aspect of tourism. It is the first step towards understanding a nation. Things will become easily clear and understandable only if the language of the common people of a place is known.

Traveling is a must for those who are interested in knowing about the world they live in. This will provide them with the maturity of judgment. Plus, tourism is the quickest and the best, if not the cheapest, method of learning new things. The experiences that you have when you travel cannot be reproduced in a book.

Tourism Segments

Religious tourism comprises many facets of the travel industry including:

- Pilgrimages
- Missionary travel
- Leisure (fellowship) vacations
- Faith-based cruising
- Crusades, conventions and rallies

- Retreats
- Monastery visits and guest-stays
- Faith-based camps
- Religious tourist attractions

Effects of Tourism

To my mind, tourism is a positive source which helps people to forget about their daily routine and to relax themselves after so many weeks or months of working. We all wait anxiously for the holidays to come and have an escapade somewhere in the mountains or even to an exotic place. We fell excited when making our luggage and start traveling together with our friends or family to spend some unforgettable moments.

Apart from this means of relaxation and enjoyment, tourism is also important for each country from the economic point of view. There are countries with a high level of tourism, especially countries with passage to sea, where visitors spend big sums of money during their holidays. This is a very positive way for the country to have large sums of money all ocated in its budget. And if tourists feel comfortable in the places they have chosen, then they will return there the next year, too and they will also show photos to their friends and will try to convince them about the beauties they have found there.

Then, tourism is very efficient because it gives us the opportunity to see unknown and uninteresting places. One can come to discover new traditions, new customs and exotic foods and drinks. Moreover, it is a great chance to meet people all over the world, make friends and enjoy at the maximum during your vacation.

Anyway, apart from all these advantages we should take into consideration two important disadvantages: one the one hand, tourism destroys the environment, as man has cut down many forests in order to build hotels or different travelers' attractions. Still, there are many associations which protect nature and try to diminish this phenomenon of destruction. On the other hand, there are many people who cannot afford to travel because their incomes are too low and the only thing they can do after a year of working is to give their children some money to travel and have fun with friends.

Positive Impacts of Tourism

- Jobs for local people
- Income for the local economy
- Helps preserve rural services like buses, village shops and post offices
- Increased demand for local food and crafts
- Tourists mainly come to see the scenery and wildlife, so there is pressure to conserve habitats and wildlife

Negative Impacts of Tourism

- Damage to the landscape: litter, erosion, fires, disturbance to livestock, vandalism
- Traffic congestion and pollution
- Local goods can become expensive because tourists will pay more
- Shops stock products for tourists and not everyday goods needed by locals
- Demand for holiday homes makes housing too expensive for local people
- Demand for development of more shops and hotels
- Jobs are mainly seasonal, low paid with long hours

Making Tourism Sustainable

National Park Authorities work with local communities and other organisations to try and make tourism more sustainable. Here are just some of the things we do:

- Show visitors how they can be responsible tourists with events, leaflets, information centres, guided walks and events, signs and websites.
- Encourage visitors to leave their cars behind and use greener travel, like bikes, buses, boats and trains.
- Support outdoor activities that don't damage the countryside or harm wildlife.
- Encourage visitors to buy local products and food.
- Run green business schemes to encourage businesses to recycle, reduce energy, conserve water and be sustainable.

- Ask local communities for their views and ideas by setting up forums, groups and consultations.
- Reduce erosion caused by visitors, by creating and repairing footpaths.
- Use planning policies to control the spread of buildings in built-up areas development.
- Encourage green energy-efficent buildings with planning policies and grant funding.
- Encourage small-scale renewable energy schemes, like woodchip boilers and solar panels, with planning policies and grant funding.

Religious Tourism International

The WTO has reported that tourist arrivals in the Middle East and Asia-Pacific region have increased at a much faster rate over the last five decades than in the rest of the world. The average annual increase in the Asia-Pacific region was some 13%, whilst this figure was 10% for the Middle East. While there are several factors behind this, religious tourism has arguably played a significant a part. Buddhists and Hindus consider India to be the most spiritual country on earth, the fact that Saudi Arabia is home to two of the holiest sites in Islam, and Israel and the Palestinian Territories comprise the Holy Land, important to Christians, Jews and Muslims throughout the world.

There are a number of forces, alongside faith itself, driving the growth of religious and pilgrimage tourism, which include:

a drive from consumers for more authentic experience, such as immersing themselves in the spiritual and cultural traditions associated with specific religions and pilgrimage sites the emergence of a more diverse tourist product as national tourist boards and tourism providers seek to extend the traditional tourist season an increasing number of travel agents offering religious tourism, pilgrimages and church tours a global culture where people seek more unusual holidays or more diversification within a trip.

Designed for travel and tourism professionals, this report provides a unique overview of this growing market. Combining the latest tourism data from the most authoritative sources and Mintel's own unique, independent analysis, it offers a level of market-explanation that can help create focused marketing and shape effective tourism policy at the highest level.

Religious Tourism in India

The international tourism market is no longer about "one shoe fitting all." It is divided into specialized segments ranging from shopping to adventure sports and from animal safaris to nightlife. Each region of the world is seeking to exploit its strengths. India's competitive advantage lies in the area of religious tourism because its religious heritage and culture is unique.

Religious tourism has a big future in India. India is richly endowed with ancient temples and religious festivals. Religions originating in India, be it Hinduism, Sikhism, Jainism or Buddhism, have a vibrant culture and spiritual philosophy. Together, they present a viable, alternative way of life as compared to the materialism and confrontation prevalent in the West.

There is a revival of religious attitudes not only in India but the world over. The second and third generations of the Indian diaspora are actively seeking out their roots in religion.

The religions of Indian origin are also proving to be an attraction to many persons of non-Indian origin because these religions advocate a pacifist and inclusive approach to life. This is evident from the posts that can be read on the numerous blog sites devoted to religion. And there can be no better way to introduce these aspirants to Indian religions than to entice them to come to India and undertake and experience religious tourism themselves.

Temples and Festivals

Within its distinct segment, religious tourism in India offers a variety to attract different kinds of tourists. In time, it has the potential to become a commercially viable endeavour. To begin with, there are pilgrimages to several world-renowned temples and shrines, such as Tirupati, Vaishno Devi and Sabarimala. For those seeking more enduring pilgrimages, there are the Char Dhams (four holy sites) at the four corners of the country and the twelve Jyotirlingas scattered across the land.

But traveling to temples and seeking the blessings of the gods is only one aspect of religious tourism and an aspect that may not interest many. Foreigners to India are fascinated by the gaiety and pomp that marks religious festivals. These can also be made nodal points for promoting religious tourism in India. Some fairs like the Kumbh at Haridwar and Pushkar camel fair already draw significant tourists, but much more can be done.

Durga Puja in Kolkata is a spectacle beyond compare. Myriad statues of Kali with her blood soaked tongue and garland of skulls in every nook and corner of the city will enthuse those not accustomed to such crowds. The Rama Lila in the hinterland of Uttar Pradesh is another experience that cannot be had anywhere in the world. The one at Ramnagar goes back two centuries without a break and can be showcased as a historical and social event as well.

Creation of Infrastructure and a Holistic Approach

While, in principle, religious tourism in India has immense potential to evolve as a niche segment, there are hurdles to be overcome. The first hurdle is the poor tourism infrastructure in general, and perhaps the even poorer infrastructure of religious centres. Adequate facilities for lodging, boarding and travel will have to be created.

What needs to be done is to create nodes near religious centers, where there is already a basic infrastructure present and plan day trips from there. For example, Chennai in South India can be a node for excursions to Madurai, Thanjavur, Trichnapalli and Pondicherry. Madurai is the home of the exquisite Meenakshi Temple, which is regarded as the holiest temple in India by many people.

The second aspect that will need to be taken care of will be to provide the tourists with a holistic religious experience. Tourists may not find it worthwhile to come all the way just for a pilgrimage.

A packaged trip that offers the different hues of religious tourism will have to be prepared. This would require blending the ritualistic part of the religious tours with informative, cultural and philosophical inputs.

Information on the mythological significance of the places of pilgrimage will need to be provided in advance so that tourists are better prepared. Traditional dances, music and theatre related to the religious shrine will have to be built into the itinerary. Discourses on the essence of the religious beliefs, workshops on yoga and ayurvedic practices can add immense value to religious tourism.

Religious tourism in India can provide an experience that cannot be had anywhere in the world. But for it to fructify, the seeds will have to be sown and the saplings will have to be nurtured.

Religious Tourism and Globalization

The Union Tourism and Housing and Urban Poverty Alleviation Minister Kumari Selja has said that it is an accepted fact that Religious Tourism has proven resilience to the pressures of Global Recession. Speaking at the inaugural session of the International Buddhist heritage Conference-2010, at Nalanda she said, not being viewed as a luxury, but as travel with a purpose, its elasticity and strength has withered the storm in the current economic scenario. She said, this has given the hope and courage and her Ministry strives to help millions of followers to achieve their life long desire to visit India and walk in the footsteps of the Great Buddha.

She said, Buddhism is a world religion today. We are proud that it arose in and around ancient Magadha. Buddhism and the numerous sites related to the life and enlightenment of Lord Buddha are spread all over India forming a set of destinations by themselves. The UNESCO World Heritage site of Ajanta & Ellora, the Sanchi monuments, the Mahabodhi Temple, along with equally stunning sites like the Amaravati, Nagarjunakonda, Sarnath, Bhagalpur, Udaigiri & Ratnagiri are great attractions for the Tourist.

Kumari Selja said, the Union Ministry of Tourism, with active involvement of concerned State Governments and Industry stakeholders, has taken up a number of initiatives to promote Tourism in these Buddhist sites steeped in culture and heritage. One of the promotional initiatives has been the launch of a special tourist train, 'The Mahaparinirvana' by the Indian Railways. The train, with an eight–day package, starts from Delhi and covers the important Buddhist sites of Bodh Gaya, Nalanda, Rajgir, Varanasi, Kushinagar and Sravasti.

She said, her Ministry has till date identified 29 mega destinations and circuits including Bodh Gaya–Nalanda–Rajgir circuit. She said, the Ministry intends to channelise quality investment in all the Mega Destinations and Circuits. Kumari Selja said that the Ajanta Ellora Conservation and Tourism Development Project is in an advanced stage of implementation. This project covers various cities with Buddhist sites in Maharashtra. It was undertaken with assistance from Japan Bank of International Cooperation. In addition to this, projects related to development of Buddhist Circuits in Uttar Pradesh and Bihar, with active assistance from Japan Bank of International Cooperation, are also in formulation.

The Minister said, while the efforts to promote tourism are doubled, we must not lose sight of the impact of unorganised and uncontrolled growth of tourism on the environment and the ecology of the destinations. She said, the true potential of tourism lies in responsible practices, enabling an effective response to climate change. This is closely interlinked with inclusive growth through sustainable community participation. India, with its abundance of bio–diversity and natural locales, is an ideal destination for eco and rural tourism. She said, our endeavor has been to formulate such policy that encourages sustainable tourism while underlining creation of environmental, social, economic and climate responsiveness. Kumari Selja said, the Ministry has adopted the 'sustainable' tourism route in the innovative Rural Tourism Projects by strengthening the skilled rural communities in association with United Nations Development Programme. Another step in the direction of sustainable tourism would be adoption of 'Green Mission Initiative' as has been done in some States. She urged all the stakeholders in tourism sector to give a thought to emulating this novel idea in their respective domains.

The Minister said, the relationship between sustainable tourism and economic growth is very intimate and delicate and requires immediate attention. She said, safety and security of tourists is an area of primary concern. Any adverse perception about safety and security of tourists would seriously affect tourist arrivals in the country. She said, she is of the firm view that security and safety of tourists is of paramount importance for sustained growth of the sector. The tourist inflow could be ensured only in a safe and secure environment. Kumari Selja said, in the Ministry of Tourism, all out efforts are being made to address this issue. The Minister announced that the center will soon launch an all India help line for tourists. She said, tourists in distress will also be able to use it.

The Minister said, while many destinations across the world reduced their marketing spends during recession, India continued with its promotional and marketing activities aggressively. The 'Incredible India' brand campaign and innovative programs like "Visit India" campaign have contributed to revival of international tourism in the country. During December 2009, the foreign tourist arrivals in India saw a 21% increase over the same period in 2008. She said, the future looks bright and we expect buoyancy to return to the sector soon.

The Minister said, introduction of "Visa on Arrival" for tourists coming from potentially source market countries free from security concerns has come into force from 1st January 2010 and presently, the Scheme is applicable for tourists from five countries, viz., Singapore, Finland, New Zealand, Luxembourg and Japan on a pilot basis for a period of one year. She said, we expect that this move will send positive signals to source markets and give a tremendous boost to inbound tourism.

Kumari Selja said, tourism works in synergy. All components of the Sector have to work together harmoniously to deliver positive experiences to the travelers. She said, an integrated balanced growth of the Sector is essential to ensure India the pedestal that it deserves on the global tourism map.

The Deputy Chief Minister, Bihar Sushil Kumar Modi asked the Union Tourism Ministry to provide more funds for tourism projects in the state. He assured that such funds will be utilized properly. The two-day conference is being organized by ministry of tourism in collaboration with the state government of Bihar with an aim to promote Buddhist Circuits in India. The theme for the conference is "experience buddhism in the land of origin"

More than 110 eminent monks and erudite scholars, reputed academicians, tour operators as well as Media representatives (mainstream media and travel journalists) from the relevant markets overseas are participating in the Conference through the Indiatourism Offices Overseas. The delegates have come from 18 countries including China, Japan, Malayasia, Cambodia, Thailand, Vietnam, Indonesia, Korea, France, USA and UK. Bihar, Andhra Pradesh, Arunachal Pradesh, Sikkim, Assam, Jammu & Kashmir, Madhya Pradesh, Maharashtra, Orissa and Uttar Pradesh are also being represented at the conference.

Statistics

Although no definitive study has been completed on worldwide religious tourism, some segments of the industry have been measured:

- According to the World Tourism Organization, an estimated 300 to 330 million pilgrims visit the world's key religious sites every year.
- According to the U.S. Office of Travel and Tourism Industries, Americans traveling overseas for "religious or pilgrimage" purposes has increased from 491,000 travelers in 2002 to 633,000 travelers in 2005 (30% increase).
- According to the Religious Conference Management Association, in 2006 more than 14.7 million people attended religious meetings

(RCMA members), an increase of more than 10 million from 1994 with 4.4 million attendees.

- The United Methodist Church experienced an increase of 455% in mission volunteers from 1992 with almost 20,000 volunteers compared to 110,000 volunteers in 2006.
- The Christian Camp and Conference Association states that more than eight million people are involved in CCCA member camps and conferences, including more than 120,000 churches.
- Religious attractions including Sight & Sound Theatre attracts 800,000 visitors a year while the Holy Land Experience and Focus on the Family Welcome Center each receives about 250,000 guests annually. **Religious tourism**, also commonly referred to as *faith tourism*, is a form of tourism whereby people of faith travel individually or in groups for pilgrimage, missionary, or leisure (fellowship) purposes. The International Conference on Religious Tourism estimates the worldwide faith tourism industry at $18 billion.
- 50,000 churches in the United States with religious travel programs
- One-quarter (25%) of travelers said they were currently interested in taking a spiritual vacation (e.g., religious retreat, pilgrimage). More than one in ten travelers (12%) said they were more interested now compared to five years ago in taking a spiritual vacation. The appeal of a spiritual vacation spans the ages, with approximately one-third of each age group (18-34 years old, 35-54 years old and 55+) expressing current interest in taking such a vacation.

In the News

- CBS Early Show: Rest, relaxation, & religion
- TIME Magazine: Spirit and adventure
- USA TODAY: On a wing and a prayer
- The New York Times: 21st-century religoius travel, Leave the sackcloth at home
- The Los Angeles Times: More agencies are serving the flock - religious travelers
- Belief.net: Companies see increased interest in spiritual tours
- Rocky Mountain News: In the footsteps of the faithful
- The Grand Rapids Press: Spiritual journeys take off in the travel industry

- Yahoo! Business Traveler: Keeping the Faith
- Washington Post: Seeking answers with field trips in faith
- Nassau Guardian (Bahamas): Religious niche being targeted by Bahamas Ministry

Countries, Tourist Boards & Religious Tourism

- Jordan: Promoting niche markets such as religious tourism is a large part of Jordan's overall tourism strategy
- Cypress: Launching new marketing efforts to increase religious tourism of its current 100,000 faith-based visitors annually
- Italy: Religious tourism in Italy alone generates over $4.5 billion each year.
- Vatican:
- Bahamas: One of the few countries with a Director of Religious Tourism and staff dedicated to attracting faith-based visitors ;
- Scotland: Projected to triple from religious tourism dollars of GBP 80-100 to GBP 300 million by 2014
- Switzerland: Seeking to highlight its religious sites and attract more visitors.
- India: Largest portion of visitors are religious pilgrims
- Israel: Tourism ministry looks to boost tourism from North America

2 An International Perspective

World Tourism Organization

The **World Tourism Organization (UNWTO)**, based in Madrid, Spain, is a United Nations agency dealing with questions relating to tourism. It compiles the World Tourism rankings. The World Tourism Organization is a significant global body, concerned with the collection and collation of statistical information on international tourism. This organization represents public sector tourism bodies, from most countries in the world and the publication of its data makes possible comparisons of the flow and growth of tourism on a global scale. The official languages of UNWTO are Arabic, English, ýFrench, Russian, and ýSpanish.

Organizational Aims

The World Tourism Organization plays a role in promoting the development of responsible, ýsustainable and universally accessible tourism, paying particular attention to the ýinterests of developing countriesý.

The Organization encourages the implementation ýof the Global Code of Ethics for Tourism, with a view to ensuring that member ýcountries, tourist destinations and businesses maximize the positive economic, ýsocial and cultural effects of tourism and fully reap its benefits, while minimizing its ýnegative social and environmental impacts.

UNWTO is committed to the United Nations Millennium Development Goals, geared ýtoward reducing poverty and fostering sustainable development.

History

The origin of the World Tourism Organization stems back to 1925 when the International Congress of Official Tourist Traffic Associations (ICOTT) was formed at The Hague. Some articles from early volumes of the Annals of Tourism Research, claim that the UNWTO originated from the International Union of Official Tourist Publicity Organizations (IUOTPO), although the UNWTO states that the ICOTT became the International Union of Official Tourist Propaganda Organizations first in 1934.

Following the end of the Second World War and with international travel numbers increasing, the IUOTPO restructured itself into the International Union of Official Travel Organizations (IUOTO). A technical, non-governmental organization, the IUOTO was made up of a combination of national tourist organizations, industry and consumer groups. The goals and objectives of the IUOTO were to not only promote tourism in general but also to extract the best out of tourism as an international trade component and as an economic development strategy for developing nations.

Towards the end of the 1960's, the IUOTO realized the need for further transformation to enhance its role on an international level. The 20th IUOTO general assembly in Tokyo, 1967, declared the need for the creation of an intergovernmental body with the necessary abilities to function on an international level in cooperation with other international agencies, in particular the United Nations. Throughout the existence of the IUOTO, close ties had been established between the organization and the United Nations (UN) and initial suggestions had the IUOTO becoming part of the UN. However, following the circulation of a draft convention, consensus held that any resultant intergovernmental organization should be closely linked to the UN but preserve its "complete administrative and financial autonomy".

It was on the recommendations of the UN that the formation of the new intergovernmental tourism organization was based. Resolution 2529 of the XXIVth UN general assembly stated:

" The general assembly believes that a formula that would allow agreement to be reached more readily among governments for the establishment of an international tourism organization of an intergovernmental, particularly to assist the developing countries would be: (a) The conversion of the International Union of Official Travel

Organizations into an intergovernmental organization through a revision of its statutes: (b) The establishment of operational links between the United Nations and the transformed Union by means of a formal agreement."

In 1970, the IUOTO general assembly voted in favor of forming the World Tourism Organization (WTO), based on statutes of the IUOTO, and after ratification by the prescribed 51 states, the WTO came into operation on November 1, 1974.

Most recently, at the fifteenth general assembly in 2003, the WTO general council and the UN agreed to establish the WTO as a specialized agency of the UN. The significance of this collaboration, WTO Secretary-General Mr. Francesco Frangialli claimed, would lie in "the increased visibility it gives the WTO, and the recognition that will be accorded to [it].Tourism will be considered on an equal footing with other major activities of human society".

As of 2010, its membership included 154 member states, seven associate members (Flemish Community, Puerto Rico, Aruba, Hong Kong, Macau, Madeira, Netherland Antilles), two observers (Holy See, Palestine). 15 of these members have withdrawn from the organization for different periods in the past: Australia, Bahamas, Bahrain, Canada, Costa Rica, El Salvador, Honduras, Kuwait, Malaysia, Nicaragua, Panama, Philippines, Qatar, Thailand and Puerto Rico.

Non-members are: Suriname, Guyana, United States, Belize, Trinidad and Tobago, Dominica, Grenada, Barbados, Antigua and Barbuda, Saint Lucia, Saint Kitts and Nevis, Saint Vincent and the Grenadines, Liberia, Somalia, Comoros, Ireland, Iceland, United Kingdom, Denmark, Sweden, Finland, Belgium, Luxembourg, Liechtenstein, Estonia, United Arab Emirates, Myanmar, Singapore, New Zealand, Palau, Micronesia, Marshall Islands, Cook Islands, Tuvalu, Nauru, Niue, Kiribati, Solomon Islands, Samoa, Tonga and the rest of states with limited recognition.

Additionally there are some 350 affiliate members, representing the private sector, educational institutions, tourism associations and local tourism authorities. The frequent confusion between the two WTOs – World Tourism Organization and the Geneva-based World Trade Organization – officially ended on 1 December 2005, when the General Assembly approved to add the letters UN (for United Nations) to the start of abbreviation of the leading international tourism body in English and in Russian. UNWTO abbreviation remains OMT in French and

Spanish. UNWTO General Assembly concluded its work at its 16th session in Dakar, Senegal, on 2 December 2005.

Secretaries-General of UNWTO

- **1975–1985** — Robert Lonati (France)
- **1986–1989** — Willibald Pahr (Austria)
- **1990–1996** — Antonio Enriquez Savignac (Mexico)
- **1998–2009** — Francesco Frangialli (France)
- **2010–*present*** — Taleb Rifai (Jordan)

Structure

General Assembly

The General Assembly is the supreme organ of the Organization. Its ordinary ýsessions, held every two years, are attended by delegates of the Full and Associate ýMembers, as well as representatives from the Business Council.ý It is the most important meeting of senior tourism officials and high-level ýrepresentatives of the private sector from all over the world.

Regional Commissions

Established in 1975 as subsidiary organs of the General Assembly, the six Regional Commissions normally meet once a year. They enable member States to maintain ýcontact with one another and with the Secretariat between sessions of the General ýAssembly, to which they submit their proposals and convey their concerns. Each ýCommission elects one Chairman and its Vice-Chairmen from among its Members ýfor a term of two years commencing from one session to the next session of the ýAssembly.ýý

Executive Council

The Executive Council's task is to take all necessary measures, in consultation with ýthe Secretary-General, for the implementation of its own decisions and ýrecommendations of the Assembly and report thereon to the Assembly.ý The Council meets at least twice a year.ý ýThe Council consists of Full Members elected by the Assembly in the proportion of ýone Member for every five Full Members, in accordance with the Rules of Procedure ýlaid down by the Assembly with a view to achieving fair and equitable geographical ýdistribution.ý The term of office of Members elected to the Council is four years and elections for ýone-half of the Council membership are held every two years. Spain is a Permanent ýMember of the Executive Council.ý

Committees

*World Committee on Tourism Ethics ý*Programme Committee ý*Committee on Budget and Finance ý*Committee on Market and Competitiveness

- Committee on Statistics and the Tourism Satellite account
- Sustainable Development of Tourism Committee
- Committee on Poverty Reduction
- Committee for the Review of Applications for Affiliate Membership

Secretariat

The Secretariat is led by Secretary-General ad interim Taleb Rifai of Jordan, who ýsupervises about 110 full-time staff at UNWTO's Madrid Headquarters. He is assisted ýby the Deputy Secretary-General. These officials are responsible ýfor implementing UNWTO's programme of work and serving the needs of Members. ýThe Affiliate Members are supported by a full-time Executive Director at the ýMadrid Headquarters. The ýSecretariat also includes a regional support office for Asia-Pacific in Osaka, Japan, ýfinanced by the Japanese Government.

American Bus Association

The **American Bus Association**, or **ABA**, is a trade association for motorcoach operators and tour companies in the United States and Canada. Its membership consists of about 1,000 companies that operate buses or bus-based tours, about 2,800 organizations representing the travel and tourism industry, and several hundred suppliers of buses and related products and services. Its headquarters is in Washington, D.C.

The organization was founded in 1926 as the Motor Bus Division of the American Automobile Association. It was reorganized in 1930 as the National Association of Motor Bus Operators, and in 1960 changed its name to National Association of Motor Bus Owners. It adopted its present name in 1977.

To the public at large, the ABA is best known for its **Top 100 Events in North America**, an annual compendium of the best events for group travel in the United States and Canada. Each year, 100 U.S. and Canadian events are selected for the program. One event from each country is singled out for top honors. The program was begun in 1982, and today, the Top 100 Events get worldwide attention via television, radio and print media. The prime source for information about these events is *Top 100 Events in North America* magazine, distributed to ABA members and thousands of travelers worldwide.

Members

The organization has four types of members:

Motorcoach Operators - Companies that own motorcoaches and provide privately-contracted services such as charters, tours, sightseeing, scheduled service, airport express service, school bus service, and/or local receptive operations. (The membership does not include public transport bus services.)

Tour Operators - Companies that organize tours without owning equipment. They offer packaged travel by arranging transportation for hotels, attractions and other travel suppliers. Their tours are primarily to locations away from the company's hometown.

Travel Industry Members - Tourism-related companies and organizations that work in partnership with the North American motorcoach industry. They include travel and tourism companies, convention and visitor bureaus, destination marketing organizations, accommodations, attractions, food service organizations, and tourism service professionals such as receptive operators who specialize in tour planning for a local area.

Associate Members - Manufacturers and suppliers of buses and bus-related products and services.

Top 100 Events in North America

The ABA compiles an annual list of its selections as the best events for group travel in the United States and Canada. The events include celebrations, festivals, parades, fairs, exhibits, shows, commemorative events, etc. They are chosen by a committee of ABA-member motorcoach and tour operators from hundreds of events that have been nominated by ABA members. From among the winners, ABA names a Number One Event for the United States, and another one for Canada. The list and its members get worldwide publicity through television, radio, and print media.

The Top 100 Events for the coming year are published in a full-color *Top 100 Events in North America* magazine which is distributed with the September/October issue of ABA's *Destinations* magazine. ABA distributes the magazine to all its members and to thousands of travelers worldwide. ABA's Web site also lists the winners and has links directly to the events.

American Bus Marketplace. Holds this annual convention, which is a major event for the group travel industry. It is held in a different city each year, with a typical attendance of about 3,000 people. The meeting presents an annual opportunity for members of the group travel and motorcoach industry to build business relationships, view new products and services, learn about the latest industry trends, and develop personal networks. The Marketplace features a highly organized series of opportunities for attendees to meet face-to-face in prescheduled seven-minute appointments. Other Marketplace events include professional education seminars, exhibits provided by suppliers, and familiarization tours of attractions in the host city.

Bus Industry Safety Council. Sponsors this organization, whose mission is to develop and promote motorcoach safety. The 200-member council meets regularly to discuss issues and innovations in areas of safety, regulatory compliance, mechanics, technology and security.

Publications. Publishes Destinations magazine, an important glossy magazine in the tour and travel industry, and The Insider, a biweekly newsletter for members and others. Compiles and distributes The ABA Motorcoach Marketer, an annual member directory and travel guide.

Continuing education. Sponsors the Certified Travel Industry Specialist (CTIS) program, providing motorcoach and group travel professionals with industry-specific education and credentialing. The education is provided through correspondence courses at Indiana University - Purdue University Indianapolis and attendance at specialized ABA educational seminars. Conducts webinars online, and educational talks and seminars at its annual Marketplace event.

Awards. Sponsors a Lifetime Achievement Award for individuals who have made major contributions to the motorcoach, tourism, and hospitality industry, and a Kaleidoscope Award for individuals or organizations that have directly impacted the advancement of diversity within the industry.

Code of Ethics. Sponsors a code of ethics for its members. The code was adopted to promote and maintain high standards of business and personal conduct. Its ten points cover general business integrity and several specific items of financial behavior.

Government Affairs. Represents the industry before elected officials and regulatory bodies. Monitors pertinent legislative and regulatory activity, and keeps members informed of developments in these areas. These activities have helped in securing Americans with Disabilities Act grants to assist coach operators in equipping coaches with wheelchair lifts, and Transportation Security Administration funds in support of industry efforts to improve security measures for drivers and passengers.

Affiliated Organizations

The ABA sponsors the ABA Foundation, which funds research, scholarships, and internships related to its mission. It supports BUSPAC, a political action committee that works to advance the interests of the industry and the traveling public.

The ABA maintains strategic partnerships with about twenty other industry organizations and a similar number of state and provincial bus associations.

Tour Guide

A tour guide (or tourist guide) provides assistance, information and cultural, historical and contemporary heritage interpretation to people on organized tours, individual clients, educational establishments, at religious and historical sites, museums, and at venues of other significant interest. They (normally) have a recognized national or regional tourist guide qualification.

The CEN (European Committee for Standardization) definition for "tourist guide" (part of the work by CEN on definitions for terminology within the tourism industry) is:

Tourist guide = person who guides visitors in the language of their choice and interprets the cultural and natural heritage of an area, which person normally possesses an area-specific qualification usually issued and/or recognized by the appropriate authority, March 2010

CEN also produced a definition for "tour manager": Tour manager = person who manages and supervises the itinerary on behalf of the tour operator, ensuring the programme is carried out as described in the tour operator's literature and sold to the traveller/consumer and who gives local practical information

In Europe, tourist guides (tour guide being initially a term primarily used in the US market) are represented by FEG, the European Federation of Tourist Guide Associations and outside Europe by WFTGA.

The tourist guiding qualification is specific to each and every country; in some cases the qualification is national, in some cases it is broken up into regions. In all cases it is embedded in the educational and training ethic of that country. The Art of Guiding is a skill; it is the skill of selecting information and varying it for different audiences; it is the skill of presenting it in a simple and precise way; it is the skill of allowing the visitor to see and to understand; it is a skill which, if well performed, is invisible.

Tourist Trap

A tourist trap is an establishment, or group of establishments, that has been created with the aim of attracting tourists and their money. Tourist traps will typically provide services, entertainment, souvenirs and other products for tourists to purchase.

While the term may have negative connotations for some, such establishments may be viewed by tourists as fun and interesting diversions.

Travel Behavior

Large metropolitan areas typically only do such surveys once every decade, though some cities are conducting panel surveys, which track the same people year after year.

That data is generally used to estimate transportation planning models, so that transport analysts can make predictions about people who haven't been surveyed. This is important in forecasting traffic, which depends on future changes to road networks, land use patterns, and policies.

Some years ago it was recognized that behavioral research was limited by data, and a special data set was developed to aid research: The Baltimore Disaggregate Data Set which is the result an in depth survey, ca. 1977. Its title indicates today's emphasis on disaggregated rather than aggregated data. This particular data set is believed lost. A small program to preserve and make available on the web these travel behavior surveys, the Metropolitan Travel Survey Archive, is now under way at the University of Minnesota. There is also the National Personal Transportation Survey (later National Household Travel Survey), conducted every five years or so, but with much less spatial detail.

Travel Behavior and Aactivity Analysis

Analysis of travel behavior from the home can answer the question: How does the family participate in modern society. Consider two non-observable extremes. At one extreme we have the non-specialized household. It does everything for itself, and no travel is required. Ultimate specialization is the other extreme; travel is required for all things. Observed households are somewhere in between. The "in between" position of households might be thought of as the consequence of two matters.

1. There is social and economic structure - the organization of society. To participate in this society, the household specializes its occupations, education, social activities, etc.
2. The extent to which members of the household specialize turns on their attributes and resources.

Moore (1964) has observed that increasing specialization in all things is the chief feature of social change. Considering social changes, one might observe that 100 years ago things were less specialized compared to today. So we would expect lots of change in household travel over the time period. Data are not veıy good, but the travel time aspect of what's available seems contrary to the expectation, travel hasn't changed much. For instance, the time spent on the journey to work may have been stable for centuries (the travel budget hypothesis). Here are some travel time comparisons from John Robinson (1986).

Table: Minutes per day spent in travel

	Men		Women	
Activity	1975	1985	1975	1985
Work Travel	25	31	9	17
Family Travel	33	31	33	33
Leisure Travel	27	33	21	23
Total	85	94	63	73

Most travel behavior analysis concerns demand issues and do not touch very much on supply issues. Yet when we observe travel from a home, we are certainly observing some sort of market clearing process - demand and supply are matched.

History of Travel Behavior Analysis

Analytic work on travel behavior can be dated from Liepmann (1945). Liepmann obtained and analyzed 1930s data on worker travel in England. Many of the insights current today were found by Liepmann: time spent, ride sharing, etc. Most academics date modern work from advances in mode choice analysis made in the 1970s. This created much excitement, and after some years an International Association for Travel Behaviour Research emerged. There are about 150 members of the Association; it holds a conference every three years. The proceedings of those conferences yield a nice record of advances in the field. The proceedings also provide a record of topics of lasting interest and of changing priorities. Mode choice received priority early on, but in the main today's work is not so much on theory as it is on practice. Hagerstrand (1970) developed a time and space path analysis, often called the time-space prism.

Caribbean Tourism Organization

The Caribbean Tourism Organization's main objective is the development of sustainable tourism for the economic and social benefit of Caribbean people. The CTO provides to and through its public and private sector members, the services and information to accomplish this goal.

Operations

The CTO, with headquarters in Barbados, comprises 32 member countries, including English, French, Spanish and Dutch countries and territories, as well as private sector allied members. These include the Caribbean Hotel Association, companies, organizations and persons providing products and services to the Caribbean tourism industry. CTO's offices are located in the USA, UK, Canada and Barbados. CTO Chapters are located in France, Germany, Holland, across the U.S. and in the Caribbean.

History

CTO was established in 1989 with the merger of the Caribbean Tourism Association (founded in 1951) and the Caribbean Tourism Research and Development Center (founded in 1974).

The body is primarily involved in the joint promotion and marketing of Caribbean tourist destinations in North America and Europe.

Member Countries

- Antigua and Barbuda
- Bahamas
- Barbados
- Belize
- Cuba
- Dominica
- Dominican Republic
- French overseas departments:
  Guadeloupe
  Martinique
  Saint Barthelemy
  Saint Martin
- Grenada
- Guyana
- Haiti
- Jamaica
- Kingdom of the Netherlands:
  Aruba
  Bonaire
  Curaçao
  Saint Eustatius
  Saint Maarten
- Saint Kitts and Nevis
- Saint Lucia
- Saint Vincent & the Grenadines
- Suriname
- Trinidad & Tobago
- British overseas territories:

Anguilla

Bermuda

British Virgin Islands

Cayman Islands

Montserrat

Turks & Caicos Islands

- United States territories:

Puerto Rico

U.S. Virgin Islands

- Venezuela

Convention and Visitor Bureau

A convention and visitor bureau (CVB) is the dominant form of destination marketing organization in the United States, but is found in other countries as well. Destination marketing organizations have many names - convention and visitors bureaus, visitors' bureaus, welcome centers, tourism bureaus, travel and tourism bureaus, information centers and more. Regardless of the name, these organizations offer many services to the traveling public. While each U.S. state has a department of travel and tourism, most counties and/or cities also have their own CVB, to promote a narrower geographical area.

Mission

Although there are many government and chamber of commerce bodies that have responsibility for marketing a destination to visitors and selling to conventions and meeting planners, most convention and visitors bureaus (CVBs) are non-profit organizations, working independently under the direction of a board of elected directors. The fundamental mission of a convention and visitor bureau is the promotion of the economic development of a destination through increasing visits from tourists and business travelers, which generates overnight lodging for a destination, visits to restaurants, and shopping revenues. Convention and visitor bureaus are the most important tourism marketing organizations in their respective tourist destinations, as they are directly responsible for marketing the destination brand through travel and tourism "product awareness" to visitors. While they primarily are funded through the collection of "bed taxes" on visitors, convention and visitors bureuas produce billions of dollars in direct and indirect revenue and taxes for their state and local economies with their marketing and sales expertise.

Services

Typically, a convention and visitors bureau provides information about a destination's lodging, dining, attractions, events, museums, arts and culture, history and recreation. Some even provide bus services, insider tips, top ten attraction and activity lists, blogs, photos, forums, free things to do, season-specific activity suggestions and more. The organization works with tourists and meeting planners to provide valuable information on their local area. Their goal is to help make a visitor's trip or a conference attendees' meeting a much more enjoyable and rewarding experience. In many locations, they work closely with a convention center that will offer large spaces for larger meetings, trade shows, and conventions than can be accommodated in a single hotel. Usually, these organizations also have a local office where one can find maps, brochures, travel professionals, local insight, visitors guides, souvenirs and more.

Marketing Initiatives

A convention and visitor bureau's marketing initiatives are typically achieved through the following: trade association marketplaces, web pages, advertising, distribution of promotional and collateral material, direct sales, hosting familiarization tours for journalists and travel industry personnel, and sponsoring other hospitality functions. The target decision maker of these marketing initiatives is not typically a resident in the community. Most often, if visitors are going to spend the night in a hotel, they reside at least 100 miles away. Thus, the marketing activity usually takes place or is directed outside the convention and visitors bureau's community. Convention and visitors bureaus in larger destinations often will market nationally and globally, while smaller cities may focus just on their state or region.

Destination Marketing Organization

A destination marketing organization is an entity or company, which is promoting a tourist destination, in order to increase the amount of visitors to this destination. They promote the long-term development and marketing of a destination, focusing on convention sales, tourism marketing and services.

Australia

The Association of Australian Convention Bureaux (AACB) consists of 15 city and regional bureaux, dedicated to marketing their specific region as premier Business Events destinations to intrastate, interstate and international markets. The bureaux also recognise their responsibility to promote Australia as a whole.

Germany

The German Convention Bureau (GCB) represents the interests of the German tourism industry. The GCB markets Germany as a destination for conventions, meetings, events and incentives, both on a national and international level and is the place to contact for anybody planning an event in Germany.

Korea

Korea Tourism Organization (KTO) is a statutory organization of the Republic of Korea (South Korea), under the Ministry of Culture and Tourism and is commissioned to promote tourism in South Korea.

United States

DMO's are represented in the United States by convention and visitor bureaus (CVBs), which are paid by bed taxes or just from their members. Every U.S. state and almost every larger city and county has its own CVB.

Examples of United States DMOs:

- Baton Rouge Area Convention and Visitors Bureau(BRACVB)
- Panama City Beach Convention & Visitors Bureau(PCBCVB)
- Fairfax County, Virginia Convention & Visitors Corporation (Visit Fairfax)
- Loudoun Convention & Visitors Association(LCVA)
- Bradenton Area Convention & Visitors Bureau(BACVB)
- Minneapolis, Official Convention + Visitors Association
- River Parishes Tourist Commission
- Auburn-Opelika Tourism Bureau
- Tunica Convention & Visitors Bureau (TCVB)
- North Carolina Division of Tourism
- Ventura California Visitors & Convention Bureau

- Oakland Convention & Visitors Bureau
- Jersey Shore Convention & Visitors Bureau(JSCVB)

Puerto Rico

The Puerto Rico Convention Bureau (PRCB) is a non-profit organization that markets tourism in Puerto Rico, as a meetings and conventions destination.

Scandinavia

TravelG8 and Travelgate.net, Destination Marketing anno 1994, promotes all major countries looking for Scandinavian travellers. Scandinavia & Nordic countries (Sweden, Norway, Denmark, Finland and Iceland) is the third largest market in Europe.

- Travelgate.net - The Gateway to The World
- TravelG8 - Show Yourself

European Travel Commission

The European Travel Commission (ETC) is the organization responsible for the promotion of Europe as a tourist destination. Its members are the national tourism organisations (NTOs) of thirty-eight European countries, including all EU member states, as well as Croatia, Georgia, Iceland, Monaco, Montenegro, Norway, San Marino, Serbia, Switzerland, Turkey and Ukraine. The national tourism organizations of all sovereign states in Europe are eligible for full membership of the European Travel Commission. Regional cross-border organizations and tourism-related bodies may join as associate members. The European Travel Commission is neither part of the European Commission nor an institution of the European Union.

History

ETC was established in 1948 in Norway. Between World War I and World War II, Europe became aware of the importance of tourism.

1925

The establishment of national tourism organizations rapidly led to the creation of the "International Union of Official Tourist Publicity Organizations": its first mission was the launch of a joint publicity campaign named "Europe Calling".

1947

This union became the International Union of Official Travel Organisations (IUOTO), which is today known as the World Tourism Organization, WTO.

1948

In its first General Assembly, the IUOTO adopted the principle of Regional Commissions: 19 European countries were represented and those countries decided to establish the first such Commission. Since its creation, ETC, has been a results-oriented organisation working closely with government agencies and all segments of the industry to achieve practical objectives. First priority was given to making governments aware of the importance of tourism in their national economies, which had been deeply disturbed by World War II. That is why ETC has always supported an international co-operation, a collective action and the building of a European solidarity.

Constitution

Henri Ingrand (France), the first chairman of the ETC had settled the basic principles for its operations. The second one, Arthur Haulot (Belgium) drafted in 1958, its official statutes in accordance with the Belgium law. When the Commission was transferred to Dublin in 1965 with Timothy O'Driscoll as chairman, these statutes remained the only "legal" constitution of the ETC. New statutes were drafted in 1987 when the headquarters were transferred to Paris under the chairmanship of Walter Leu (Switzerland). In 1996, when the ETC moved to Brussels a new version was adopted to the Belgian legislation under the chairman Walter Leu (Switzerland). Constitution was modified and adopted at the General Meeting n°66 following the 2002 law.

Membership

In 1948, the original membership of the European Travel Commission was 19 countries. At that time Eastern European countries, members of IUOTO were invited to participate. None of these countries accepted, apparently due to political reasons. Germany, Yugoslavia, Malta and Cyprus joined the Commission a few years later.

Mission

ETC sees itself as a virtual organisation marketing Europe as a tourist destination in global markets, primarily by means of the internet. The three principal focuses of the Commission's work are electronic marketing, market intelligence and operational excellence. ETC seeks to provide added value to members by encouraging exchange of information and management expertise and promoting awareness about the role played by national tourism organisations.

Organisation & Budget

The members elect a President, three Vice-Presidents, a Board of Directors, a Chairman of the Market Intelligence Group and a Chairman of the Marketing & Technology Network for revolving two years terms.

ETC is entirely financed by Members' contributions, calculated according to a set of agreed criteria. Additional financial support for specific campaigns is raised overseas. Long-standing local industry support for ETC's activities is proof of its credibility in the field.

ETC is registered in Belgium as an 'association internationale sans but lucratif' (or aisbl) - a non-profit making international association.

Overseas

The representatives of the overseas offices of the European national tourism organisations operating in the various long-haul markets join together to form an ETC Operations Group and elect a Chairman. They decide on a programme of joint activities for the promotion of Europe for the year ahead, propose a budget, and seek local industry support.

In Europe

This programme is submitted for approval to ETC's Members in Europe, who meet twice a year (in Spring and Autumn) for a General Meeting.

Activities

ETC currently promotes and markets "Destination Europe" around the world through its operations groups in the United States, Canada, Asia (Japan) and Latin America (Brazil). ETC also plans to extend its activities to emerging markets such as China, India and Russia.

Vital to ETC activities are its Market Intelligence Group and Marketing & Technology Network. The Market Intelligence Group commissions and produces market intelligence studies, handbooks on methodologies and best practice, and facilitates the exchange of European tourism statistics on "TourMIS".

The Marketing & Technology Network provides information and expertise about the use of digital media by national tourism organisations, produces the "New Media Review", and organises an e-Business Academy once a year. The work of all operations groups is carried out by experts from member NTOs.

visiteurope.com is the official website of the European Travel Commission (ETC). ETC markets Europe as tourist destination on behalf of its 38 member countries. Under a pair of soaring wings, a symbol of travel and discovery deeply rooted in Europe's myths and history, visiteurope.com brings the excitement of a European vacation to potential guests around the world with localised versions in a number of major languages. The content of visiteurope.com is brought jointly by ETC and the 38 national tourism organisations.

South-East Asian Tourism Organisation

The South-East Asian Tourism Organisation (SEATO) is a working group formed by both government and non-government tourism organizations operating in Southeast Asia. SEATO was formed in late 2009 with the aim of spreading the financial impacts of tourism more widely into the kampongs and villages of the region.

Travel and Tourism Competitiveness Report

The Travel and Tourism Competitiveness Report was first published in 2007 by the World Economic Forum. The 2007 report covered 124 major and emerging economies. The 2008 report covered 130 countries, and the 2009 report expanded to 133 countries. The index is a measurement of the factors that make it attractive to develop business in the travel and tourism industry of individual countries, rather than a measure of a country attractiveness as a tourist destination. The report ranks selected nations according to the Travel and Tourism Competitiveness Index (TTCI), which scores from 1 to 6 the performance of a given country in each specific subindex. The overall index is made of three main subindexes: (1) regulatory framework; (2) business environment and infrastructure; and (3) human, cultural, and natural resources. The Report also includes a specific Country Profile for each of the nations evaluated, with each of the scores received to estimate its TTCI, and complementary information regarding key economic indicators from the World Bank, and country indicators from the World Travel and Tourism Council.

Variables

For the 2008 index, each of the three main subindexes is made of the scoring of the following 14 variables, called pillars in the TTC Report. Several changes were introduced in the 2008 TTCI in the definition of the variables as compared to the definitions of the 2007 TTCI. First, the "environmental regulation" pillar was improved with help from the IUCN and the UNWTO, and for the 2008 index was re-named the "environmental sustainability" pillar to "better reflect its components and to capture the increasingly recognized importance of sustainability in the sector's development." Second, the original pillar "natural and cultural resources" was divided into two separate subcomponents: "natural resources" and "cultural resources", thus, allowing to differentiate those countries which do not necessarily have the same strengths or weaknesses in these two different resources. In general, the model was improved with better data and new concepts were introduced. The 2009 report kept the same 14 variables.

Visitor Center

A visitor center or centre (see American and British English spelling differences), visitor information center, tourist information center, is a physical location that provides tourist information to the visitors who tour the place or area locally [clarification needed]. It may be:

- A visitor center at a specific attraction or place of interest, such as a landmark, national park, national forest, or state park, providing information (such as trail maps, and about camp sites, staff contact, restrooms, etc.) and in-depth educational exhibits and artifact displays (for example, about natural or cultural history). Often a film or other media display is used. If the site has permit requirements or guided tours, the visitor center is often the place where these are coordinated.
- A tourist information center, providing visitors to a location with information on the area's attractions, lodgings, maps, and other items relevant to tourism. Often, these centers are operated at the airport or other port of entry, by the local government or chamber of commerce. Often a visitor center is called simply an information center.

Europe

In the United Kingdom, there is a nationwide network of Tourist Information Centres run by the British Tourist Authority (BTA), represented online by the VisitBritain website and public relations organisation. Other TICs are run by local authorities or through private organisations such as local shops in association with BTA.

The English Tourism Council is a subsidiary part of the British Tourist Authority and promotes domestic tourism under the Enjoy England banner.

In Wales, the National Assembly for Wales supports TICs through Visit Wales.

In Scotland, the Scottish Government supports VisitScotland, the official tourist organization of Scotland, which also operates Tourist Information Centres across Scotland.

North America

In North America, a welcome center is a rest area with a visitor center, located after the entrance from one state or province to another state or province or in some cases another country, usually along an interstate highway. These information centers are operated by the state they are located in.

South America

Peru features iperu, tourist information and assistance, a free service that provides tourist information for domestic and foreign travelers, the information covers destinations, attractions, recommended routes and licensed tourism companies in Peru. It also provides assistance on various procedures or where tourists have problems of various kinds. iperu receive complaints and suggestions for destinations and tourism companies operating in Peru (lodging, travel agencies, airlines, buses, etc.).

iperu, tourist information and assistance has a nationwide network represented online by the Peru.info website, the 24/7 line (51 1) 5748000, and 31 local offices in 13 regions in all over Peru: Lima-Callao, Amazonas, Piura, Lambayeque, La Libertad, Ancash, Arequipa, Tacna, Puno, Ayacucho, Cusco, Tumbes and Iquitos.

The official tourist organization or national tourist board of Peru is PromPerú, a national organization that promotes both tourism and international commerce of this country worldwide.

World Travel and Tourism Council

The World Travel & Tourism Council (WTTC) was conceptualized in the early 1980s when a group of CEOs came to the realization that although Travel & Tourism was the largest service industry in the world and the biggest provider of jobs, nobody knew it. There was no consolidated data or voice for the industry to give the message to elected official and policy makers.

WTTC was established in 1990 and today the Council is positioned as the global business leaders' forum for Travel & Tourism, comprising the Chairmen and Chief Executives of 100 of the world's foremost organizations, representing all regions and sectors of the industry; a membership list is attached.

Mission

WTTC works to raise awareness of Travel & Tourism as one of the world's largest industries, employing approximately 235 million people and generating 9.3 per cent of world GDP, WTTC works together with governments to raise awareness of the economic and social importance of the industry across the world.

WTTC's mission focuses on three main areas:

Driving the Agenda: Raising awareness of the impact of Travel & Tourism and working with governments to make the industry an economic and job-creating priority

The Facilitator: Helping industry participants to understand, anticipate, interpret and act on global key regional development

The Networking Forum: WTTC is the business leaders' forum to which Travel & Tourism players aspire

Blueprint for New Tourism

By 2003, events around the world such as the September 11th attacks, war in Iraq, the SARS crisis and increased terrorism meant that WTTC had to work to rebuild confidence among travellers. The Global Travel & Tourism Summit in 2003 was opened up to global press and media for the first time and the theme - Building New Tourism - came out of the atmosphere at the time. The outcome of the Summit shaped the Council's future vision and led to the launch of the Blueprint for New Tourism. The Blueprint for New Tourism provides a new strategic framework to ensure that Travel & Tourism works for everyone in the future. It promotes Travel & Tourism as a partnership between the private and public sectors, matching the needs of economies, local and regional authorities and local communities with those of business. The three main messages that form the framework for the Blueprint for New Tourism are: 1. Governments recognizing Travel & Tourism as a top priority 2. Business balancing economics with people, culture and environment 3. A shared pursuit of long-term growth and prosperity See below for external links to the full Blueprint for New Tourism.

Activities

WTTC Research

When the World Travel & Tourism Council (WTTC) was established in 1990, the founding Members decided that the quantification of Travel & Tourism's impact on world and national economies would be the most important contribution they could make to achieve their goal of raising awareness among policy leaders and decision-makers of Travel & Tourism's economic contribution and its potential for creating wealth and employment around the world. The subsequent 19 years of investment in research made a significant contribution to the development of the new international standard for Tourism Satellite Accounting (TSA) research, adopted in 2001 by the United Nations Statistical Commission. WTTC has also developed a Crisis Impact Forecasting Model to assess the potential impact of a crisis on the industry within 48 hours. It was put into place following the crises of the London and Egypt bombings in 2005.

TSA Commissioned Reports

Over the years, WTTC and its research partner, UK-based Oxford Economics (OE), have endeavoured to create a system of Tourism Satellite Accounting research, which now covers 181 economies around the world. Using a combination of macro-economic research and forecasts, national accounting data/information, Travel & Tourism variables and econometric modelling, WTTC/OE have produced a system of research covering many concepts of Travel & Tourism 'Demand', from personal consumption to business purchases, capital investment, government spending and exports. This information is then translated into economic concepts of production, such as gross domestic product (GDP) and employment, which can be compared with other industries and the economy as a whole to provide statistical information that can assist in policy- and business decision-making. Today, WTTC produces annual TSA forecasts for 181 countries and 13 regions and carries out commissioned TSA reports for a growing number of countries, regions, and cities each year..

Regional Initiatives

WTTC has established two Regional Initiatives in India and China and is now working more extensively in China. Due to a consensus from Members of the Council, a Middle East Chapter has been founded to work together on region-specific issues, and similarly in Europe, an EU Steering Committee has been meeting regularly to drive WTTC's lobbying in Brussels. The purpose of these initiatives is to bring together key players from across the region to work together to accelerate industry growth.

Policy Reports and Initiatives

The Council works with and consults with its Members to produce policy papers covering a wide variety of topical issues facing the industry. These papers are produced with the aim of presenting the Council's collective stance and putting forward guidelines on how to best meet challenges or optimise opportunities. WTTC's Policy statements can be region-specific or globally applicable, setting out strategies for areas of business ranging from corporate social responsibility to tackling infrastructure, human resources, and climate change. WTTC also launched the Green Globe environmental awareness programme which became an autonomous organization in 1998.

Global Travel & Tourism Summit

The Global Travel & Tourism Summit is an annual WTTC gathering for both public and private sector leaders of travel and tourism. The Summit aims to facilitate meaningful dialogue among the world's Travel & Tourism industry and government leaders. Past locations of the Summit include Vilamoura, Doha, New Delhi, Washington D.C., Lisbon, and Dubai. The 9th Global Travel & Tourism Summit took place from 14-16 May 2009 in Florianópolis, Brazil.

Tourism for Tomorrow Awards

The Tourism for Tomorrow Awards were set up in 1989 by the Federation of Tour Operators to encourage action from all sectors of the industry to protect the environment. WTTC took over the Awards in 2004. Awarded annually, they recognise and promote the world's leading examples of best practice in responsible tourism development across four categories:

Destination Stewardship Award, Conservation Award, Community Benefit Award, Global Tourism Business Award

Winners and finalists are taking the stage in a Awards special session during WTTC's Global Travel & Tourism Summit.

3 Pilgrimage Management

A pilgrimage is a very long journey or search of great moral significance. Sometimes, it is a journey to a shrine of importance to a person's beliefs and faith. Members of many major religions participate in pilgrimages. A person who makes such a journey is called a pilgrim.

The Holy Land acts as a focal point for the pilgrimages of the Abrahamic religions such as Judaism, Christianity, Islam and the Bahá'í Faith.

In the kingdoms of Israel and Judah, the visitation of certain ancient cult-centers was repressed in the 7th century BCE, when worship was restricted to the YHWH at the Temple in Jerusalem. In Syria, the shrine of Astarte at the headwater spring of the river Adonis survived until it was destroyed by order of Emperor Constantine in the 4th century.

In mainland Greece, a stream of individuals made their way to Delphi or the oracle of Zeus at Dodona, and once every four years, at the period of the Olympic games, the temple of Zeus at Olympia formed the goal of swarms of pilgrims from every part of the Hellenic world. When Alexander the Great reached Egypt, he put his whole vast enterprise on hold, while he made his way with a small band deep into the Libyan desert, to consult the oracle of Ammun. During the imperium of his Ptolemaic heirs, the shrine of Isis at Philae received many votive inscriptions from Greeks on behalf of their kindred far away at home.

As a common human experience, pilgrimage has been proposed as a new Jungian archetype by Wallace Clift and Jean Dalby Clift.

Pilgrimage centres

Antiquity

Many ancient religions had sacred sites, temples, oracles and sacred groves to which pilgrimages were made.

- Karnak, Egypt.
- Thebes, Egypt.
- Kurukshetra, India.
- Delphi, Greece. Oracle.
- Dodona, Epirus, Greece. Oracle.
- Ephesus, Temple of Artemis (Diana), Turkey.
- Baalbek Lebanon.
- Jerusalem, Israel.

Bahá'í Faith

Bahá'u'lláh decreed pilgrimage to two places in the Kitáb-i-Aqdas: the House of Bahá'u'lláh in Baghdad, Iraq, and the House of the Báb in Shiraz, Iran. Later, `Abdu'l-Bahá designated the Shrine of Bahá'u'lláh at Bahji, Israel as a site of pilgrimage.

Bahá'í pilgrimage consists of visiting the holy places in Haifa, Acre, and Bahjí at the Bahá'í World Centre in northwest Israel, and Bahá'ís can apply to join an organized nine-day pilgrimage where they are taken to visit the various holy sites, or attend a shorter three-day pilgrimage.

Buddhism

There are four places that Buddhists make pilgrimage to:

- Lumbini: Buddha's birth place (in Nepal)
- Bodh Gaya: place of Enlightenment
- Sarnath: where he delivered his first teaching
- Kusinara: (now Kusinagar, India) where he attained mahaparinirvana (died).

Other pilgrimage places in India and Nepal connected to the life of Gautama Buddha are: Savatthi, Pataliputta, Nalanda, Gaya, Vesali, Sankasia, Kapilavastu, Kosambi, Rajagaha, Varanasi.

Other famous places for Buddhist pilgrimage include:

- India: Sanchi, Ellora, Ajanta.
- Thailand: Sukhothai, Ayutthaya, Wat Phra Kaew, Wat Doi Suthep.
- Tibet: Lhasa (traditional home of the Dalai Lama), Mount Kailash, Lake Nam-tso.
- Cambodia: Angkor Wat, Silver Pagoda.
- Sri Lanka: Polonnaruwa, Temple of the Tooth (Kandy), Anuradhapura.
- Laos: Luang Prabang.
- Myanmar: Bagan, Sagaing Hill.
- Nepal: Bodhnath, Swayambhunath.
- Indonesia: Borobudur.
- China: Yung-kang, Lung-men caves. The Four Sacred Mountains
- Japan: Kansai Kannon Pilgrimage, Chagoku 33 Kannon Pilgrimage, Shikoku Pilgrimage, Mount Kaya.

Christianity

Christian pilgrimage was first made to sites connected with the birth, life, crucifixion and resurrection of Jesus. Surviving descriptions of Christian pilgrimages to the Holy Land date from the 4th century, when pilgrimage was encouraged by church fathers like Saint Jerome. Pilgrimages also began to be made to Rome and other sites associated with the Apostles, saints and Christian martyrs, as well as to places where there have been apparitions of the Virgin Mary.

Hinduism

Kumbh Mela is the largest pilgrimage recorded in history. Kumbh Mela is also credited with the largest gathering of humans in the entire world.

Most Hindu places of pilgrimage are associated with legendary events from the lives of various gods. Almost any place can become a focus for pilgrimage, but in most cases they are sacred cities, rivers, lakes, and mountains. Hindus are encouraged to undertake pilgrimages during their lifetime. Most Hindus visit sites within their region or locale. Those who can afford to go may journey to more popularly known and visited sites, such as those in the following list.

- Allahabad
- Amarnath
- Arunachala
- Ayodhya
- Chitrakut
- Bhavani, Erode
- Benares
- Chidambaram
- Dakshineshwar
- Dharmasthala
- Kedarnath
- Kumbh Mela
- Ganga Talao
- Gaya
- Guruvayoor
- Hampi
- Haridwar
- Kalahasti
- Kanchipuram
- Kanyakumari
- Kateel
- Kollur
- Kumbakonam
- Kukke Subramanya
- Kunrakudy
- Madurai
- Mahabalipuram
- Maihar
- Marudamalai
- Mathura
- Mandher Devi temple in Mandhradevi

- Mayapur
- Mount Kailash
- Nashik
- Nathdwara
- Palani
- Pazhamudircholai
- Gangotri
- Pushkar
- Puttaparthi
- Yamunotri
- Rishikesh
- Sabarimala
- Shakumbhri Devi
- Shirdi
- Sikkal
- Sivagiri, Kerala
- Somnath
- Sringeri
- Srirangam
- Swamimalai
- Swamithope
- Talapady
- Tanjavur
- Thiruchendur
- Tiruchirappalli
- Thiruparamkunram
- Thiruthani
- Thiruvannamalai
- Tirupati
- Ujjain
- Udupi

- Malai Mandir
- Vaishno Devi
- Vayalur
- Vindhyachal
- Viralimalai
- Virpur
- Vrindavan
- Badrinath
- Dwarka
- Puri
- Rameshwaram

The last four sites in the list together comprise the Chardham, or four holy pilgrimage destinations. It was traditionally believed that one who undertakes a pilgrimage to all four sites will attain moksha, the release from samsara (cycle of rebirths), at the time of death. The holy places of pilgrimage for the Shaktism sect of Hinduism are the Shakti peethas (Temples of Shakti).

Islam

The pilgrimage to Mecca (the Hajj) is one of the Five Pillars of Islam. It should be attempted at least once in the lifetime of all able-bodied Muslims who can afford to do so. It is the most important of all Muslim pilgrimages, and is the largest pilgrimage for Muslims.

Another important place for Muslims is the city of Medina, the second holiest place in Islam, in Saudi Arabia, where Muhammad rests, in Al-Masjid al-Nabawi (the Mosque of the Prophet).

The Ihram (white robes of pilgrimage) is meant to show equality of all pilgrims in the eyes of God: that there is no difference between a prince and a pauper. Ihram is also symbolic for holy virtue and pardon from all past sins.

While wearing the Ihram in Mecca, a pilgrim may not shave, clip their nails, wear perfume, swear or quarrel, hunt, kill any creature, uproot or damage plants, cover the head for men or the face and hands for women, marry, wear shoes over the ankles, perform any dishonest acts or carry weapons. If they do their pilgrimage is uncompleted.

Judaism

The Temple in Jerusalem was the center of the Jewish religion, until its destruction in 70 CE, and all adult men who were able were required to visit and offer sacrifices (korbanot), particularly during Passover, Shavuot and Sukkot.

Following the destruction of the Second Temple and the onset of the diaspora, the centrality of pilgrimage to Jerusalem in Judaism was discontinued. In its place came prayers and rituals hoping for a return to Zion and the accompanying restoration of regular pilgrimages.

Until recent centuries, pilgrimage had been a fairly difficult and arduous adventure. But now, Jews from many countries make periodic pilgrimages to the holy sites of their religion.

The western retaining wall of the original temple, known as the Wailing Wall, or Western Wall remains in the Old City of Jerusalem and this has been the most sacred site for religious Jews. Pilgrimage to this area was off-limits from 1948 to 1967, when East Jerusalem was controlled by Jordan.

Many Jews still enjoy visiting Israel even if it is not an official "pilgrimage." There are numerous lesser Jewish pilgrimage sites, mainly tombs of tzadikim, throughout the Land of Israel and all over the world, including: Hebron; Bethlehem; Mt. Meron; Netivot; Uman, Ukraine; Silistra, Bulgaria; Damanhur, Egypt; and many others.

Sikhism

The Sikh religion does not place great importance on pilgrimage. Guru Nanak Dev was asked "Should I go and bathe at pilgrimage places?" and replied: "God's name is the real pilgrimage place which consists of contemplation of the word of God, and the cultivation of inner knowledge."

Eventually, however, Amritsar and Harmandir Saheb (the Golden Temple) became the centre of the Sikh faith, and if a Sikh goes on pilgrimage it is usually to this place.

Zoroastrianism

The Zoroastrians take pilgrimage trips in India to the eight Atash Behrams in India and one in Yazd.

Secular Pilgrimage

In modern usage, the terms pilgrim and pilgrimage have developed in sense to include sites of secular importance. For example, fans of Elvis Presley may choose to visit his home, Graceland, in Memphis, Tennessee. Visits to war memorials such as the Vietnam Veterans Memorial are often seen as pilgrimages. Similarly one may refer to a cultural center such as Venice as a "tourist Mecca".

Paris Commune

The Père Lachaise Cemetery, where the defenders of the Paris Commune made their last stand and many of them were afterwards summarily executed, is the focus of annual pilgrimages by parties and organizations of the French Left.

Communism

In a number of Communist countries, secular pilgrimages were established as an "antidote" to religious pilgrimages, the most famous of which are:

- USSR: Mausoleum of Lenin in Red Square, Moscow
- PRC: Mausoleum of Mao Zedong in Tiananmen Square, Beijing
- Germany: Birthplace of Karl Marx, Trier

Fascism

The mausoleum of Italian Dictator Benito Mussolini in Predappio, Italy serves as a pilgrimage site for Italian Neo-Fascists. In post-World War II Germany, considerable efforts were made to prevent Hitler's bunker in Berlin from becoming a similar place of pilgrimage for Neo-Nazis.

Catholic Association Pilgrimage

The Catholic Association of the UK, abbreviated to the CA, has been around in one form or another since 1881 and ran its first pilgrimage to Lourdes in 1901. Its objects are set out in the Memorandum and Articles but its main purpose is to mastermind the CA Annual Pilgrimage to Lourdes, currently incorporating the diocesan pilgrimages of Clifton Diocese, East Anglia Diocese, Northampton Diocese, Portsmouth Diocese, Southwark Archdiocese, and the Stonyhurst College Lourdes Pilgrimage and British Province of the Carmelites Pilgrimage. Each of these groups is overseen by a Diocesan Director. The entire Pilgrimage is coordinated by the Pilgrimage Director (currently Mgr Bill Saunders from Southwark

Archdiocese)and the Pilgrimage Management Committee, and takes place at the end of August.

The CA is a registered charity. The Catholic Association was originally founded in 1891, with the approval and blessing of Cardinal Manning. Its original objects are stated in its Rules as being;

To promote unity and good fellowship among Catholics by organising lectures, concerts, dances, whist tournaments, excursions, and other gatherings of a social character, and to assist, whenever possible, in the work of Catholic organization, and in the protection and advancement of Catholic interests.

It was particularly successful in the organization of pilgrimages to Rome and other places of Catholic interest. The first pilgrimage to Lourdes took place in September 1901 and became the forerunner of what nowadays is known as the CA Annual.

The Second World War brought the activities of the Association to a halt. However in 1947 the organisation of pilgrimage resumed with the first to Lourdes in that year. The Catholic Association was responsible for organising the HCPT pilgrimage at Easter until that pilgrimage separated to make its own arrangements. A similar situation arose when the pilgrimage of the burgeoning diocese of Arundel and Brighton was removed from the Catholic Association by the Bishop, Michael Bowen. That Diocese now has a very successful pilgrimage to Lourdes in July each year. A list of previous officials is available on their website. The charity now organises an annual pilgrimage to Lourdes.

How the Pilgrimage Works

The CA is a 'Company Limited by Guarantee and not having a Share Capital.' It is also a Registered Charity (number 1071120). The Catholic Association is a company and the Directors are registered as such, although the Directors refer to themselves as Trustees.

Catholic Association Trust

The Trustees fulfill the usual role of Trustees, which is to guard the funds.

The Trustees appoint Pilgrimage Officers (the heads of the different service sections including doctors, nurses, brancardiers, handmaids, youth group etc.). The Pilgrimage Officers, together with the Diocesan Directors, make up the Pilgrimage Management Committee (PMC). Trustees are permitted to attend meetings of the PMC but, apart from two or three who have specific functions there, it is generally thought that the PMC should be allowed to manage itself. There is some overlap of membership and responsibilities between the Trustees, the PMC, and the Hospitalité Council.

Pilgrimage Management Committee

The Trustees appoint Pilgrimage Officers (the heads of the different service sections including doctors, nurses, handmaids, youth group etc.). The Pilgrimage Officers, together with the Diocesan Directors, make up the Pilgrimage Management Committee (PMC). Trustees are permitted to attend meetings of the PMC but, apart from two or three who have specific functions there, the PMC should be allowed to manage itself. There is some overlap of membership and responsibilities between the Trustees, the PMC, and the Hospitalité Council. The PMC is responsible for the actual organisation and practicalities of the annual Lourdes pilgrimage.

As at November 2010, the membership of the PMC consists of:

- Rt Rev Paul Hendricks, (Auxiliary Bishop of Southwark) (Chairman)
- Mgr Bill Saunders (Pilgrimage Director)
- Steve Gill (Treasurer)
- Chris Thorpe (Secretary)
- Heads of Service (Currently, Matt Betts, Anna Jackson, Sue Woodford, Adam Farmer)
- Chris Buller (President Hospitalité)
- Tina Walker (Young Helpers' Group Leader)
- Fr Simon Blakesley (Chaplain to the Sick & Hospitalité)
- Judy Ball (Director of Music)
- Mike Carter ('Accueil pilgrims' bookings)
- A Director or Co-ordinator from each of the Diocesan and other participating groups (Stonyhurst College, Glanfield Children's Group & British Province of Carmelites)

Catholic Association Hospitalité

The Catholic Association Hospitalité of Our Lady of Lourdes - CA Hospitalité for short - exists to bind together the volunteer pilgrims, known in French as Hospitalier(e)s, who help in the service of all pilgrims - especially 'sick pilgrims' - during the Pilgrimage; doctors, nurses, handmaids (female helpers), brancardiers (male helpers), chaplains, and praying members. The Hospitalité is a religious sodality in the Catholic Church, with a strong social and spiritual element and it is affiliated to the Hospitalité Notre Dame de Lourdes (the central Hospitalité coordinating most volunteers in Lourdes throughout the year).

The CA Hospitalité is governed by a Council consisting of some ex-officio members who are Pilgrimage Officers (on the Pilgrimage Management Committee), and three members elected each for three years on a 'rolling' programme. The Council elects its own Officers, the President has a seat on the PMC, and the Council has power to co-opt members for a specific purpose. The Council is the driving force of the Hospitalité and looks after everything connected to the Sick Pilgrims.

The principal aims and objects of the CA Hospitalité are set out in the Constitution (and summarised above the application for membership) as follows:

a. To serve sick pilgrims going to Lourdes on the Catholic Association Pilgrimage and to help in the smooth running of religious and other activities involving sick pilgrims on that Pilgrimage under the direction of and in collaboration with the Pilgrimage Directors and Heads of Service.

b. To strengthen the bonds of fraternal life between its members and to help them maintain their obligations as Christians, their responsibilities in the Church and their devotion to Our Lady. This service consists especially of looking after the material needs of the sick pilgrims although the obligation of a member of the Hospitalité is not limited to material work. Members will be expected to help all pilgrims to benefit fully from the religious and social benefits of a pilgrimage to Lourdes.

Volunteer pilgrims may apply for membership of the Hospitalité on conclusion of their first pilgrimage. The Hospitalité Council may admit to the membership any class of person or individual who, in their opinion, renders suitable services to the sick. Following approval by the Hospitalité Council, applicants will be admitted to ordinary membership during their next pilgrimage to Lourdes, having made an Act of Consecration before the Patron or Chaplain. After working with the Pilgrimage for a further two years as members, helpers may apply for admission to full membership of the Hospitalité the following year. The Hospitalité Council may also invite 'Sick Pilgrims' to become full members of the Hospitalité who support the organization through their prayers.

It is worth remembering that members are encouraged to take the Spirit of Lourdes home with them and to promote the pilgrimage, in particular by recruiting other volunteers and by making known the facilities provided for Sick Pilgrims, both those who need to stay in an Accueil (house of welcome for the sick) and others who would be better served in a hotel.

As at October 2010 the CA Hospitalité Council consists of:

- Crispian Hollis, Bishop of Portsmouth (Patron)
- Chris Buller (President)
- Nimal Hemelge (Secretary)
- Richard Long-Fox (Treasurer)
- Fr Simon Blakesley (Chaplain)
- Dr Adam Farmer (Chief Medical Officer)
- Sue Woodford (Chief Nurse)
- Matt Betts (Chief Brancardier)
- Anna Jackson (Chief Handmaid)
- Tina Walker (Leader of the Young Helpers' Group)
- Andy Joyce (Elected Member 2008 - 2011)
- Vicki Gale (Elected Member 2010 - 2012)
- David Ball (Elected Member 2010 - 2013)

More information: CA Hospitalité Newsletter

The CA Hospitalité is also affiliated to the Association of British Lourdes Pilgrimage Hospitalités.

UK Hospitalité Events

- Each year the Catholic Association holds an AGM for all members.
- Every two years the Catholic Association runs a retreat at Walsingham.

Volunteering

The CA relies on volunteer helpers to work with the various assisted pilgrims (sick) who come to Lourdes each year. The CA divides their volunteers up in services (with a Head of Service for each of these):

- Brancardiers (male non medical helpers). The Chief Brancardier is their Head of Service.
- Handmaids (female non medical helpers). The Chief Handmaid is their Head of Service.
- Nurses. The Chief Nurse is their Head of Service.
- Doctors. The Chief Medical Officer is their Head of Service.

Each service works in teams to look after the assisted pilgrims in the Accueil and in hotels. The brancs and handmaids are in mixed teams; and the two heads of service work together in various areas of assisted pilgrim care.

Helpers Children's Programme (HCP)

The CA also organises their Helpers' Children's Programme (HCP), which offers a programme of activities for any helpers with children working on the Pilgrimage. HCP is open over various periods of the day and allows for helpers to be free to do a lot more work with the assisted pilgrims.

Music Group

The CA also searches for volunteers to be part of their music group, which plays at all the services and events during the Pilgrimage. The group look for singers and those who can play musical instruments. Volunteers must always bring their own instruments.

Pilgrimage Main Events

Whilst small details will change from year to year, like most of the large-scale pilgrimages to Lourdes, the Catholic Association pilgrimage includes certain recurring events:

- Pilgrimage Candle
- Opening Mass
- Prayer on the Prairie
- Opening Party

- Mass at the Grotto
- Blessed Sacrament Procession
- Marian Torchlight Procession
- Sacrament of Reconciliation
- Baths
- Outing
- Anointing of the Sick
- Hospitalite Service
- Children's Mass
- Stations of the Cross
- Pilgrimage Photos
- Diocesan Events
- Passage through the Grotto
- Accueil Party
- Going Forth Mass

Health & Safety

Like all pilgrimages the CA has an extensive Health & Safety Policy.

Travel

The Catholic Association, for a number of years, has appointed Tangney Tours as their official travel agent, although a number of pilgrims travel independently.. Most of the Pilgrimage travels from Stansted airport, but many also travel by train from St Pancras and other airports like Manchester.

Accommodation

The Catholic Association tends to stay at hotels to the St Joseph Gate side of Lourdes. These include:

A Hotel Beau Site

B Hotel St Clair

C Hotel Tara

D Hotel Mediterranee

E Hotel De La Grotte

F Hotel Miramont

G St Georges Hotel

H Hotel Moderne

I Notre Dame De France

J Hotel St Saveur

K Solitude Hotel

L Petit Languedoc

M Hotel Irlande

N Hotel Arcade

O Hotel Alba

P Hotel Christ Roi

R Hotel Gallia Londres

4 Religious Tourism Segments

Pilgrimages

A pilgrimage is a term primarily used in religion and spirituality of a long journey or search of great moral significance. Sometimes, it is a journey to a sacred place or shrine of importance to a person's beliefs and faith. Members of every religion participate in pilgrimages. A person who makes such a journey is called a pilgrim.

Secular and civic pilgrimages are also practiced, without regard for religion but rather of importance to a particular society. For example, many people throughout the world travel to the City of Washington in the United States for a pilgrimage to see the Declaration of Independence and the Constitution of the United States. British people often make pilgrimages to London for public appearances of the monarch of the United Kingdom.

Pilgrimages were first made to sites connected with the life, birth and crucifixion of Jesus. Surviving descriptions of Christian pilgrimages to the Holy Land date from the 4th century, when pilgrimage was encouraged by church fathers like Saint Jerome. Pilgrimages also began to be made to Rome and other sites associated with the Apostles, Saints and Christian martyrs, as well as to places where there have been alleged apparitions of the Virgin Mary.

The second largest single pilgrimage in the history of Christendom was to the Funeral of Pope John Paul II after his death on April 2, 2005. An estimated four million people traveled to Vatican City, in addition to the almost three million people already living in Rome, to see the body of Pope John Paul II lie in state.

World Youth Day is a major Catholic Pilgrimage, specifically for people aged 16-35. It is held internationally every 2-3 years. In 2005, young Roman Catholics visited Cologne, Germany. In 1995, the largest gathering of all time was to World Youth Day in Manila, Philippines, where four million people from all over the world attended.

Missionary Travel

Wilcox World Travel and Tours / American Express has been working with missionaries, both short term and long term, for 46 years. We are one of the few agencies in the United States able to offer missionary rates, and we have the experience to help plan your trip and avoid costly mistakes. Missionary travel has been at the core of Wilcox World Travel and Tours/American Express Travel since its inception in 1953.

Air travel has made the ends of the earth nearer. Wilcox World Travel and Tours/American Express is your partner for church travel, medical mission, or world missions. One of the few agencies in American authorized to offer missionary rates, we work closely with you to determine your best options.

Do you need to arrive on a certain day? Travel with excess baggage? Need a layover included in the price? Concerned about possible change fees? After a consultation with one of our agents, we can offer you the best options and value for your missionary travel. Our keen attention to detail and decades of experience will help you and your team sort through all of the details for the best price, itinerary, and terms.

If you are a missionary traveling to Asia, Europe, South or Central America, Africa or Oceania, you will be looking to find the least expensive way to reach your destination. As published airfare can be very expensive for most people, you should consider consolidator airfare to help keep the cost of travel down.

By using our consolidator flights, you can save up to 60% off of conventional published airfare. It's fast and easy to find prices and then book your flights using our consolidator database. If you compare our prices to the large travel sites, you will find that many times our prices are less the half of theirs.

If you're involved in or interested in mission work around the world, OSCAR is an important reference web site that has useful information, advice and resources. This site has listings for job opportunities and mission events, there are also news articles, and an area reserved with resources for those people that wish to be involved in supporting world missions.

If you are planning a missionary trip to Mexico, the GoMissionsToMexico.com web portal can provide you with the opportunity to see and experience another culture up close. You'll be immersed in the culture, language and people of Mexico all while being provided with a clean, safe, ministry base for your group to stay at while serving on your short term missions trip to Mexico.

If you are not sure about where you wish to go for your next mission, you may wish to consult the Christian Mission Trips search engine. At the time of this writing, they had mission opportunities with over 90 organizations that include over 1,300 short term mission trips. This helpful site also has a community forum and articles for your enjoyment.

Another good resource for mission trips is Adventures In Missions, which is an interdenominational missions organization focusing on discipling. Here you can find trips for adult and family, college-age, teen and youth group missions.

If you are Premed or a medical student looking to experience a medical mission, the Mission Finder web site can help you find a mission where your talents can help the spiritual and medical needs of people around the globe.

Make sure to plan accordingly and have some specialized missionary travel insurance arranged in case of an emergency. This site has excellent explanations of their travel insurance plans which include not only individual plans but also group plans.

As with any type of travel, it's important to check the consular information sheets for your destination.

Finally, the U.S. passport services office will provide you with information on obtaining, replacing or changing a U.S. passport.

Leisure (fellowship) Vacations

If you're ready for a vacation, then you might consider embarking on a fellowship vacation- a trip that combines the best of rest, relaxation, and play with a Christian group or within a Christian setting. Fellowship vacation options feature everything from leisure travel to cruising to adventures trips. Fellowship vacation appeals to a range of Christian-individuals, couples, churches and groups, families, youth, young adults, and senior citizens. If you really want to get away, "put your feet up," and let go of all the worries and cares of life, then a Christian leisure vacation is for you.

Faith-based Cruising

Such trips are also known as fellowship cruising, and their primary purpose is often sharing faith and friendship. You not only enjoy the religious aspects with your group, but share in the many enjoyments of a cruise vacation.

Today there's more itinerary options and more varied activities than ever before. For instance there's specialty cruises designed to educate and entertain, by bringing along popular leaders and entertainers, as well as providing ample opportunities for networking.

Sometimes these cruises even raise money for worthwhile causes through donations, like on Royal Caribbean's "Cruise with a Cause," a five-day cruise to the Bahamas featuring an all-star lineup of Christian pop stars and inspirational speakers. There's a "Girl's Get-a-Way Cruise," Christian Family Cruises, Singles Cruises, Retreat Cruise and Reunion Cruises, offering Christian music, Christian TV channels, family movies, religious-themed shore excursions, clean comedy, inspirational lectures and speakers and Pilgrimages can even be arranged.

Other Cruise lines like Windstar and Clipper make every aspect of the cruise ship fully kosher for the Jewish faith-based cruise community. Holland America Line will donate a certain amount of money per group cabin booked toward the chartering company's designated charitable cause. This cause can be anything from a local church to a national ministry effort.

Cruising with a Purpose is the catch phrase applied to religious cruising today as the experience really brings believers together, whether it is for learning, preaching or enjoying Christian or spiritual music together with your group. Social exchange and enrichment programs while on a cruise vacation is quite appealing to many different types of people. It's one of the most popular vacation options, with more and more faith-based groups of all religions discovering the convenience of organizing a group cruise vacation for their families, their friends and their fellow parishioners.

You can enjoy a religious-based cruise to anywhere in the world that appeals to you; the Caribbean, Hawaii and the South Pacific, a Transatlantic crossing, South America, Bermuda, the Mediterranean or Scandinavia/ Russia, just to name a few. If you prefer, you can stay closer to home and do an Alaska cruise or a New England/Canada itinerary.

If you are considering bringing your kids, cruising is great for children! Cruising offers a wonderful opportunity for the entire family to connect while sharing a unique faith-based experience.

Fundraising

Faith-based cruises also offer religious groups the perfect setting for a fundraiser. Everything is done for you; there are wonderful restaurants open at all hours and a lot of onboard flexibility. Out at sea, you can combine business and fun, while sailing to some of the most beautiful destinations in the world. These cruises offer powerful fundraising tool, where you can expect a big response.

A Group Cruise Retreat or Conference

There are many advantages to selecting a cruise ship for as your religious retreat or conference. The relaxed environment will encourage camaraderie among your religious group as you share an exciting travel experience.

Other advantages include multi-choice dining options, diverse menu selections and endless buffets. Additionally, because it is a self-contained environment with a variety of function rooms for private events, it is easier to get people to attend.

Our cruise specialists can help you with any questions you may have in organizing your faith-based group sailing. If you need assistance making arrangements for your religious or faith-based cruise, Call or Email Us and we'll help you select the perfect cruise package for you and your group.

Faith Based Cruise Programs

The acronym CRUISE provides a good foundational outline for launching a faith-based cruise program at your church or religious organization:

Contact a trusted cruise travel planner with specific Faith Based Cruise experience and inquire about initial information.

Review your cruise line options, the benefits of using that agency, cruise destination choices, itineraries, prices, etc.

Understand how a cruise theme, such as a biblical seminar cruise, Christian entertainment, etc., will affect your cruise.

Implement your chosen cruise theme into your travel information, your ministry and all cruise program offerings.

Sell, sell, sell your cruise to your church, religious group, members, community, etc..

Emphasize the enjoyment and experience of sharing faith, fun and fellowship; this will make the cruise memorable.

By doing the above, you will be off to a great start. Keep in mind that the most critical components in launching a successful faith-based cruise are finding the right travel specialist and agency and finding the right cruise line. Fortunately we have travel planners that specialize in this form of travel.

No matter what cruise you choose, though, you are sure to wow your members. Cruising remains one of tourism's most popular forms of travel today, with almost 20 percent of Americans having already taken a cruise, and such a trip will attract many in your faith community.

And, possibly best of all, it's a kind of vacation for any age group. Grandparents, parents, young adults and children can all come along. Offer your group a water-filled, spiritual vacation getaway. Call us today or email us to start planning your next faith based cruise.

Crusades, Conventions and Rallies

The Crusades were a series of religiously sanctioned military campaigns, waged by much of Roman Catholic Europe, particularly the Franks of France and the Holy Roman Empire. The specific crusades to restore Christian control of the Holy Land were fought over a period of nearly 200 years, between 1095 and 1291. Other campaigns in Spain and Eastern Europe continued into the 15th century. The Crusades were fought mainly by Roman Catholic forces (taking place after the East-West Schism and mostly before the Protestant Reformation) against Muslims who had occupied the near east since the time of the Rashidun Caliphate, although campaigns were also waged against pagan Slavs, pagan Balts, Jews, Russian and Greek Orthodox Christians, Mongols, Cathars, Hussites, Waldensians, Old Prussians, and political enemies of the various popes. Orthodox Christians also took part in fighting against Islamic forces in some Crusades. Crusaders took vows and were granted a plenary indulgence.

The Crusades originally had the goal of recapturing Jerusalem and the Holy Land from Muslim rule and their campaigns were launched in response to a call from the Christian Byzantine Empire for help against the expansion of the Muslim Seljuk Turks into Anatolia. The term is also used to describe contemporaneous and subsequent campaigns conducted through to the 16th century in territories outside the Levant usually against pagans, heretics, and peoples under the ban of excommunication for a mixture of religious, economic, and political reasons. Rivalries among both Christian and Muslim powers led also to alliances between religious factions against their opponents, such as the Christian alliance with the Sultanate of Rûm during the Fifth Crusade.

The Crusades had far-reaching political, economic, and social impacts, some of which have lasted into contemporary times. Because of internal conflicts among Christian kingdoms and political powers, some of the crusade expeditions were diverted from their original aim, such as the Fourth Crusade, which resulted in the sack of Christian Constantinople and the partition of the Byzantine Empire between Venice and the Crusaders. The Sixth Crusade was the first crusade to set sail without the official blessing of the Pope. The Seventh, Eighth and Ninth Crusades resulted in Mamluk and Hafsid victories, as the Ninth Crusade marked the end of the Crusades in the Middle East.

A convention, in the sense of a meeting, is a gathering of individuals who meet at an arranged place and time in order to discuss or engage in some common interest. The most common conventions are based upon industry, profession, and fandom. Trade conventions typically focus on a particular industry or industry segment, and feature keynote speakers, vendor displays, and other information and activities of interest to the event organizers and attendees. Professional conventions focus on issues of concern to the profession and advancements in the profession. Such conventions are generally organized by societies dedicated to promotion of the topic of interest. Fan conventions usually feature displays, shows, and sales based on pop culture and guest celebrities. Science fiction conventions traditionally partake of the nature of both professional conventions and fan conventions, with the balance varying from one to another. Conventions also exist for various hobbies, such as gaming or model railroads.

Conventions are often planned and coordinated, often in exacting detail, by professional meeting and convention planners, either by staff of the convention's hosting company or by outside specialists. Most large cities will have a convention center dedicated to hosting such events. The term MICE - meetings Incentives Conventions and Exhibitions - is widely used in Asia as a description of the industry. The Convention ("C") is one of the most dynamic elements in the M.I.C.E. segment. The industry is generally regulated under the tourism sector.

In the technical sense, a convention is a meeting of delegates or representatives. The 1947 Newfoundland National Convention is a classic example of a state-sponsored political convention. More often, organizations made up of smaller units, chapters, or lodges, such as labor unions, honorary societies, and fraternities and sororities, meet as a whole in convention by sending delegates of the units to deliberate on the organization's common issues. This also applies to a political convention, though in modern times the common issues are limited to selecting a party candidate or party chairman. In this technical sense, a congress, when it consists of representatives, is a convention. The British House of Commons is a convention, as are most other houses of a modern representative legislature. The National Convention or just "Convention" in France comprised the constitutional and legislative assembly which sat from September 20, 1792 to October 26, 1795.

Many sovereign states have provisions for conventions besides their permanent legislature. The Constitution of the United States of America has a provision for the calling of a constitutional convention, whereby delegates of the states are summoned to a special meeting to amend or draft the constitution. This process has never occurred, save for the original drafting of the constitution, although it almost happened in several cases. The US Constitution also has provisions for constitutional amendments to be approved by state conventions of the people. This occurred to ratify the original constitution and to adopt the twenty-first amendment, which ended prohibition.

Con is a common abbreviation for convention, and some conventions (such as DEF CON and Gen Con) use it in their names.

A demonstration or street protest is action by a mass group or collection of groups of people in favor of a political or other cause; it normally consists of walking in a mass march formation and either beginning with or meeting at a designated endpoint, or rally, to hear speakers.

Actions such as blockades and sit-ins may also be referred to as demonstrations. Demonstrations can be nonviolent or violent (usually referred to by participants as "militant"), or can begin as nonviolent and turn violent dependent on circumstances. Usually, if a demonstration begins as or becomes violent, riot police or other forms of law enforcement become involved in order to try to prevent the protest from spreading and turning into a riot.

For example- The protesters, mostly ethnic Indians, were against the introduction of the Malay language novel 'Interlok' in the senior school curriculum.

A section of the minority community, including the Malaysian Indian Congress (MIC) -- the country's largest ethnic Indian political party, believes the book contains offensive words like 'pariah' which they say connotes a caste system that they claim does not exist in this country.

The protest came despite the government's assurance that the book would be introduced in the curriculum only after amendments were made.

Meanwhile, Prime Minister Najib Tun Razak said the protesters wanted to grab media attention.

"We do not want to be hard on them but they are hoping that the police will use violence against them and when that happens, it will be good stuff for the international media to exploit. Their intention is to paint a bad image for the country," Najib said.

The group can always submit their memorandum or meet him to settle any problem without resorting to illegal demonstration, he added.

City police chief, Deputy Commissioner Zulkifli Abdullah, had earlier said the 109 persons were held to maintain order and security within the city.

The arrested people were in the age group of 18-66 and eight of the group's leaders are believed to be among them.

Zulkifli said that those who participated in today's "illegal" gathering to protest against the novel were an isolated group.

"It does not speak for the whole Indian community as we have been approached by about 13 Indian NGOs supporting our stance against the illegal gatherings," he said.

The arrests were made as the protesters walked from the Rennaisance Hotel to the Kuala Lumpur City Centre (KLCC) outside the iconic Petronas Twin Towers, the tallest building in the world a few years ago.

Though the main group of protesters was stopped by the police near the hotel before they could march to the Petronas twin towers, a section managed to evade police to make their way to the protest venue.

Retreats

The meaning of a spiritual retreat can be different for the many variegated religious communities that participate in them around the world. Spiritual Retreats are an integral part of many Buddhist, Christian and Sufi (Islamic) groups. In Buddhism, retreats are seen by some as integral for reconnection to one's self. Retreats are also popular in many Christian churches, dating back to the beginning of Christianity itself, and popularised in the Middle Ages by St. Ignatius of Loyola. In Christianity, retreats find their Biblical grounding in mirroring Christ's forty days in the desert, an understanding shared by many within Protestantism, Roman Catholicism and Orthodox Christianity. Meditative retreats are an important practice in Sufism, the mystical path of Islam. The Sufi teacher Ibn Arabi's book Journey to the Lord of Power (Risalat al-Anwar) is a guide to the inner journey that was published over 700 years ago.

Buddhism

A retreat can either be a time of solitude or a community experience. Some retreats are held in silence, and on others there may be a great deal of conversation, depending on the understanding and accepted practices of the host facility and/or the participant(s). Retreats are often conducted at rural or remote locations, either privately, or at a retreat centre such as a monastery. Some retreats for advanced practitioners may be undertaken in darkness, a form of retreat that is common as an advanced Dzogchen practice in the Nyingma school of Tibetan Buddhism.

Spiritual retreats allow time for reflection, prayer, or meditation. They are considered essential in Buddhism, having been a common practice since the Vassa, or rainy season retreat, was established by the founder of Buddhism, Gotama Buddha. In Zen Buddhism retreats are known as sesshin.

Christianity

The Christian retreat can be defined in the most simplest of terms as a definite time (from a few hours in length to a month) spent away from one's normal life for the purpose of reconnecting, usually in prayer, with God. Although the practice of leaving one's everyday life to connect on a deeper level with God, be that in the desert (as with the Desert Fathers), or in a monastery, is as old as Christianity itself, the practice of spending a specific time away with God is a more modern phenomenon, dating from the 1520s and St. Ignatius of Loyola's composition of the Spiritual Exercises.

Roman Catholicism

The Retreat was popularised in Roman Catholicism by the Society of Jesus (Jesuits), whose founder, St. Ignatius of Loyola, as a layman began, in the 1520s, directing others in making (participating in) the exercises. The Spiritual Exercises were, in full, a series of four 'weeks'. During each week, the retreatant reflects and prays upon a specific topic; the topic of the First Week is God's love and humanity's sinfulness in the first week; the topic of the Second Week is Jesus' early life and Ministry; the topic of the Third Week is Jesus' Passion and Death; and the topic of the Fourth Week is Jesus' Resurrection. In Ignatius' early days of directing the exercises, he would, so as to keep the retreat to its bare essentials, usually lead a particular individual or group of people, in the first week, ending with a General Confession. Another form the Exercises came in, which became known as the nineteenth "Observation", 'allowed continuing one's ordinary occupations with the proviso of setting aside a few hours a day for this special purpose.' Hence, the retreat, as it was popularised by St. Ignatius, came in many forms, though was singular in purpose, that is, to come closer to God through prayer.

The theological rooting of all retreats in the story of Jesus' forty days in the desert is illustrated by Johann Baptist Metz in his book 'Poverty of Spirit', in which he writes, 'becoming human involves more than conception and birth. It is a mandate and a mission, a command and a decision.' He goes on to write that '(the temptation in the desert is) the biblical way of presenting the spiritual process of God's assumption of humanity.' So, in the same way that Christ had to overcome temptations on his 'poverty' as a simple human being, so too we must overcome the same temptations, though this time, in us asserting ourself as God, and denying the reality of the God of Abraham and Isaac. The only path to greater authenticity in human life is connection with God, as Metz writes: 'prayer is the ultimate realisation of humanity.' Hence, it is in retreats that one seeks to reconnect and deepen one's prayer life.

Sufi Retreats or Spiritual Khalwa

The literal meaning of khalwa is seclusion or retreat, but it has a different connotation in Sufi terminology: It is the act of total self-abondonment in desire for the Divine Presence. In complete seclusion, the Sufi continuously repeats the name of God as a highest form of dhikr (remembrance of God meditation). In his book, Journey to the Lord of

Power, Muhiyid-Did ibn Arabi (1165-1240 A.D.) discussed the stages through which the Sufi passes in his khalwa.

Ibn Arabi suggested: "The Sufi should shut his door against the world for forty days and occupy himself with remembrance of Allah, that is to keep repeating, "Allah, Allah..." Then, "Almighty God will spread before him the degrees of the kingdom as a test. First, He will discover the secrets of the mineral world. If he occupies himself with dthikr, He (God) will unveil to the secrets of the vegetable world, then the secrets of the animal world, then the infusion of the world of life-force into lives, then the "surface sign" (the light of the Divine Names, according to Abdul-Karim al-Jeeli, the book's translator), then the degrees of speculative sciences, then the world of formation and adornment and beauty, then the degrees of the qutb (the soul or pivot of the universe-see #16) (59) Then he will be given the divine wisdom and the power of symbols and authority over the veil and the unveiling. The degree of the Divine Presence is made clear to him, the garden (of Eden) and Hell are revealed to him, then the original forms of the son of Adam, the Throne of Mercy. If it is appropriate, he will know his destination. Then he will reveal to him the Pen, the First Intellect (as it is called by Sufi philosophers), then the Mover of the Pen, the right hand of the Truth. (The "Truth" as defined by al-Jeeli is that by which everything is created, none other than God most High.) (60)

The practice of khalwah is regularly followed by the Sufis, with the permission and the supervision of a Sufi authority.

The Sufis base the assigning of forty days of khalwa period on the forty days Allah had appointed for Musa (Moses) as a fasting period before speaking to him, as mentioned in different chapters in the Qur'an. One of them is from surat al-Baqarah.

Khalwa is still practiced today amongst authorized Sheikhs, such as Mawlana Sheikh Nazim Al-Haqqani, Lefka, Cyprus.

Monastery Visits and Guest-stays

Monastery (plural: monasteries) denotes the building, or complex of buildings, that houses a room reserved for prayer (e.g. an oratory) as well as the domestic quarters and workplace(s) of monastics, whether monks or nuns, and whether living in community or alone (hermits).

The earliest extant use of the term monast?rion is by the 1st century AD Jewish philosopher Philo (On The Contemplative Life, ch. III).

Monasteries may vary greatly in size - a small dwelling accommodating only a hermit, or in the case of communities anything from a single building housing only a one senior and two or three junior monks or nuns, to vast complexes and estates housing tens or hundreds.

In English usage, the term "monastery" is generally used to denote the buildings of a community of monks. The name convent tends to be used (inaccurately) for the buildings accommodating female monastics (nuns). (The term "nunnery" for the latter is outmoded and considered offensive). It may also be used to reflect the Latin usage for houses of friars, more commonly called a friary, or for communities of teaching or nursing Religious Sisters. Various religions may use these terms in more specific ways.

In most religions the life inside monasteries is governed by community rules that stipulates the sex of the inhabitants and requires them to remain celibate and own little or no personal property. The degree to which life inside a particular monastery is socially separate from the surrounding populace can also vary widely; some religious traditions mandate isolation for purposes of contemplation removed from the everyday world, in which case members of the monastic community may spend most of their time isolated even from each other. Others focus on interacting with the local communities to provide services, such as teaching, medical care, or evangelism. Some monastic communities are only occupied seasonally, depending both on the traditions involved and the local weather, and people may be part of a monastic community for periods ranging from a few days at a time to almost an entire lifetime.

The life within the walls of a monastery may be supported in several ways: by manufacturing and selling goods, often agricultural products such as cheese, wine, beer, liquor, and jellies; by donations or alms; by rental or investment incomes; and by funds from other organizations within the religion, which in the past formed the traditional support of monasteries. However, today Christian monastics have updated and adapted themselves to modern society by offering computer services, accounting services, and management as well as modern hospital administration in addition to running schools, colleges and universities.

There were many buildings in a monastery, including a: church, chapter house, dormitory, infirmary, cloister, smithy, stable, balneary and pigsties. Another building which might be in a monastery is a school.

For a discussion of the history and development of the life inside hermit cottages see monasticism and abbey.

Monastery Stays is a worldwide web based booking service for monastery and convent accommodation in Italy. Commenced in 2005 and launched and operated since 2006 by a group of four friends all who had the experience of visiting Italy and enjoyed the experience at various depths of staying in monastery and convent guest houses.

Monastery and convent accommodation in Italy is available for all to enjoy. Visiting a monastery may begin as a stopover, but one cannot ignore the presence of peace in these places and its associated 'wellness'. It is a place for restoration of the body with a good nights sleep but also for the inner self, an experience that you will not find in Europe's best Resort, Spa or Wellness Centre!

The team at Monastery Stays solved the problems they personally encountered in dealing with monastery and convent accommodation in Italy - where are they... what is the quality of accommodation... is there availability when I want to travel... will I have an ensuite or a private bathroom... is it possible to travel with a family... what are the up to date prices... what are the facilities... what is the curfew... is there a lift for disabled access... is there parking on site... how do I book a room... they only speak Italian and I do not.... how do I know that I will have a reservation on arrival... how will I receive a confirmation... how do I find the monastery once booked... how do I get from the airport in Rome to the monastery...etc?

So was born Monastery Stays to centralise into one place answering all these questions and take the difficulties out of making a reservation at monastery and convent accommodation in Italy.

The leadership team involved with Monastery Stays - John Clayton, a practising marketing consultant, Angela Hoban, lawyer and her husband David Hoban, hospitality industry consultant and Mark Logan, who until 2006 spent many years in the City of London's financial and technology sector. All have been friends and work colleagues in their professional lives for 10 to 20 years.

Faith-based Camps

"Some faith-based camps will be stronger on faith, while others are designed to be an alternative to broken homes," says Derrick Mueller, the national director of Christian Camping International in Canada. "How that faith is actualized will be different for each camp."

Some Christian camps like Camp Hyanto, a coed residential camp in Gananoque, offer a more structured faith-based experience, with morning worship and chapel sessions each day. Others, like Fraser Lake Camp, take campers on a less traditional Christian journey, bringing the Bible's messages to life through ongoing skits rather than structured readings and teachings.

"We aim to teach the campers without them realizing it's a lesson," says Eric Musselman, director of Fraser Lake Camp. "We don't have a lot of specific teaching time. Instead, we like to have all aspects of the camp operate within a Christian context." The camp begins and ends with a chapel session, but throughout the week the children watch educational skits.

Fraser Lake Camp, a non-denominational Christian camp in Bancroft, reduces social barriers by eliminating the need for money at camp. "We don't have a camp store-we don't want to be in a situation where one child has $100 to spend for the week, while another has just $10," says Musselman. "We take away factors that would label the kids."

For some children, going to one of Ontario's Christian kids camps allows them and others to see who they really are. "Troubled kids that find their way to a faith-based camp experience love as opposed to programs," says Mueller. "The atmosphere of love develops a love of who you are."

Operated by the Anglican Church of Canada, Camp Hyanto accepts campers of all faiths. "We allow kids who are struggling that a lot of other camps can't accommodate. We offer guidance and love, and we show them that they are special," says Laura Morrison, the camp's director. "We want to share the love that God gives us."

Religious Tourist Attractions

A tourist attraction is a place of interest where tourists visit, typically for its inherent or exhibited cultural value, historical significance, natural or built beauty, or amusement opportunities. Some examples include historical places, monuments, zoos, aquaria, museums and art galleries, botanical gardens, buildings and structures (e.g., castles, libraries, former prisons, skyscrapers, bridges), national parks and forests, theme parks and carnivals, living history museums, ethnic enclave communities, historic trains and cultural events. Many tourist attractions are also landmarks.

Tourist attractions are also created to capitalise on legends such as a supposed UFO crash site near Roswell, New Mexico and the alleged Loch Ness monster sightings in Scotland. Ghost sightings also make tourist attractions. Ethnic communities may become tourist attractions, such as Chinatowns in the United States and the black British neighborhood of Brixton in London, England.

In the US, owners and marketers of attractions advertise tourist attractions on billboards along the side of highways and roadways, especially in remote areas. Tourist attractions often provide free promotional brochures and flyers in information centres, fast food restaurants, hotel and motel rooms or lobbies, and rest areas. While some tourist attractions provide visitors a memorable experience for a reasonable admission charge or even for free, others can have a tendency to be of low quality and to overprice their goods and services (such as admission, food, and souvenirs) in order to profit from tourists excessively. Such places are commonly known as tourist traps.

5 Sikh Religious Tourism Spots

There are many beautiful Gurdwaras around the world. The Harmandir Sahib in Amritsar, India - also known as the Golden Temple - is the most visited Gurdwara in the world. There are no idols, statues, or religious pictures in a gurdwara, but the essential feature of a gurdwara is the presiding presence of the holy book, the Guru Granth Sahib. The Sikhs hold high respect for the commandments laid down in the Guru Granth Sahib.

A gurdwara has a darbar (main) hall, a free community kitchen langar, and other facilities. A gurdwara is identified from a far away place by nishan sahib. Many of the gurdwaras in Punjab have a pool (sarovar) for bathing in. The Sikh marriage, called Anand Karaj is performed inside gurdwara. The first gurdwara was built in Kartarpur, Pakistan Kartarpur in the year 1521 by the first Sikh guru, Guru Nanak Dev.

Gurdwaras are open to everyone regardless of faith. Visitors remove their shoes, wash their hands and cover their head with a cloth before entering the darbar sahib. Visitors are also forbidden to go into the gurdwara while they are inebriated or possess alcohol, cigarettes or any intoxicating substances. They may give some money for the upkeep of the gurdwara.

Devotees will sit cross-legged on the floor. On entering the hall, devotees walk slowly and respectfully to the main throne (called the takht) on which the Guru Granth Sahib rests. Devotees then stand before the holy scriptures, often say a silent prayer, then bow.

Many gurdwaras are designed to seat men on one side and women on the other, although designs vary and the divide is far from mandatory.

Worshippers are offered kara parshad (sweet flour and oil based food offered as prashad) in the worship hall, which is usually given into cupped hands by a sewadar (volunteer).

Langar communal vegetarian food made by volunteers and funded by the worshippers themselves. There is no meat served in the langar hall so that vegetarians will not be offended by or restricted by the food available. Langar is always served to the Sangat (the langar congregation) sitting on the ground, as equality amongst all members of the community is a tenet of Sikhism.

Many Gurdwaras also have other facilities for Sikhs to learn more about their religion, such as libraries, complexes for courses in Punjabi and Sikhism, meeting rooms, and room-and-board accommodation for those who need it (serais).

ll religions have temples where people can gather together to contemplate on God and pray. The Sikh temple is called a Gurdwara. The word 'Gurdwara' means 'Gateway to the Guru'. In Sikhism ones personal dedication to living a good life is important but another important aspect of Sikhism is the Sangat (congregation). Not only should one meditate on God on their individual level but also on a corporate level. There are thousands of Gurdwaras throughout Punjab and the rest of the world. They serve as community centers for the Sikh's. There are no restrictions on who may enter a Gurdwara for prayer. People of all religions are welcome to attend. Another common feature of all Gurdwaras around the world is Langer, the free community kitchen. Here food is served to all people who sit together to enjoy a communal meal. It is a symbol of the Sikh belief in a non-sexist, non-racist society where all people of all casts, religions are equal and can share a common meal in the true spirit of unity.

Many of the Gurdwaras in Punjab have a pool (sarovar) for bathing in. In Sikhism one can bath in these pools if they wish, but they should be pure inside in order to accomplish anything. For the water may clean you on the outside, but it cannot clean you on the inside if your heart is not pure. Unlike some religions, pilgrimages is not a part of Sikhism. Sikhs may visit any Gurdwara as they are all considered equal because in all the living Guru, Sri Guru Granth Sahib (the Sikh Holy Scriptures), is installed as the spiritual head of the Sikh religion.

Akal Takht

The Akal Takht of the Timeless One or Seat (Throne) of God. It is one of the five seats of temporal physical religious authority of the Sikhs.

Akal means The Timeless One - another term for God. Takht means 'seat' or 'throne' in Persian. Akal Takht is located in the Harmandir Sahib complex in Amritsar, Punjab, and faces the Darshani Deohri.

The Akal Takht was begun by the sixth Sikh Guru, Guru Har Gobind as a symbol for political sovereignty of Sikhs. It stood as a symbol of political and military resistance against the tyranny and cruelity of the rulers the 17th and 18th century. In the 18th century, Ahmed Shah Abdali led a series of attacks on the Akal Takht and Harmandir Sahib.

On June 4, 1984, the Akal Takht building was destroyed during Operation Bluestar launched by the Indian Army on controversial orders of Prime Minister Indira Gandhi to evict a group of armed Sikhs that had fortified the buildings as they had received inside information that the Indian Army was going to attack Harimandir Sahib on orders of the Prime Minister.

The Akal Takhat was founded by Guru Hargobind on June 15, 1606 (now celebrated on 2 July) and was established as the place from which the spiritual and temporal concerns of the Sikh community could be acted upon.

It stood as a symbol of political bulwark against the Mughal Emperors in the 17th and 18th century. Various attacks on the Akal Takhat and Harimandir Sahib have been led in past by Ahmed Shah Abdali and Massa Rangar in the 18 century. On June 4, 1984, the Indian Army did more than just damage the outer facade of the Akal Takhat, they destroyed the sancitity of the Akal Takht with tanks and reduced it to rubble, while attempting to take out Sikh militants in a controversial military operation known as Operation Bluestar.

It is the most supreme of all the Takhats. There are four other takhats established by the panth (community) during the last century:

- Keshgarh Sahib (Anandpur)
- Patna Sahib
- Hazur Sahib
- Damdama Sahib

Often, Amritsar is considered a takht.

The Jathedar of the Akal Takhat is the highest spokesperson of the Sikh Panth and is meant to be a spiritual leader without control or influence from any outside, politically motivated sources.

Khande-Bate-Dee-Pahul or the initiation with the sword, initiated by Guru Gobind Singh, continues to be routinely performed at the Akal Takht. Hari Singh Nalwa, a General under Maharaja Ranjit Singh the leader of the Sikh Kingdom, wished to make the Akal Takht resplendent with gold and had donated a part of his wealth for this purpose.

On the original plot of land of the Akal Takhat, there only existed a high mound of earth across a wide open space, where Guru Hargobind as a child used to play. The Gurus original Takhat is said to have been a simple platform, 3.5 metres high, on which the Guru would sit like a king at court, surrounded by insignia of royalty such as the parasol and the flywhisk, and perform kingly tasks of receiving petitions and administrating justice. Today's Akal Takhat is a large 5-storey modern structure (3 storeys were added by Maharaja Ranjit Singh) with inlaid marble and a gold-leafed dome, that does not convey the design of Guru Hargobind's simple Takht or plinth. However, recent restoration work has uncovered a layer of lime plaster, with painted decoration, that may have been part of the original Takhat. That plinth was far higher than the plinth of the Harimandir; yet the absence of a superstructure kept the original Akal Takhat at a level lower than the shrine.

The elaboration of the structure on marble pillars, as a semi-circular platform with an open view to the courtyard, reminiscent of an air-house, must have grown from the use to which the Durbar hall was put.

The gilding of the ceiling with ornamentations like those in the interior of the Hari Mandir is perhaps later than in the holy of holies. The wall paintings apparently belong to a later period, as there are panels showing Europeans.

The total effect of the Akal Takhat and the open courtyard, in front of the Darshani Deori and the viewa of the Amritsar beyond, is of a unique and noble structure remenisant of the of the piazza Saint Marco in Venice where the Doge's Palace faces the Grand Canal.

Gurdwara Baba Atal

Many of the millions of pilgrims that visit the Harimandir Sahib every year do not realise that one of Amritsar's finest architectural marvels and one of the Sikh religions most poignant places of worship is just a short walk from the famous Harimandir Sahib

Built some two centuries ago, the Baba Atal Gurdwara is a touching commemoration of the young life of Baba Atal Rai, the son of Guru

Hargobind. Its nine storeys echo his nine years of life before his death in 1628.

Gurdwara Sri Tarn Taran Sahib

Gurdwara Sri Tarn Taran Sahib is a Gurdwara established by the fifth guru, Guru Arjan Dev. It is situated in the city of Tarn Taran Sahib. It has the distinction of having the largest sarovar (Water pond) of all the gurudwaras. Also it is famous for the month gathering of pilgrims on day of Amavas (No moon night). It is near Harmandir Sahib, Amritsar.

Golden Temple

The Golden Temple, or Harmandir Sahib, in Amritsar in Punjab is famous not only for its religious relevance but also for its architecture--a mix of Hindu and Muslim designs especially prominent in its golden dome. Constructed in the 14th century, it is one of India's most popular religious spots. Considered one of the most sacred sites for the Sikh religion, the temple stands for the valor and honor of the Sikhs. Its four doorways on all sides symbolize the overall tolerance of Sikhism, which greets all four religions' worshippers--Hinduism, Islam, Christianity and Sikhism--with open arms. Completed in 1601, the temple's most holy part is the Hari Mandir or Divine Temple, which is the golden structure at the center of a large body of water. Its design uses white marble encrusted with precious stones and verses from the holy book of the Sikhs decorate the structure. The temple's staff also feeds 35,000 people a day for free in the dining hall, inviting everyone and turning away no one in this communal sharing of food. International visitors can secure accommodations in the complex for a minimal fee, and the complex sets aside 400 rooms to Sikh pilgrims free of charge.

Its name literally means Temple of God. The fourth guru of Sikhism, Guru Ram Das, excavated a tank in 1577 AD which subsequently became known as Amritsar (meaning "Pool of the Nectar of Immortality"), giving its name to the city that grew around it. In due course, a splendid Sikh edifice, Harmandir Sahib (meaning "the abode of God"), rose in the middle of this tank and became the supreme centre of Sikhism. Its sanctum came to house the Adi Granth comprising compositions of Sikh gurus and other saints considered to have Sikh values and philosophies, e.g., Baba Farid, and Kabir. The compilation of the Adi Granth was started by the fifth guru of Sikhism, Guru Arjan Dev.

Originally built in 1574, the site of the temple was surrounded by a small lake in a thin forest. The third of the six grand Mughals, Emperor Akbar, who visited the third Sikh guru, Guru Amar Das, in the neighbouring town of Goindval, was so impressed by the way of life in the town that he gave a jagir (the land and the revenues of several villages in the vicinity) to the guru's daughter Bhani as a gift on her marriage to Bhai Jetha, who later became the fourth Sikh guru, Guru Ram Das. Guru Ram Das enlarged the lake and built a small township around it. The town was named after Guru Ram Das as Guru Ka Chak', Chak Ram Das or Ram Das Pura.

During the leadership of the fifth guru, Guru Arjan Dev (1581-1606), the full-fledged Temple was built. In December 1588, the great Muslim Sufi saint of Lahore, Hazrat Mian Mir, who was a close friend of Guru Arjan Dev Ji, initiated the construction of the temple by laying the first foundation stone (December 1588 AD). A mason then straightened the stone but Guru Arjan Dev told him that, as he had undone the work just completed by the holy man, a disaster might come to the Harmandir Sahib. It was later attacked by the Mughals.

The temple was completed in 1604. Guru Arjan Dev, installed the Guru Granth Sahib in it and appointed Baba Buddha Ji as the first Granthi (reader) of it on August 1604. In the mid-18th century it was attacked by the Afghans, by one of Ahmed Shah Abdali's generals, Jahan Khan, and had to be substantially rebuilt in the 1760s. However, in response a Sikh Army was sent to hunt down the Afghan force. They were under orders to show no mercy and historical evidence suggests the Sikh Army was decisively victorious in the ensuing battle. Both forces met each other five miles outside Amritsar; Jahan Khan's army was destroyed. He himself was decapitated by commander Sardar Dayal Singh.

The temple is surrounded by a large lake, known as the Sarovar, which consists of Amrit ("holy water" or "immortal nectar"). There are four entrances to the temple, signifying the importance of acceptance and openness; ostensibly, this concept is reminiscent of the tent of the Old Testament patriarch Abraham, whose tent was open on all four sides in order to be able to welcome travelers from all directions. Inside the temple complex there are many shrines to past Sikh gurus, saints and martyrs (see map). There are three holy trees (bers), each signifying a historical event or Sikh saint. Inside the temple there are many memorial plaques that commemorate past Sikh historical events, saints, martyrs and includes commemorative inscriptions of all the Sikh soldiers who died fighting in World Wars I and II.

In 1988, after Operation Black Thunder, the government acquired a narrow peripheral strip of land (including buildings) in order to use their space as a security buffer. The acquisition process involved the displacement and relocation of a large number of residences and businesses. However, the project met with a strong resistance from both moderate and militant Sikh organisations and had to be abandoned following the murder of a senior government-employed engineer connected with the project. The project was revived only in 1993 by the Deputy Commissioner Karan Bir Singh Sidhu, who was also appointed as the project director of what became popularly known as the Galliara Project. He changed the concept of the periphery from that of a security belt to that of a second parikarma and created a serene landscape that was fully consistent with the ethereal beauty of the Harmandir Sahib. This was done in quiet consultation with the Shiromani Gurdwara Prabandhak Committee (SGPC). Present-day pilgrims can travel by foot in the Galliara; no vehicles are permitted.

In keeping with the rule observed at all Sikh temples (gurdwaras) worldwide, the Harmandir Sahib is open to all persons regardless of their religion, colour, creed, or sex. The only restrictions on the Harmandir Sahib's visitors concern their behavior when entering and while visiting:

- Maintaining the purity of the sacred space and of one's body while in it:
  - o Upon entering the premises, removing one's shoes (leaving them off for the duration of one's visit) and washing one's feet in the small pool of water provided;
  - o Not drinking alcohol, eating meat, or smoking cigarettes or other drugs while in the shrine
- Dressing appropriately:
  - o Wearing a head covering (a sign of respect) (the temple provides head scarves for visitors who have not brought a suitable covering);
  - o Not wearing shoes (see above).

First-time visitors are advised to begin their visit at the information office highlighted in the map and then proceed to the Central Sikh Museum near the main entrance and clock tower.

Much of the present decorative gilding and marblework dates from the early 19th century. All the gold and exquisite marble work were conducted under the patronage of Hukam Singh Chimni and Emperor Ranjit Singh, Maharaja of the Sikh Empire of the Punjab. The Darshani Deorhi Arch stands at the beginning of the causeway to the Harmandir Sahib; it is 202 feet (62 m) high and 21 feet (6 m) in width. The gold plating on the Harmandir Sahib was begun by Emperor Ranjit Singh and was finished in 1830. The Sher-e-Punjab (Lion of the Punjab) was a major donor of wealth and materials for the shrine and is remembered with much affection by the Punjabi people in general and the Sikh community in particular. Maharaja Ranjit Singh also built two of the other most sacred temples in Sikhism. This was because Maharaja Ranjit Singh had a deep love for the tenth guru of Sikhism Guru Gobind Singh. The other two most sacred temples in Sikhism, which he built, are Takht Sri Patna Sahib (intiation or birth place of Guru Gobind Singh) and Takht Sri Hazur Sahib, the place of Guru Gobind Singh's Sikh ascension into heaven.

For the global Sikh pilgrim or international tourist visitor the fastest way to reach the Harmandir Sahib is by air travel. The holy city of Amritsar, where the Harmandir Sahib is located, has a rapidly expanding modern airport called Amritsar International Airport. The airport can be reached directly by the international traveller from most major cities of the world including London and Toronto. Moreover, there is a rapidly expanding array of international hotels in the holy city that can be booked for overnight stays. Lonely Planet Bluelist 2008 has voted the Harmandir Sahib as one of the world's best spiritual sites.

Baba Deep Singh

Baba Deep Singh (1682-1757) is revered among Sikhs as one of the most hallowed martyrs in Sikhism and as a highly religious person. He is remembered for his sacrifice and devotion to the teachings of the Sikh Gurus. He was the first jathedar(Head) of Damdami Taksal a 300 years old religious school of the Sikhs which was allegedly founded by last Sikh Guru, Guru Gobind Singh(although no research or historical document supports this was founded by Guru Gobind Singh). His name is also found as Deep Singh (without the "Baba" honorific) and Baba Deep Singh Ji.

Baba Deep Singh was born in 1682 to a Sikh couple, Bhagata(father) and Jioni(mother). He lived in the village of Pohuwind in the district of Amritsar. He went to Anandpur on the day of Vaisakhi in 1699, where he was baptized as Khalsa by Guru Gobind Singh. Deep Singh took Khande di Pahul or Amrit Sanchar (ceremonial initiation into Khalsa). As a youth, he spent considerable time in close companionship of Guru Gobind Singh. He started learning weaponry, riding and other martial skills. From Bhai Mani Singh, he began learning, reading and writing Gurmukhi and the interpretation of the Gurus' words. After spending two years at Anandpur, he returned to his village in 1702 and married and settled down. He was summoned by Guru Gobind Singh at Talwandi Sabo in 1705, where he helped Bhai Mani Singh in making copies of the Guru Granth Sahib. Before departing for Deccan, Guru Gobind Singh installed him as the caretaker of Gurdwara Damdama Sahib.

In 1709, Baba Deep Singh joined Banda Bahadur during the assaults on the towns of Sadhaura and Sirhind. In 1733, Nawab Kapur Singh appointed him a leader of an armed squad(jatha). On the Vaisakhi of 1748, at the meeting of the Sarbat Khalsa in Amritsar, the 65 jathas of the Dal Khalsa were reorganized into twelve Misls. Baba Deep Singh was entrusted with the Leadership of the Shaheedan Misl.

In April 1757, Ahmad Shah Durrani raided Northern India for the fourth time. While he was on his way back to Kabul from Delhi with precious booty and young men and women as captives, the Sikhs made a plan to relieve him of the valuables and free the captives. The squad of baba Deep Singh was deployed near Kurukshetra. His squad freed a large number of prisoners and raided Durrani's considerable treasury. On his arrival in Lahore, Durrani, embittered by his loss, ordered the demolition of the Harimandir Sahib. The shrine was blown up and the sacred pool filled with the entrails of slaughtered cows. Durrani assigned the Punjab region to his son, Prince Timur Shah, and left him a force of ten thousand men under General Jahan Khan.

Baba Deep Singh, aged 75-years old, felt that it was up to him to atone for the sin of having let the Afghans desecrate the shrine. He emerged from scholastic retirement (he had been making copies of the Guru Granth Sahib), and declared to a congregation at Damdama Sahib that he intended to rebuild the temple. Five hundred men came forward to go with him. Deep Singh offered prayers before starting for Amritsar: "May my head fall at the Darbar Sahib." As he went from hamlet to hamlet, many villagers joined him. By the time baba Deep Singh reached Tarn Taran Sahib, ten miles from Amritsar, over five thousand peasants armed with hatchets, swords, and spears accompanied him.

Takht Sri Damdama Sahib

The Takht Sri Darbar Sahib Damdama Sahib, one of the Five Takhts or Seat of Temporal Authority of Sikhism, Takht Sri Damdama Sahib is situated at Bathinda in Punjab, India and is the place where Guru Gobind Singh, the tenth Sikh Guru, prepared the full version of the Sikh Scriptures called Sri Guru Granth Sahib in 1705. The other four Takhts are the Akal Takht, Takht Sri Keshgarh Sahib, Takht Sri Patna Sahib and Takht Sri Hazur Sahib.

The Takht is located at the village of Talwandi Sabo, 28 km Southeast of Bathinda. Literally, Damdama means breathing place. Guru Gobind Singh stayed here after the Sikhs had fought several defensive battles. A combination of Mughals and hillmen besieged Anandpur Sahib on the orders of emperor Aurangzeb. Finally the stock of food in the town ran out. The Mughals promised safe passage to Punjab for the Sikhs if they would hand over the fortress of Anandpur. At first Guru Gobind tested their promise of safe passage by staging a test which the attackers failed miserably, later with promises written in the margins of the Muslims Holy Qur'an and some of the sacred writings of the Hindu elements of the army that had all but starved his small contingent of family and Sikhs and a personal promise of safety by Aurangzeb sent by an ajent of the Emperor who was fighting in the distant Deccan, the Guru was persuaded to agree to their offer, leaving Anandpur with his family and a small band of retainers. During the flight from Anandpur, when the Sikhs, having been promised safe passage to Punjab, Sahibzada Fateh Singh was, along with his elder brother Zorawar Singh, put under the care of his grandmother, Mata Gujari Kaur ji, Unfortunately in the confusion of the rain swollen Sarsa (normally little more than a creek) and an attack by Muslim pursuers, the Guru's two youngest sons and their Grandmother were separated from the main body of Sikhs. However, managing to get across they were befriended by one of the Guru's former cooks. Later betrayed and handed off by the authorities of the small village where they had been given sanctuary, they were handed over to agents of Wazir Khan and carted off to Sirhind and placed under arrest in the Khan's Thanda Burj (cold tower). While the Thanda Burj was built to capture the cool night breezes of air drawn over water channels in the areas hot summers, during the dead of winter the unheated burj offered no comfort for the Guru's mother and sons.

On 26 December 1705, Fateh Singh and his elder brother, Zorawar Singh were martyred at Sirhind. Fateh Singh is probably the youngest recorded martyr in history who knowingly laid down his life at the very tender age of 6 years. Sahibzada Fateh Singh and his older brother, Sahibzada Zorawar Singh are among the most hallowed martyrs in Sikhism.

The mind boggles to understand how children of such young age had the guts, courage, bravery and focus to refuse the promise of many lavish gifts and a future of cosy comforts of royalty that were being offered by the Mughals.

Today, the place is known as Fatehgarh Sahib). An unequal but grim battle commenced with the sunrise on 7 December 1705 in the words of Guru Gobind Singh's Zafamamah, a mere forty defying a hundred thousand (lakh). The besieged, after they had exhausted the meagre stock of ammunition and arrows, made sallies in batches of five each to engage the encircling host with sword and spear. Sahibzada Ajit Singh led one of the sallies and laid down his life fighting in the thick of the battle. He was 18 years old at the time of his supreme sacrifice for his faith. Gurdwara Qatalgarh now marks the spot where he fell, followed by Sahibzada Jujhar Singh, who led the next sally. The Sahibzadas lead two such successive sallies, Ajit Singh and Jujhar Singh, 18 and 14 years old respectively, who like the other Sikhs fell fighting heroically. The valour displayed by the young sons of Guru Gobind Singh has been poignantly narrated by a modern Muslim poet Allahyar Khan Jogi who used to recite his Urdu poem entitled, "ShahidaniWafa" from Sikh pulpits during the second and third decades of the twentieth century. By nightfall Guru Gobind Singh was left with only five Sikhs in the fortress. These five urged him to escape so that he could rally his followers again and continue the struggle against oppression. The Guru agreed. He gave his own attire to Sangat Singh who resembled him somewhat in features and physical stature, and, under cover of darkness, made good his way through the encircling host slackened by the fatigue of the day's battle. Daya Singh, Dharam Singh and Man Singh also escaped leaving behind only two Sikhs, Sangat Singh and Sant Singh. Next morning as the attack was resumed, the imperial troops entered the garhi without much resistance, and were surprised to find only two occupants who, determined to die rather than give in, gave battle till the last. Later having reached safety he wrote a letter in Persian prose, called the Zafarnamah (Epistle of Victory), to the Mughal Emperor Aurangzeb-calling him to task as he had guaranteed safe passage to the Punjab for the Sikhs who had abandoned the city of Anandpur and its forts only to be attacked. Guru Gobind Singh fought a successful battle at Muktsar and then moved towards Talwandi Sabo.

Sang Dhesian

Sang Dhesian (Dhesian Sang) is a village in Phillaur tahsil of Jalandhar district of Punjab state of India known for Baba Sang ji Gurdwara. Sang Dhesian village is named after Baba Sang Ji who was very devoted disciple of Guru Arjun Dev. Sang Dhesian village is known for 'Baba Sang Ji

Gurdwara' which is one of the most famous Gurdwara in India. Baba Sang Gurdwara is 125 feet high and 90 feet long. Devotees around the area helped to build Gurdwara. Approximately 25 ounces of gold was donated by devotees to the Gurdwara. Baba Sang Ji Gurdwara has been a congregation since 1991.

Manji Sahib

Gurdwara Manji sahib also known as Alamgir Sahib, situated near village named alamgir, Ludhiana. Guru Gobind Singh ji, tenth gurus of Sikhs stayed here for few days. On reaching alamgir, guru gobind singh ji shot an arrow into ground and spring appeared from that place. That place still their and called Tirsar. Also, one devoted sikh presented a horse to guru gobind singh ji.

Tenth of the Sikh Gurus, Guru Gobind Singh (1666-1708 C.E.) lived during an extremely dangerous time. His father, Guru Teg Bahadur, had sacrificed his own head to protect freedom of religion for Hindus, who were being threatened with conversion or death by zealous Muslim rulers. Abduction of women and pillage of goods were rampant, but the people were too timid and terrorized to resist. In the midst of this political situation, Guru Gobind Singh gained great stature as both saint and soldier: a leader of firm spiritual principles and intense devotion to God, and at the same time, fearless dedication to protecting all people from oppression and injustice. In 1699, he dramatically initiated five men from the lower castes as his Five Beloveds, blessing them with great courage as well as nearness to God.

They became models for the Khalsa, the order of the pure which Guru Gobind Singh created to stand on the front line against injustice. The Khalsa were held to a very strict moral and spiritual discipline and under Guru Gobind Singh's courageous inspiration, helped to turn the tide against Mughal oppression in India. In addition to his spiritual and military leadership, Guru Gobind Singh was a gifted intellectual, and had many poets in his court. He was inspired to write many powerful spiritual compositions, including Jaap Sahib, but did not include them in the Sikh scripture, the Guru Granth Sahib. His writings have instead been collected in a separate volume, called the Dasam Granth.

Upon his passing away, he instructed his Sikhs to regard the Guru Granth Sahib as their teacher. Guru Gobind Singh is greatly revered at Gobind Sadan, for he is one of the two figures who began appearing in vision to Baba Virsa Singh when he was a boy and who continues to guide and bless his work. Use Gobind Sadan search engine to find what Baba Virsa Singh says about these: Guru Gobind Singh, Guru Teg Bahadur, Five Beloveds, Khalsa, Jaap Sahib, Guru Granth Sahib, Dasam Granth

Gurdwara Dukh Nivaran Sahib

Gurdwara Dukh Nivaran Sahib is situated in what used to be the village of Lehal, now part of Patiala city. According to local tradition, supported by an old handwritten document preserved in the Gurdwara, one Bhag Ram, a jhivar of Lehal, waited upon ninth guru of Sikhs Guru Tegh Bahadur during his sojourn at Saifabad (now Bahadurgarh), and made the request that he might be pleased to visit and bless his village so that its inhabitants could be rid of a serious and mysterious sickness which had been their bane for a long time.

The Guru visited Lehal on Magh sudi 5, 1728 Bikram/24 January 1672 and stayed under a banyan tree by the side of a pond. The sickness in the village subsided. The site where Guru Tegh Bahadur had sat came to be known as Dukh Nivaran, literally meaning eradicator of suffering. Devotees have faith in the healing qualities of water in the sarovar attached to the shrine.

Raja Amar Singh of Patiala (1748-82) had a garden laid out on the site as a memorial which he entrusted to Nihang Sikhs. Records of a court case in 1870 mention a Guru's garden and a Nihangs' well being in existence here.In 1920, during a survey for the proposed construction of Sirhind-Patiala-Jakhal railway line, it appeared that the banyan tree under which had sat Guru Tegh Bahadur would have to be removed. But men charged with felling it refused to touch it.

Ultimately, Maharaja Bhupinder Singh ordered cancellation of the entire project. No gurudwara building had, however, been raised. It was only in 1930 that a committee was formed to collect funds and commence construction and was completed twelve years later in the year 1942. Maharaja Yadavindra Singh who was a devout Sikh built the present building and sarovar. The Gurdwara when completed passed under the administrative control of the Patiala state government. It was later transferred to the Dharam Arth Board of the Patiala and East Punjab States Union and eventually to the Shiromani Gurudwara Prabandhak Committee.

Gurdwara Fatehgarh Sahib

Gurudwara Fatehgarh Sahib is named so, because it marks the conquest of the Sikhs in 1710 when under the leadership of Banda Bahadur, the Sikhs ran over the area and razed the fort (built by Ferozshah Tughlaq) to the ground. To commemorate the martyrdom of younger sons of Guru Gobind Singh who were bricked alive in 1704 by Wazir Khan, the then Fauzdar of Sirhind, a magnificent Gurudwara has been constructed.

Takht Sri Patna Sahib

The Gurdwara at Patna Sahib was in remembrance of the birth place of Guru Gobind Singh, the tenth Guru of the Sikhs on 22 December 1666, and like many historical Gurdwara's in India and Pakistan, this Gurdwara too, was built by Maharaja Ranjit Singh (1780-1839), the first Maharaja of the Sikh Empire, on the banks of Ganges river, in Patna, Bihar.

It was here at Takhat Patna Sahib, that Guru Gobind Singh, the tenth Sikh Guru was born in 1666. He also spent his early years here before moving to Anandpur. Besides being the birthplace of Guru Gobind Singh, Patna was also honored by visits from Guru Nanak as well as Guru Tegh Bahadur.

This is one of only five Takhats or Holy Seats of Authority of the Sikhs. The Gurdwara Patna Sahib is in remembrance of the birthplace of Guru Gobind Singh, the tenth Guru of the Sikhs. Like many historical Gurdwara's in India and Pakistan, this Gurdwara was built by Maharaja Ranjit Singh.

Originally,this is the place where Guru Nanak visited before going to the holy place Gaya.He was a great scholar of history and knew the importance of Pataliputra, which already was almost forgotten by Hindus. He tried to revive the glory of Indian culture.At this place stood the haveli of Salis Rai Jouri, who was a great devotee of Guru Nanak. He was so much influenced by the teachings of the Guru that he converted his palatial home into a dharamsala (place where dharam is learned). When Guru Tegh Bahadur visited Patna, he stayed in this exact site. A magnificent house was built above the dharamsala of Salis Rai. Mullah Ahmed Bukhari, the author of Mirat-ul-Ahwal Jahan Nama, who stayed at Patna for some time at the close of 18th century, has made a reference to Harmandir Sahib. He writes, "Over the birthplace of Guru Gobind Singh, the Sikhs have raised a public edifice, made it a place of power and strength, and call it 'Harmandir'. It is also called 'Sangat' and is held in great esteem and veneration. They have made it a place of pilgrimage. Maharaja Ranjit Singh started the work of reconstructing the Harmandir in 1839 following destruction by fire, but did not survive to see the new structure. Again in 1934, when an earthquake rocked the entire state of Bihar, some portions of the Harmandir fell down. Construction of the present building was taken up on November 19, 1954 and was completed in about three years.

"As described by Charles Wilkins" By Professor Kirpal Singh, Punjabi University Charles Wilkins was one of the pioneering orientalists of the 18th century. With his help Sir William Jones, founder of the Asiatic Society, Calcutta, learnt Sanskrit. Later, he earned the title of "Father of Sanskrit" in the eyes of his contemporaries by writing grammar of Sanskrit language. He was the first to design and manufacture the type for production of Sanskrit and Persian grammars and proved to be a pioneer in the typographic art in the oriental language.

Born in 1749 in England, Wilkins joined the service of the East India Company at the age of twenty. He suggested to the Governor General, Warren Hastings, to establish a printing press in 1778. Wilkins translated Manusmriti, Mahabharat and Hitopdesh and the later years of his life were devoted to the revision of Richardson's Persian, Arabic and English Dictionary. He died in 1836 in England.

Charles Wilkins was one of the earliest Europeans to write about the Sikhs. He wrote on March 1, 1781:

"Before I left Calcutta a gentleman with whom I chanced to be discoursing of that sect of people who are distinguished from worshippers of Brahm and followers of Mohomed by the appellation 'Seek' (meaning Sikhs) informed me that there was a considerable number of them settled in the city of Patna."

Since he was proceeding on leave to Benaras he stopped at Patna. Following is the description of Gurdwara Patna Sahib and the daily routine there:

" I found the College of the Seeks (Sikhs) situated in one of the narrow streets of Patna, at no very considerable distance from the custom house. I was permitted to enter the outward gate; but as soon as I came to the steps which led up into the Chapel, or public hall, I was civilly accosted by two of the Society, I asked them if I might ascent into the hall. They said it was a place of worship open to me and to all men; but at the same time, intimated that I must take off my shoes.. I did not hesitate to comply, and I was then politely conducted into the hall, and seated upon a carpet, in the midst of the assembly, which was so numerous as almost to fill the room.

Gurudwara Bangla Sahib

Gurudwara Bangla Sahib is the most prominent Sikh gurdwara, or Sikh house of worship, in Delhi, known for its association with the eighth Sikh Guru, Guru Har Krishan, and the pond inside its complex, known as the "Sarovar", whose water is considered holy by Sikhs and is known as "Amrit". It was built by Sikh General, Sardar Bhagel Singh in 1783, who supervised the construction of nine Sikh shrines in Delhi in the same year, during the reign of Mughal Emperor, Shah Alam II.

It is situated near Connaught Place, New Delhi and is instantly recognisable by its stunning golden dome and tall flagpole, Nishan Sahib. Gurdwara Bangla Sahib was originally a bungalow belonging to Raja Jai Singh, an Indian ruler in the seventeenth century, and was known as Jaisinghpura Palace.

The eighth Sikh Guru, Guru Har Krishan resided here during his stay in Delhi in 1664. During that time, there was a smallpox and cholera epidemic, and Guru Har Krishan helped the suffering by giving aid and fresh water from the well at this house. Soon he too contracted the illness and eventually died on March 30, 1664. A small tank was later constructed by Raja Jai Singh over the well, its water is now revered as having healing properties and is taken by Sikhs throughout the world back to their homes. The Gurdwara and its Sarovar are now a place of pilgrimage for both Sikhs and Hindus, and a place for special congregation on birth anniversary of Guru Har Krishan and death anniversary of Maharaja Ranjit Singh.

Gurudwara Sis Ganj Sahib

The Gurdwara Sis Ganj Sahib is built at the site in the Chandni Chowk area of Old Delhi, where the ninth Sikh Guru, Guru Tegh Bahadur was beheaded on the orders of the Mughal emperor in 1675 AD, Aurangzeb, for refusing to convert to Islam. Before his body could be quartered and exposed to public view, it was stolen under the cover of darkness by one of his disciples, Lakhi Shah Vanjara, who then burnt his house to cremate the Guru's body. This place is marked by another Gurdwara, Gurdwara Rakab Ganj Sahib. The severed head ("Sis") of Guru Tegh Bahadur was brought to Anandpur Sahib by Bhai Jaita, another disciple of the Guru. It was cremated by the Guru's son, Gobind Rai, who would later become Guru Gobind Singh, the tenth and last Guru of the Sikhs. The Gurdwara at this place is also called Gurdwara Sis Ganj Sahib.

Nankana Sahib

Nankana Sahib was earlier known as 'Rai-Bhoi-Di-Talwandi' is a city in the Pakistani province of Punjab named after the first Guru of the Sikhs Guru Nanak Dev. Located at 31°26'51N 73°41'50E - about 80 kilometers south west of Lahore and about 75 kilometres East from Faisalabad, with a population of approx. 60,000, it is also the capital of Nankana Sahib District and Tehsil. Because Nankana Sahib is the birthplace of Guru Nanak Dev, the central figure in Sikhism, it is a city of high historic and religious value and is a popular pilgrimage site for Sikhs from all over the world.

About thirty miles south-west of the city of Lahore, the capital of the Punjab district of Pakistan. Called Talwandi in the 15th century, this town was surrounded by a deep Bar (a raised forest tract) in the centre of Punjab (the Land of 5 Rivers). Today the town is surrounded by a broad expanse of agricultural vegetation that wears a cheerful appearance through each season. The jal or arak tree Salvadora persica, (the toothbrush tree) predominates, but there are also found the phulahi (Acacia modesta) and the jand (Prosopis spicigera). The wild deer, though not seen anymore, were seen occasionally to appear startled at the travellers who disturbed the solitude of its domain, and the hare and the partridges used to cower cautiously among the thickets, deprecating molestation.

Talwandi is said to have been originally built by a Hindu king called Raja Vairat. It was sacked and destroyed by fire and crowbar. The Punjab was parcelled out to Muslim warrior chiefs in exchange for peace by the sovereigns of Delhi (Delhi Sultanate). One of these chiefs was Rai Bhoi Bhatti, a Muslim of the Bhatti Rajput tribe. Rai Bhoi along with his son salvaged Talwandi and restored it and built a fort on the summit of the tumulus, in which he lived the secure and happy ruler of his estate with several thousand acres of cultivated land, and a boundless wilderness. Nankana was subsequently known then as Rai-Bhoi-Di-Talwandi (or Rai Bhoi's Talwandi). After Rai Bhoi's death, his heritage descended to his only son Rai Bular Bhatti, who governed the land and town at the birth and during the youth of Nanak.

During Rai Bular's rule, Talwandi did not share the tumults and excitements of the outer political world. Rai Bular was a 'gentle giant', towering in stature, but quiet and solitary. Talwandi became a reflection of his personality. It was a quiet place for the training of a prophet, a religious teacher who lead his countrymen to the sacred path of truth, freeing their minds from the superstitions of ages. In this retreat was born Guru Nanak, the founder of the Sikh religion. His was born on the third day of the light half of the month of Baisakh (April-May) in the year 1526 of the Vikramaditya era, corresponding to A.D. 1469.

Now people of many castes are living here but most dominant are Bhatti because they are well educated and financially very strong. They support political candidates in the region.

Sikh Temple Makindu, Makindu

Sikh Temple Makindu is located about 104 miles (170km) from Nairobi on the main Nairobi to Mombasa Road. It was built in 1926 by the Sikhs who were working on the construction of the Uganda railway line from the coast (Mombasa) inland to Lake Victoria and beyond to Uganda. Today, all types of people visit this Gurdwara everyday and it is a 'must-see' Gurdwara for any Sikh travelling to Kenya and East Africa.

This holy Sikh shrine provides a peaceful atmosphere where one can meditate and calm ones mind before proceeding to join the "rat-race" again on the busy coastal road, the main arterial road from the coast to the capital, Nairobi. The Gurdwara complex is very large spanning an estimated 5000 square meters and has facilities for langar (free food) around the clock and living accommodation for travellers.

Set in the forest off the main road, the Makindu Gurdwara is the only convenient rest stop for weary motorists on this busy and long road to and from Mombasa. So the Sikh community of Kenya has done something special by building such a beautiful edifice and campus where anyone of any religion or of no religion can withdraw from the mundane and reflect on the spiritual. This large complex houses a huge dining facility which provides free langar 24 hours a day as determined by their founder Guru, Guru Nanak.

Rooms with beds - several with attached bathrooms - are available for tourists to stay for up to two nights. Everyone in Kenya seems to know of it and most tourists stay to rest and eat. Most are non-Sikhs. There is no charge for this service, but most people donate to the Gurdwara. Apparently it is run by a consortium of the Nairobi Gurdwaras. The aura at Makindu would calm the most tormented mind; one automatically drifts away from the mundane and towards the spiritual and peaceful.

Although the Sikh Temple Makindu was built in 1926, its roots are believed to have been present way before then. When the Uganda Railway was completed in 1902 at Port Florence (which is now Kisumu, Kenya), Makindu played a prominent role as a service point on the railway's advance from Mombasa. Dozens of artisans and train drivers were Sikhs and the station at Makindu became a place of religious fervour.

Sikhs, Hindus and Muslims would gather together in the evenings and sing the praises of God. They did so under a tree, the spot where the current Gurdwara now stands. It is also believed that the Gurdwara was funded by non-Sikhs along with Sikhs.

In the years before 1926, the Gurdwara was a tin-roof little hut where the Sikhs used to pray everyday, and the Guru Guru Granth Sahib was housed there. But when the Railway moved on from Makindu, the service point went into disuse and became unimportant. The Sikhs naturally moved along too, leaving the tiny Gurdwara behind, under the watchful eye of an African servant who would clean the Gurdwara. Sikh devotees who passed along the Gurdwara would leave offerings of money by dropping it through the locked Gurdwara's window.

Gurdwara Karte Parwan

Karte Parwan Gurdwara in the Karte Parwan section of Kabul, Afghanistan, is one of the main Gurdwaras in the region. Gurdawara means the Gateway to the Guru, and is a place of worship for Sikhs. There were thousands of Sikhs living in Kabul before the Saur Revolution of 1978 and the Soviet war in Afghanistan. Many of them fled among the Afghan refugees in the 1980s and 90s to India and neighboring Pakistan. After the US invasion in late 2001, some of them decided to return. As of 2008, there are approximately 300 Sikhs in the area.

Khalsa Diwan Sikh Temple

Khalsa Diwan Sikh Temple is a gurdwara in the Wan Chai District of Hong Kong, on the junction of Queen's Road East and Stubbs Road, Hong Kong Island.

This Gurdwara functions as its role of providing religious, social, practical and cohesive support to generations of Sikhs in Hong Kong and continue to do so. It is also the center of Sikh community activities. The need for a proper Gurdwara was evident in the early days of Hong

Kong and the government allocated land at Happy Valley for building the Gurdwara. Sikh Soldiers of the British Army helped build the Gurdwara in 1901.

In the 1930's the number of Sikhs kept on increasing the Gurudwara was required to be rebuilt. In the early 1940s during the World War II, the Gurudwara was bombed twice, sustaining extensive damage. The then Gurudwara Granthi (priest), Bhai Nand Singh, was sitting in the main hall reading the Sri Guru Granth Sahib (the Sikh holy scripture) when he was fatally injured In one of the attacks. However, the Guru Granth Sahib was not damaged. Many Sikhs and Non-Sikhs had sought refuge in the Gurudwara and some of them sustained injuries. After the war, the damaged areas of the Gurudwara were rebuilt by the Sikhs and Sindhi Hindus.

Again in 1980's the Gurudwara's main hall was extended and linked with Queens' Road East by a covered bridge, which provides easy access for the devotees.

Central Sikh Temple

Central Sikh Temple is the first Sikh gurdwara in Singapore. Established in 1912, the temple had relocated several times before moving to its current site at Serangoon Road at the junction of Towner Road and Boon Keng Road in the Kallang Planning Area in 1986. The gurdrawa is the main place of worship for the 15,000 Sikhs in the country, and is also known as Wada Gurdrawa.

In 1849, after the British conquered the Indian state of Punjab, many Punjabis began to migrate overseas, to places such as Singapore. The British decided to recruit Sikh migrants as security forces in the Straits Settlements. Sikhs began to arrive in Singapore in 1881, to form a Sikh Contingent of the Straits Settlements police force.

The first Sikh temple, or gurdwara, was set up in the police barracks, but it soon could not accommodate the growing Sikh community. A bungalow was purchased for a new temple at Queen Street in 1912, with the assistance of Sindhi merchant by the name of Wassiamull. The Sikhs used the land to build a gurdwara. The gurdwara later became known as "Central Sikh Temple" when other temples were established. The name Wada Gurdwara means the "Big Temple" in English. Central Sikh Temple was reconstructed in 1921, and the congregation hall was located on the first floor and other facilities on the first floor. It is a custom for gurdwaras to provide food and lodging for their guests. Besides being a place of worship, the temple was also used for welfare and education services.

Internal conflicts between the Sikh communities plagued the temple's congregation, which was later divided into three factions from different areas of Central Punjab, namely the Majha, Malwa and Doabha. Their fighting for leadership resulted led to a split in the temple leadership. In 1917, the temple's management was handed over to the Muslim and Hindu Endowment Board, which the Sikhs took it as an insult. The Sikh community publicly protested in the 1930s against the management of the Muslim and Hindu Endowment Board. In 1940, the colonial government created the Queen Street Gurdwara Ordinance, under which Sikhs were allowed to appoint their own board of trustees, and each of the three factions had equal representation of the board.

An all-faction building committee was formed in 1955 to build a new temple. In 1959, the committee acquired a property comprising nine houses adjoining the Central Sikh Temple. There were also plans to build a new temple at Newton, though many preferred to remain at Queen Street. Architectural plans were drawn up and approved by the government in 1963. However, plans were shelved for a new temple following an internal disagreement. In 1976, the government acquired the land where the nine houses stood as part of an urban redevelopment programme and the temple was asked to vacate a year later. The Queen Street site was later gazetted as a historical site. The temple temporarily moved to Seng Poh Road at Tiong Bahru Estate in December 1979, occupying the old building of Bukit Ho Swee Community Centre. An alternative site was found near Towner Road and construction began in 1984 and was completed in 1986. The temple was opened in November 1987, coinciding with the 518th anniversary of Guru Nanak, the first Sikh Gurus.

Khalsa Diwan Society Vancouver

The Khalsa Diwan Society Vancouver is a Sikh society based at a gurdwara in Vancouver, British Columbia, Canada. The current site is located at 8000 Ross St, Vancouver, BC. It was the largest gurdwara in North America.

The Khalsa Diwan Society was founded on July 22, 1906 and was registered on March 13, 1909. The corporate name was "The Khalsa Diwan Society". Their first site and gurdwara was built in 1908 at 1866 West 2nd Avenue. It was inaugurated on January 19, 1908. The financial situation of the society depended on the number of Sikhs living in British Columbia. Donations rose considerably as more Sikhs came to British Columbia. The population of Sikhs rose in the period of 1904-1908, the population being 5,185. It fell to 2,342 in 1911. The Sikh population dwindled even more, to 1,099, as the year 1918 approached. The society decided to build a new gurdwara in 1969. The society purchased 2.75 acres (11,100 m2) of city land in 1968. Construction was completed in the first week of April 1970 for a price of $6,060. Sri Guru Granth Sahib was moved from the 2nd Avenue gurdwara to the Ross Street gurdwara on Vasakhi Day 1970.

In the early 1950s, a serious split occurred in the Canadian Sikh community, when the Khalsa Diwan Society elected a clean-shaven Sikh to serve on its management committee. Although most of the early Sikh immigrants to Canada were non-Khalsa, and a majority of the members of the society were clean-shaven non-Khalsa Sikhs, a faction objected to the election of a non-Khalsa to the management committee. The factions in Vancouver and Victorial broke away from the Khalsa Diwan Society, and established their own gurdwara society called Akali Singh.

Gurdwara Sri Guru Singh Sabha

Gurdwara Sri Guru Singh Sabha Southall (SGSS) is a Sikh Gurdwara situated in the London suburb of Southall on Havelock Road and Park Avenue. It is the largest Sikh temple in Europe. Building work at the Havelock Road site commenced in March 2000 and the Gurdwara opened on Sunday 30 March 2003, in order to accommodate for Southall's growing Sikh community. The Gurdwara cost £17.5 million to build. Funding came by way of donations from members of the local Sikh community and abroad.

Gurdwara Sri Guru Singh Sabha Southall was established in England by Sikhs who had emigrated in the fifties and early sixties. By the 1950s, a significant number of Sikhs were living in Britain, and the main congregational gathering was at Shepherd's Bush Gurdwara. To accommodate the Southall Sikhs, the Southall Sikh Cultural Society was established in 1960. This organisation held Sunday programmes at Shackleton Hall until it moved to 11 Beaconsfield Road.

The emigration of Malaysian and Singaporean Sikhs led to the formation of another group - Sri Guru Nanak Singh Sabha. The two groups remained independent until 1964, when they merged as Sri Guru Singh Sabha Southall. 1964 also saw the first Gurdwara built. It was situated at the Green, and was the headquarters of the Sri Guru Singh Sabha.

The Havelock Road site was purchased in 1967. The dairy was transformed into the Gurdwara in a matter of weeks. In April 1967, the Khanda was brought to England from the Tosha Khana at Darbar Sahib Amritsar for Amrit Sanchar. From those humble beginnings, Sri Guru Singh Sabha Southall emerged as the leading Gurdwara in Europe. 29 November 1997 saw Sri Guru Singh Sabha Southall move to the Park Avenue site (which was originally purchased in 1984). The move was necessary to allow for the new building at Havelock Road which opened on 30 March 2003.

Guru Nanak NSJ, Soho Road, Birmingham

The Gurdwara Sahib was built in the late 1970s under spiritual guidance of Pujey Sant Baba Puran Singh Ji Kericho Wale and under the leadership of Pujey Bhai Sahib ji Bhai Norang Singh Ji. The Spiritual leadership of the Jatha is now under the control of Bhai Sahib Ji Bhai Mohinder Singh Ji.

The total Gurdwaras spans an area of about 25,000 square metres and the building is four storeys high. There are five main Darbar Halls and three Langar Halls.

There are approximately 100 rooms most of which are for the Sangat who want to stay at the Gurdwara for the night and have facilities for sleeping and washing.

The Main Darbar Sahib is used for continuous Akhand Paath recital. A new Paath is started on Monday, Wednesday and Friday mornings, unless a Samagam is under way.

At Samagam programmes, Sampath of a Shabad is done. So each of the line of Gurbani is followed by a Sampath. A Sampath Paath usually takes eleven days of continuous reading.

6 Christianity Religious Tourism Spots

Christian tourism is a subcategory of religious tourism. As one of the largest branches of religious tourism, it is estimated that seven percent of the world's Christians -- about 150 million people -- are "on the move as pilgrims" each year. Christian tourism refers to the entire industry of Christian travel, tourism, and hospitality. In recent years it has grown to include not only Christians embarking individually or in groups on pilgrimages and missionary travel, but also on religion-based cruises, leisure (fellowship) vacations, crusades, rallies, retreats, monastery visits/guest-stays and Christian camps, as well as visiting Christian tourist attractions.

Statistics

Although no definitive study has been completed on Christian tourism, some segments of the industry have been measured:

- According to the Religious Conference Management Association, in 2006 more than 14.7 million people attended religious meetings (RCMA members), an increase of more than 10 million from 1994 with 4.4 million attendees.
- The United Methodist Church experienced an increase of 455% in Volunteers in Mission between 1992 with almost 20,000 volunteers and 2006 with 110,000 volunteers.
- The Christian Camp and Conference Association states that more than eight million people are involved in CCCA member camps and conferences, including more than 120,000 churches.

- Short-term missions draw 1.6 million participants annually.
- Christian attractions including Sight & Sound Theatre attracts 800,000 visitors a year while the Holy Land Experience and Focus on the Family welcome center each receives about 250,000 guests annually. Recently launched Christian attractions include the Creation Museum and Billy Graham Library, both of which are expected to receive about 250,000 visitors each year as well.
- 50,000 churches in the United States possess a travel program or travel ministry

Jordan

Tourism is one of the most important sectors in Jordan's economy. In 2009, 3.5 million tourists from various countries visited Jordan, with tourist receipts amounting to about 3 billion dollars.

Its major tourist attractions include visiting historical sites, like the worldwide famous Petra (UNESCO World Heritage Site since 1985, and one of New Seven Wonders of the World), the Jordan River, Mount Nebo, Madaba, numerous medieval mosques and churches, and unspoiled natural locations (as Wadi Rum and Jordan's northern mountainous region in general), as well as observing cultural and religious sites and traditions.

Jordan also offers health tourism, which is focused in the Dead Sea area, education tourism, hiking, scuba diving in Aqaba's coral reefs, pop-culture tourism and shopping tourism in Jordan's cities. More than half of the approximate 4.8 Arab tourists in 2009, mainly from the Persian Gulf, said they plan to spend their holidays in Jordan.

Religious Tourist Sites

Jordan River, which is the river where Jesus was baptised by John the Baptist according to christian tradition. The Jordan River (American English) or River Jordan (British English) is a river in Southwest Asia flowing to the Dead Sea. In Judaism, the river serves as the eastern border of the "Eretz Yisra'el", the Land of Israel. In Christian tradition, Jesus was baptised here by John the Baptist. The Hashemite Kingdom of Jordan takes its name from this river. The Jordan River is 251 kilometres (156 miles) long. In the Hebrew Bible the Jordan is referred to as the source of fertility to a large plain ("Kikkar ha-Yarden"), and it is said to be like "the garden of God" (Genesis 13:10). There is no regular description of the Jordan in the Bible; only scattered and indefinite references to it are given. Jacob crossed it and its tributary, the Jabbok (the modern Al-Zarqa), to reach Haran (Genesis 32:11, 32:23-24). It is noted as the line of demarcation between the "two tribes and the half tribe" settled to the east (Numbers 34:15) and the "nine tribes and the half tribe of Manasseh" that, led by Joshua, settled to the west (Joshua 13:7, passim). Opposite Jericho, it was called "the Jordan of Jericho" (Numbers 34:15; 35:1). The Jordan has a number of fords, and one of them is famous as the place where many Ephraimites were slain by Jephthah (Judges 12:5-6). It seems that these are the same fords mentioned as being near Beth-barah, where Gideon lay in wait for the Midianites (Judges 7:24). In the plain of the Jordan, between Succoth and Zarthan, is the clay ground where Solomon had his brass-foundries (1 Kings 7:46). In biblical history, the Jordan appears as the scene of several miracles, the first taking place when the Jordan, near Jericho, was crossed by the Israelites under Joshua (Joshua 3:15-17). Later the two tribes and the half tribe that settled east of the Jordan built a large altar on its banks as "a witness" between them and the other tribes (Joshua 22:10, 22:26, et seq.). The Jordan was crossed by Elijah and Elisha on dry ground (2 Kings 2:8, 2:14). Elisha performed two other miracles at the Jordan: he healed Naaman by having him bathe in its waters, and he made the axe head of one of the "children of the prophets" float, by throwing a piece of wood into the water (2 Kings 5:14; 6:6). The Jordan was crossed by Judas Maccabeus and his brother Jonathan Maccabaeus during their war with the Nabataeans (1 Maccabees 5:24). A little later the Jordan was the scene of the battle between Jonathan and Bacchides, in which the latter was defeated (1 Maccabees 9:42-49).

Madaba is well known for its mosaics, as well as important religious sites such as The Madaba Map, the oldest surviving original cartographic depiction of the Holy Land and especially Jerusalem. It dates to the 6th century AD. Madaba has a very long history stretching from the Neolithic period. The town of Madaba was once a Moabite border city, mentioned in the Bible in Numbers 21:30 and Joshua 13:9. Madaba dates from the Middle Bronze Age. During its rule by the Roman and Byzantine Empires from the second to the seventh centuries AD, the city formed part of the Provincia Arabia set up by the Roman Emperor Trajan to replace the Nabataean kingdom of Petra. During the rule of the Islamic Umayyad Caliphate, it was part of the southern Jund Filastin. The first witness of a Christian community in the city, with its own bishop, is found in the Acts of the Council of Chalcedon in 451, wherein Constantine, Metropolitan Archbishop of Bostra (the provincial capital) signed on behalf of Gaiano, "Bishop of the Medabeni." The resettlement of the city ruins by 90 Arab

Christian families from Kerak, in the south, led by two Italian priests from the Latin Patriarchate of Jerusalem in 1880, saw the start of archaeological research. This in turn substantially supplemented the scant documentation available.

Mount Nebo, where Moses was said to have gone to get a view of the Promised Land before he died, according to the Bible. Mount Nebo is an elevated ridge that is approximately 817 meters (2680 feet) above sea level, in what is now western Jordan. The view from the summit provides a panorama of the Holy Land and, to the north, a more limited one of the valley of the River Jordan. The West Bank city of Jericho is usually visible from the summit, as is Jerusalem on a very clear day. According to the final chapter of Deuteronomy, Mount Nebo is where the Hebrew prophet Moses was given a view of the promised land that God was giving to the Israelites. "And Moses went up from the plains of Moab to Mount Nebo, the top of Pisgah, which is opposite Jericho." (Deuteronomy 34:1).

According to Jewish and Christian tradition, Moses was buried on this mountain by God Himself, and his final resting place is unknown. Scholars continue to dispute whether the mountain currently known as Nebo is the same as the mountain referred to in the Torah.

According to the 2 Maccabees 2:4-7, the Prophet Jeremiah hid the tabernacle and the Ark of the Covenant here.

Ulm Minster

Ulm Minster is a Lutheran church located in Ulm, Germany. Although sometimes referred to as Ulm Cathedral because of its great size, the church is not a cathedral as it has never been the seat of a bishop.

Ulm Minster is a famous example of Gothic ecclesiastical architecture. Like Cologne Cathedral (Kölner Dom), also begun in the Gothic era, Ulm Minster was not completed until the 19th century. It is the tallest church in the world, and the tallest structure built before the 20th century, with a steeple measuring 160.9 metres (528 ft) and containing 768 steps. From the top level at 143 m (469 ft) there is a panoramic view of Ulm in Baden-Württemberg and Neu-Ulm in Bavaria and, in clear weather, a vista of the Alps from Säntis to the Zugspitze. The final stairwell to the top (known as the third Gallery) is a tall, spiraling staircase that has barely enough room for one person.

In the 14th century, the parish church of Ulm was located outside the walled city. The burghers of Ulm decided to erect a new church within the perimeters of the city and to finance the costs of the erection.

In 1377 the foundation stone was laid. The planned church was to have three naves of equal height, a main spire on the west and two steeples above the choir. In 1392 Ulrich Ensingen (associated with Strasbourg Cathedral) was appointed master builder. It was his plan to make the western church tower the tallest spire, which it remains in the present day.

The church, consisting of the longitudinal naves and the choir, covered by a temporary roof, was consecrated in 1405. However, structural damage, caused by the height of the naves and the weight of the heavy vaulting, necessitated a reconstruction of the lateral naves which were supported by a row of additional column in their centre.

In a referendum in 1530/31, the citizens of Ulm converted to Protestantism during the Reformation. Ulm Minster became a Lutheran Church. Although as large as many cathedrals, Ulm is not a cathedral, the responsible bishop of the Evangelical-Lutheran Church in Württemberg - member of the Evangelical Church in Germany - resides in Stuttgart.

In 1543 construction work was halted at a time when the steeple had reached a height of some 100 metres (330 ft). The halt in the building process was caused by a variety of factors which were political and religious (the Reformation, the Thirty Years' War, the War of the Spanish Succession) as well as economic (the discovery of the Americas in 1492 and of the sea route to India in 1497, leading to a shift in trade routes and commodities). One result was economic stagnation and a steady decline, preventing major public expenditure.

In 1817 work resumed and the three steeples of the church were completed. Finally, on 31 May 1890 the building was completed.

A devastating air raid hit Ulm on 17 December 1944, which destroyed virtually the entire town west of the church to the railway station and north of the church up to the outskirts. The church itself was barely damaged. However, almost all the other buildings of the town square (Münsterplatz) were severely hit and some 80% of the medieval centre of Ulm was destroyed.

Lincoln Cathedral

Lincoln Cathedral (in full The Cathedral Church of the Blessed Virgin Mary of Lincoln, or sometimes St. Mary's Cathedral) is a historic Anglican cathedral in Lincoln in England and seat of the Bishop of Lincoln in the

Church of England. It was reputedly the tallest building in the world for 249 years (1300-1549). The central spire collapsed in 1549 and was not rebuilt. It is highly regarded by architectural scholars; the eminent Victorian writer John Ruskin declared, "I have always held... that the cathedral of Lincoln is out and out the most precious piece of architecture in the British Isles and roughly speaking worth any two other cathedrals we have."

Remigius de Fécamp, first bishop of Lincoln, ordered the first cathedral to be built in Lincoln, in 1072. Before that, St. Mary's Church in Lincoln was a mother church but not a cathedral, and the seat of the diocese was at Dorchester Abbey in Dorchester-on-Thames, Oxfordshire. Lincoln was more central to a diocese that stretched from the Thames to the Humber. Bishop Remigius built the first Lincoln Cathedral on the present site, finishing it in 1092 and then dying two days before it was to be consecrated on May 9 of that year. In 1141, the timber roofing was destroyed in a fire. Bishop Alexander rebuilt and expanded the cathedral, but it was destroyed by an earthquake about forty years later, in 1185.

After the earthquake, a new bishop was appointed. The new bishop was St Hugh of Lincoln, originally from Avalon, France; he began a massive rebuilding and expansion programme. Rebuilding began at the east end of the cathedral, with an apse and five small radiating chapels. The central nave was then built in the Early English Gothic style. Lincoln Cathedral soon followed other architectural advances of the time - pointed arches, flying buttresses and ribbed vaulting were added to the cathedral. This allowed the creation and support of larger windows.

The cathedral is the 3rd largest in Britain (in floor space) after St Paul's and York Minster, being 484 feet (148 m) by 271 feet (83 m). It is Lincolnshire's largest building and until 1549 the spire was reputedly the tallest medieval tower in Europe, though the exact height has been a matter of debate. Accompanying the cathedral's large bell, Great Tom of Lincoln, is a quarter-hour striking clock. The clock was installed in the early 19th century.

There are thirteen bells in the south-west tower, two in the north west tower, and five in the central tower (including Great Tom).

The matching Dean's Eye and Bishop's Eye were added to the cathedral during the late Middle Ages. The former, the Dean's Eye in the north transept dates from the 1192 rebuild begun by St Hugh, it was finally completed in 1235. The latter, the Bishop's eye, in the south transept was re-constructed 100 years later in 1330. A contemporary record, "The

Metrical Life of St Hugh", refers to the meaning of these two windows (one on the dark, north, side and the other on the light, south, side of the building):

"For north represents the devil, and south the Holy Spirit and it is in these directions that the two eyes look. The bishop faces the south in order to invite in and the dean the north in order to shun; the one takes care to be saved, the other takes care not to perish. With these Eyes the cathedral's face is on watch for the candelabra of Heaven and the darkness of Lethe (oblivion)."

After the additions of the Dean's eye and other major Gothic additions it is believed some mistakes in the support of the tower occurred, for in 1237 the main tower collapsed. A new tower was soon started and in 1255 the Cathedral petitioned Henry III to allow them to take down part of the town wall to enlarge and expand the Cathedral, including the rebuilding of the central tower and spire. They replaced the small rounded chapels (built at the time of St Hugh) with a larger east end to the cathedral. This was to handle the increasing number of pilgrims to the Cathedral, who came to worship at the shrine of Hugh of Lincoln.

In 1290 Eleanor of Castile died. As his Queen Consort of England, King Edward I decided to honour her with an elegant funeral procession. After embalming, which in the thirteenth century involved evisceration, Eleanor's viscera were buried in Lincoln cathedral, and Edward placed a duplicate of the Westminster tomb there. The Lincoln tomb's original stone chest survives; its effigy was destroyed in the 17th century and replaced with a 19th-century copy. On the outside of Lincoln Cathedral are two prominent statues often identified as Edward and Eleanor, but these images were heavily restored in the 19th century and probably were not originally intended to depict the couple.

Between the years 1307 and 1311 the central tower was raised to its present height of 83 m (271 feet). The western towers and front of the cathedral were also improved and heightened. At this time, a tall lead-encased wooden spire topped the central tower but was blown down in a storm in 1548. With its spire, the tower reputedly reached a height of 525 feet (160 m) (which would have made it the world's tallest structure, surpassing the Great Pyramid of Giza, which held the record for almost 4,000 years). This height is agreed by most sources but has been doubted by others. Other additions to the cathedral at this time included its elaborate carved screen and the 14th century misericords, as was the Angel choir. For a large part of the length of the cathedral, the walls have arches in relief with a second layer in front giving the illusion of a passageway along the wall. However the illusion does not work, as the stonemason, copying techniques from France, did not make the arches the correct length needed for the illusion effect.

In 1398 John of Gaunt and Katherine Swynford founded a chantry there to pray for their souls, and in the 15th century the building of the cathedral turned to chantry or memorial chapels. The chapels next to the Angel Choir were built in the Perpendicular style, with an emphasis on strong vertical lines, which survive today in the window tracery and wall panelling.

St. Olaf's Church, Tallinn

St. Olaf's church or St. Olav's church (Estonian: Oleviste kirik) in Tallinn, Estonia, is believed to have been built in the 12th century and to have been the centre for old Tallinn's Scandinavian community prior to the conquest of Tallinn by Denmark in 1219. Its dedication relates to King Olaf II of Norway (a.k.a. Saint Olaf, 995-1030). The first known written records referring to the church date back to 1267, and it was extensively rebuilt during the 14th century.

A legend tells that the builder of the church, named Olaf, upon its completion, fell to his death from atop the tower. It is said that when his body hit the ground, a snake and a toad crawled out of his mouth. There is a wall-carving depicting this event in the adjoining Chapel of Our Lady.

Around 1500, the building reached a height of 159 meters. The motivation for building such an immensely tall steeple must have been to use it as a maritime signpost, which made the trading city of Tallinn visible from far out at sea. Between 1549 and 1625, when the spire burnt down after a lightning strike, it was the tallest building in the world. The steeple of St. Olav has been hit by lightning at least eight times, and the whole church has burned down three times throughout its known existence. Following several rebuildings, its overall height is now 123.7 meters.

From 1944 until 1991, the Soviet KGB used Oleviste's spire as a radio tower and surveillance point. It currently continues as an active Baptist church.

The tower's viewing platform offers panoramic views over the old town and is open to the public from April through Nov, daily 10:00 - 18:00. Admission 30kr (1.92 €).

Basilica of Our Lady of Peace of Yamoussoukro

The Basilica of Our Lady of Peace of Yamoussoukro (French: Basilique Notre-Dame de la Paix de Yamoussoukro) is a Roman Catholic minor basilica dedicated to Our Lady of Peace in Yamoussoukro, the administrative capital of Côte d'Ivoire (Ivory Coast). The basilica was constructed between 1985 and 1989 at a cost of $300 million. The design of the dome and encircled plaza are clearly inspired by those of the Basilica of Saint Peter in the Vatican City, although it is not an outright replica. The cornerstone was laid on August 10, 1985, and it was consecrated on September 10, 1990, by Pope John Paul II.

Contrary to popular belief, this particular basilica is not a cathedral. The nearby Cathedral of Saint Augustine is the principal place of worship and seat of the bishop of the Diocese of Yamoussoukro.

Guinness World Records lists it as the largest church in the world, having surpassed the previous record holder, St. Peter's Basilica, upon completion. It has an area of 30,000 sq metres (322,917 sq ft) and is 158 m (518 ft) high. However, it also includes a rectory and a villa (counted in the overall area), which are not strictly part of the church, and it can accommodate 18,000 worshippers, compared to 60,000 for St. Peter's. The Basilica is administered by Polish Pallottines.

Cologne Cathedral

Cologne Cathedral (German: Kölner Dom, officially Hohe Domkirche St. Peter und Maria) is a Roman Catholic church in Cologne, Germany. It is the seat of the Archbishop of Cologne (currently Cardinal Joachim Meisner), and is under the administration of the Archdiocese of Cologne. It is renowned as a monument of Christianity, of German Catholicism in particular, of Gothic architecture and of the continuing faith and perseverance of the people of the city in which it stands. It is dedicated to Saint Peter and the Blessed Virgin Mary. The cathedral is a World Heritage Site, one of the best-known architectural monuments in Germany, and Cologne's most famous landmark, described by UNESCO as an "exceptional work of human creative genius". It is Germany's most visited landmark, visited by 20,000 people every day.

Construction of Cologne Cathedral began in 1248 and took, with interruptions, until 1880 to complete. It is 144.5 metres long, 86.5 m wide and its towers are approximately 157 m tall. The cathedral is one of the world's largest churches and the largest Gothic church in

Northern Europe. For four years, 1880-84, it was the tallest structure in the world, until the completion of the Washington Monument. It has the second-tallest church spires, only surpassed by the single spire of Ulm Minster, completed 10 years later in 1890. Because of its enormous twin spires, it also presents the largest façade of any church in the world. The choir of the cathedral, measured between the piers, also holds the distinction of having the largest height to width ratio of any Medieval church, 3.6:1, exceeding even Beauvais Cathedral which has a slightly higher vault.

Cologne's medieval builders had planned a grand structure to house the reliquary of the Three Kings and fit its role as a place of worship of the Holy Roman Emperor. Despite having been left incomplete during the medieval period, Cologne Cathedral eventually became unified as "a masterpiece of exceptional intrinsic value" and "a powerful testimony to the strength and persistence of Christian belief in medieval and modern Europe".

Beauvais Cathedral

Beauvais Cathedral (French: Cathédrale Saint-Pierre de Beauvais) is an incomplete cathedral located in Beauvais, in northern France. It is the seat of the Bishop of Beauvais, Noyon and Senlis. It is, in some respects, the most daring achievement of Gothic architecture, and consists only of a transept (sixteenth-century) and choir, with apse and seven polygonal apsidal chapels (thirteenth century), which are reached by an ambulatory. The small Romanesque church of the tenth century, known as the Basse Œuvre, much restored, still occupies the site destined for the nave.

St. Mary's church, Stralsund

Marienkirche (St. Mary's church) is located in Stralsund, northern Germany. Built some time before 1298, it is architecturally Gothic, and was loosely modelled on St. Mary's Church in Lübeck. Between 1625 and 1647, it was the world's tallest building at 151 metres (495 ft) tall.

The bell tower collapsed in 1382, and was rebuilt by 1478. In 1495, the steeple tower blew down during a severe storm, and was then rebuilt taller. This was subsequently struck by lightning in 1647, and burned down, and was rebuilt as a baroque dome, which, completed in 1708, can be seen today. The tower is currently 104 metres (341 ft) tall

Rouen Cathedral

Rouen Cathedral (French: Cathédrale Notre-Dame de Rouen) is a Roman Catholic Gothic cathedral in Rouen, in northwestern France. It is the seat of the Archbishop of Rouen and Normandy.

Old St Paul's Cathedral

Old St Paul's Cathedral is a name used to refer to the medieval cathedral of the City of London which until 1666 stood on the site of the present St Paul's Cathedral. Built between 1087 and 1314 and dedicated to St Paul, the cathedral was the fourth church on the site at Ludgate Hill. Work began during the reign of William the Conqueror following a devastating fire in 1087 which destroyed much of the city. Work took over 200 years, and construction was delayed by another fire in 1135. The church was consecrated in 1240 and enlarged again in 1256 and the early 14th century. At its completion in the middle of the 14th century, the cathedral was one of the longest churches in the world, had one of the tallest spires and some of the finest stained glass.

The presence of the shrine of St Erkenwald made the cathedral a pilgrimage site during the Medieval period. In addition to serving as the seat of the Diocese of London, the building developed a reputation as a hub of the City of London, with the nave aisle, "Paul's walk", known as a centre for business and the London grapevine. Following the Reformation, the open air pulpit in the churchyard, St Paul's Cross, became the stage for radical evangelical preaching and Protestant bookselling.

Already severely in decline by the 17th century, restoration work by Inigo Jones in the 1620s was halted by the English Civil War. Sir Christopher Wren was attempting another restoration in 1666 when the cathedral was destroyed in the Great Fire of London. Following demolition of the old structure, the present domed cathedral was erected on the site to an English Baroque design by Wren.

Strasbourg Cathedral

Strasbourg Cathedral or the Cathedral of Our Lady of Strasbourg (French: Cathédrale Notre-Dame-de-Strasbourg, German: Liebfrauenmünster zu Straßburg) is a Roman Catholic cathedral in Strasbourg, France. Although considerable parts of it are still in Romanesque architecture, it is widely considered to be among the finest examples of high, or late, Gothic architecture. Erwin von Steinbach is credited for major contributions from 1277 to his death in 1318.

At 142 metres, it was the world's tallest building from 1647 to 1874, when it was surpassed by St. Nikolai's Church, Hamburg. Today it is the sixth-tallest church in the world.

Described by Victor Hugo as a "gigantic and delicate marvel", and by Goethe as a "sublimely towering, wide-spreading tree of God", the cathedral is visible far across the plains of Alsace and can be seen from as far off as the Vosges Mountains or the Black Forest on the other side of the Rhine. Sandstone from the Vosges used in construction gives the cathedral its characteristic pink hue.

St. Peter's Basilica

The Papal Basilica of Saint Peter (Latin: Basilica Sancti Petri), officially known in Italian as the Basilica Papale di San Pietro in Vaticano and commonly known as St. Peter's Basilica, is a Late Renaissance church located within the Vatican City. St. Peter's Basilica has the largest interior of any Christian church in the world. It is regarded as one of the holiest Catholic sites. It has been described as "holding a unique position in the Christian world" and as "the greatest of all churches of Christendom".

In Catholic tradition, the basilica is the burial site of its namesake Saint Peter, who was one of the twelve apostles of Jesus and, according to tradition, first Bishop of Rome and therefore first in the line of the papal succession. Tradition and some historical evidence hold that Saint Peter's tomb is directly below the altar of the basilica. For this reason, many Popes have been interred at St Peter's since the Early Christian period. There has been a church on this site since the 4th century. Construction of the present basilica, over the old Constantinian basilica, began on April 18, 1506 and was completed on November 18, 1626.

St. Peter's is famous as a place of pilgrimage, for its liturgical functions and for its historical associations. It is associated with the papacy, with the Counter-reformation and with numerous artists, most significantly Michelangelo. As a work of architecture, it is regarded as the greatest building of its age. Contrary to popular misconception, Saint Peter's is not a cathedral, as it is not the seat of a bishop. It is properly termed a papal basilica. The Basilica of St. John Lateran is the cathedral church of Rome.

St. Peter's Church, Riga

St. Peter's Church is a tall Lutheran church in Riga, Latvia, named after Saint Peter. First mention of the St. Peter's Church is in records dating to 1209. The church was a masonry construction and therefore undamaged by a city fire in Riga that year. The history of the church can be divided into three distinct periods: two associated with Gothic and Romanesque building styles, the third with the early Baroque period. The middle section of the church was built during the 13th century, which encompasses the first period. The only remnants of this period are located in the outer nave walls and on the inside of a few pillars in the nave, around which larger pillars were later built.

St. Martin's Church, Landshut

The Church of St. Martin in Landshut is a medieval church in that German city. St. Martin's Church, along with Trausnitz Castle and the celebration of the Landshuter Hochzeit (wedding), are the most important landmarks and historical events of Landshut. This Brick Gothic church is the tallest church in Bavaria and the tallest brick building and church, and 2nd tallest brick structure in the world (after Anaconda Smelter Stack), made without steel supports, with a height of 130.6 metres (428 ft).

St. Mary's Church, Lübeck

The Lutheran Marienkirche (St. Mary's church) in Lübeck (German: Lübecker Marienkirche or officially St. Marien zu Lübeck: St. Mary's of Lübeck) was constructed between 1250 and 1350. For many years it has been a symbol of the power and prosperity of the old Hanseatic city, and as Germany's third largest church it remains the tallest building of the old part of Lübeck. It is larger than Lübeck Cathedral . Along with the city, the church has been listed by UNESCO as of cultural significance.

It is a model for the brick Gothic style of northern Germany, reflected in approximately 70 churches in the Baltic Area. In Lübeck, the high-rising Gothic style of France was adapted to north German brick. At 38.5 meters (125 ft) the church has the highest brick vault in the world. Taking the weather vanes into account, the towers are 124.95 meters (406 ft) and 124.75 meters (405.5 ft) high.

St. Mary's is located in the merchant's borough, which stretches from the docks of the River Trave all the way up to the church itself. It is the main church of the local council and the people of Lübeck, and was erected near the market and town hall.

7 Judaism Religious Tourism Spots

Judaism is the "religion, philosophy, and way of life" of the Jewish people. Originating in the Hebrew Bible (also known as the Tanakh) and explored in later texts such as the Talmud, it is considered by Jews to be the expression of the covenantal relationship God developed with the Children of Israel. According to traditional Rabbinic Judaism, God revealed his laws and commandments to Moses on Mount Sinai in the form of both the Written and Oral Torah. This was historically challenged by the Karaites, a movement that flourished in the medieval period, retains several thousand followers today and maintains that only the Written Torah was revealed. In modern times, liberal movements such as Humanistic Judaism may be nontheistic.

Judaism claims a historical continuity spanning more than 3,000 years. It is one of the oldest monotheistic religions, and the oldest to survive into the present day. The Hebrews / Israelites were already referred to as Jews in later books of the Tanakh such as the Book of Esther, with the term Jews replacing the title "Children of Israel." Judaism's texts, traditions and values strongly influenced later Abrahamic religions, including Christianity, Islam and the Baha'i Faith. Many aspects of Judaism have also directly or indirectly influenced secular Western ethics and civil law.

Jews are an ethnoreligious group and include those born Jewish and converts to Judaism. In 2010, the world Jewish population was estimated at 13.4 million, or roughly 0.2% of the total world population. About 42% of all Jews reside in Israel and about 42% reside in the United States and Canada, with most of the remainder living in Europe. The largest Jewish religious movements are Orthodox Judaism (Hareidi Judaism and Modern Orthodox Judaism), Conservative Judaism and Reform Judaism. A major source of difference between these groups is their approach to Jewish law. Orthodox Judaism maintains that the Torah and Jewish law are divine in origin, eternal and unalterable, and that they should be strictly followed. Conservative and Reform Judaism are more liberal, with Conservative Judaism generally promoting a more "traditional" interpretation of Judaism's requirements than Reform Judaism. A typical Reform position is that Jewish law should be viewed as a set of general guidelines rather than as a set of restrictions and obligations whose observance is required of all Jews. Historically, special courts enforced Jewish law; today, these courts still exist but the practice of Judaism is mostly voluntary. Authority on theological and legal matters is not vested in any one person or organization, but in the sacred texts and the many rabbis and scholars who interpret these texts.

At its core, the Tanakh is an account of the Israelites' relationship with God from their earliest history until the building of the Second Temple (c. 535 BCE). Abraham is hailed as the first Hebrew and the father of the Jewish people. As a reward for his act of faith in one God, he was promised that Isaac, his second son, would inherit the Land of Israel (then called Canaan). Later, Jacob and his children were enslaved in Egypt, and God commanded Moses to lead the Exodus from Egypt. At Mount Sinai they received the Torah - the five books of Moses. These books, together with Nevi'im and Ketuvim are known as Torah Shebikhtav as opposed to the Oral Torah, which refers to the Mishna and the Talmud. Eventually, God led them to the land of Israel where the tabernacle was planted in the city of Shiloh for over 300 years to rally the nation against attacking enemies. As time went on, the spiritual level of the nation declined to the point that God allowed the Philistines to capture the tabernacle. The people of Israel then told Samuel the prophet that they needed to be governed by a permanent king, and Samuel appointed Saul to be their King. When the people pressured Saul into going against a command conveyed to him by Samuel, God told Samuel to appoint David in his stead.

Once King David was established, he told the prophet Nathan that he would like to build a permanent temple, and as a reward for his actions, God promised David that he would allow his son, Solomon, to build the first permanent temple and the throne would never depart from his children.

Rabbinic tradition holds that the details and interpretation of the law, which are called the Oral Torah or oral law, were originally an unwritten tradition based upon what God told Moses on Mount Sinai. However, as the persecutions of the Jews increased and the details were in danger of being forgotten, these oral laws were recorded by Rabbi Judah haNasi (Judah the Prince) in the Mishnah, redacted circa 200 CE. The Talmud was a compilation of both the Mishnah and the Gemara, rabbinic commentaries redacted over the next three centuries. The Gemara originated in two major centers of Jewish scholarship, Palestine and Babylonia. Correspondingly, two bodies of analysis developed, and two works of Talmud were created. The older compilation is called the Jerusalem Talmud. It was compiled sometime during the 4th century in Israel. The Babylonian Talmud was compiled from discussions in the houses of study by the scholars Ravina I, Ravina II, and Rav Ashi by 500 CE, although it continued to be edited later.

Some critical scholars oppose the view that the sacred texts, including the Hebrew Bible, were divinely inspired. Many of these scholars accept the general principles of the documentary hypothesis and suggest that the Torah consists of inconsistent texts edited together in a way that calls attention to divergent accounts. Many suggest that during the First Temple period, the people of Israel believed that each nation had its own god, but that their god was superior to other gods. Some suggest that strict monotheism developed during the Babylonian Exile, perhaps in reaction to Zoroastrian dualism. In this view, it was only by the Hellenic period that most Jews came to believe that their god was the only god, and that the notion of a clearly bounded Jewish nation identical with the Jewish religion formed.

John Day argues that the origins of biblical Yahweh, El, Asherah, and Ba'al, may be rooted in earlier Canaanite religion, which was centered on a pantheon of gods much like the Greek Pantheon.

Jerusalem

Jerusalem is the capital of Israel, though not internationally recognized as such.[iii] If the area and population of East Jerusalem is included, it is Israel's largest city in both population and area, with a population of 763,800 residents over an area of 125.1 km2 (48.3 sq mi).[iv] Located in the Judean Mountains, between the Mediterranean Sea and the northern edge of the Dead Sea, modern Jerusalem has grown far beyond the boundaries of the Old City.

Jerusalem is a holy city to the three major Abrahamic religions- Judaism, Christianity and Islam. In Judaism, Jerusalem has been the holiest city since, according to the Torah, King David of Israel first established it as the capital of the united Kingdom of Israel in c. 1000 BCE, and his son Solomon commissioned the building of the First Temple in the city. In Christianity, Jerusalem has been a holy city since, according to the New Testament, Jesus was crucified in c. 30 CE and 300 years later Saint Helena found the True Cross in the city. In Sunni Islam, Jerusalem is the third-holiest city. It became the first Qibla, the focal point for Muslim prayer (Salah) in 610 CE, and, according to Islamic tradition, Muhammad made his Night Journey there ten years later. As a result, and despite having an area of only 0.9 square kilometres (0.35 sq mi), the Old City is home to sites of key religious importance, among them the Temple Mount, the Western Wall, the Church of the Holy Sepulchre, the Dome of the Rock and al-Aqsa Mosque.

During its long history, Jerusalem has been destroyed twice, besieged 23 times, attacked 52 times, and captured and recaptured 44 times. The oldest part of the city was settled in the 4th millennium BCE, making Jerusalem one of the oldest cities in the world. The old walled city, a World Heritage site, has been traditionally divided into four quarters, although the names used today-the Armenian, Christian, Jewish, and Muslim Quarters-were introduced in the early 19th century. The Old City was nominated for inclusion on the List of World Heritage Sites in Danger by Jordan in 1982.

Today, the status of Jerusalem remains one of the core issues in the Israeli-Palestinian conflict. After the 1967 Arab Israeli War, Israel annexed East Jerusalem (which was controlled by Jordan following the 1948 war) and considers it a part of Israel, although the international community has rejected the annexation as illegal and considers East Jerusalem to be Palestinian territory held by Israel under military occupation. Israel, however, considers the entire city to be a part of Israel following its annexation of East Jerusalem through the Jerusalem Law of 1980.

According to Palestinian Central Bureau of Statistics 208,000 Palestinians live in East Jerusalem, which is sought as a future capital of a future Palestinian state.

All branches of the Israeli government are located in Jerusalem, including the Knesset (Israel's parliament), the residences of the Prime Minister and President, and the Supreme Court. Jerusalem is home to the Hebrew University and to the Israel Museum with its Shrine of the Book. The Jerusalem Biblical Zoo has ranked consistently as Israel's top tourist attraction for Israelis.

Given the city's central position in both Israeli nationalism (Zionism) and Palestinian nationalism, the selectivity required to summarise more than 5,000 years of inhabited history is often influenced by ideological bias or background (see Historiography and nationalism). For example, the Jewish periods of the city's history are important to Israeli nationalists (Zionists), whose discourse suggests that modern Jews descend from the Israelites and Maccabees, whilst the Islamic, Christian and other non-Jewish periods of the city's history are important to Palestinian nationalism, whose discourse suggests that modern Palestinians descend from all the different peoples who have lived in the region. As a result, both sides claim the history of the city has been politicized by the other in order to strengthen their relative claims to the city, and that this is borne out by the different focuses the different writers place on the various events and eras in the city's history.

Ceramic evidence indicates the occupation of City of David, within present-day Jerusalem, as far back as the Copper Age (c. 4th millennium BCE), with evidence of a permanent settlement during the early Bronze Age (c. 3000-2800 BCE). The Execration Texts (c. 19th century BCE), which refer to a city called Roshlamem or Rosh-ramen and the Amarna letters (c. 14th century BCE) may be the earliest mention of the city. Some archaeologists, including Kathleen Kenyon, believe Jerusalem as a city was founded by Northwest Semitic people with organized settlements from around 2600 BCE. According to Jewish tradition, the city was founded by Shem and Eber, ancestors of Abraham. In the biblical account, Jerusalem ("Salem") when first mentioned is ruled by Melchizedek, an ally of Abraham (identified with Shem in legend). Later, in the time of Joshua, Jerusalem lay within territory allocated to the tribe of Benjamin (Joshua 18:28), but continued to be under the independent control of the Jebusites until it was conquered by David and made into the capital of the united Kingdom of Israel (c. 11th century BCE). Recent excavations of a Large Stone Structure and a nearby Stepped Stone Structure are widely believed[by whom?] to be the remains of King David's palace. The excavations have been interpreted by some archaeologists as lending credence to the biblical narrative.[51]

According to Hebrew scripture, King David reigned until 970 BCE. He was succeeded by his son Solomon, who built the Holy Temple on Mount Moriah. Solomon's Temple (later known as the First Temple), went on to play a pivotal role in Jewish history as the repository of the Ark of the Covenant. For more than 400 years, until the Babylonian conquest in 587 BCE, Jerusalem was the political capital of the united Kingdom of

Israel and then the Kingdom of Judah. During this period, known as the First Temple Period, the Temple was the religious center of the Israelites. On Solomon's death (c. 930 BCE), the ten northern tribes split off to form the Kingdom of Israel. Under the leadership of the House of David and Solomon, Jerusalem remained the capital of the Kingdom of Judah.

When the Assyrians conquered the Kingdom of Israel in 722 BCE, Jerusalem was strengthened by a great influx of refugees from the northern kingdom. The First Temple period ended around 586 BCE, as the Babylonians conquered Judah and Jerusalem, and laid waste to Solomon's Temple. In 538 BCE, after 50 years of Babylonian captivity, Persian King Cyrus the Great invited the Jews to return to Judah to rebuild the Temple. Construction of the Second Temple was completed in 516 BCE, during the reign of Darius the Great, 70 years after the destruction of the First Temple. In about 445 BCE, King Artaxerxes I of Persia issued a decree allowing the city and the walls to be rebuilt. Jerusalem resumed its role as capital of Judah and center of Jewish worship.

When Macedonian ruler Alexander the Great conquered the Persian Empire, Jerusalem and Judea came under Macedonian control, eventually falling to the Ptolemaic dynasty under Ptolemy I. In 198 BCE, Ptolemy V lost Jerusalem and Judea to the Seleucids under Antiochus III. The Seleucid attempt to recast Jerusalem as a Hellenized city-state came to a head in 168 BCE with the successful Maccabean revolt of Mattathias the High Priest and his five sons against Antiochus Epiphanes, and their establishment of the Hasmonean Kingdom in 152 BCE with Jerusalem again as its capital. In 63 BCE, Pompey the Great intervened in a Hasmonean struggle for the throne and captured Jerusalem, incorporating Judea into the Roman Republic.

As Rome became stronger it installed Herod as a Jewish client king. Herod the Great, as he was known, devoted himself to developing and beautifying the city. He built walls, towers and palaces, and expanded the Temple Mount, buttressing the courtyard with blocks of stone weighing up to 100 tons. Under Herod, the area of the Temple Mount doubled in size. Shortly after Herod's death, in 6 CE Judea came under direct Roman rule as the Iudaea Province, although Herod's descendants through Agrippa II remained client kings of neighbouring territories until 96 CE. Roman rule over Jerusalem and the region began to be challenged with the First Jewish-Roman War, which resulted in the destruction of the Second Temple in 70 CE. Jerusalem once again served as the capital of Judea during the three-year rebellion known as the Bar Kokhba revolt, beginning in 132 CE. The Romans succeeded in suppressing the revolt in 135 CE. Emperor Hadrian romanized the city, renaming it Aelia Capitolina, and banned the Jews from entering it. Hadrian renamed the entire Iudaea Province Syria Palaestina, after the biblical Philistines, in an attempt to de-Judaize the country. The enforcement of the ban on Jews entering Aelia Capitolina continued until the 4th century CE.

In the five centuries following the Bar Kokhba revolt, the city remained under Roman then Byzantine rule. During the 4th century, the Roman Emperor Constantine I constructed Christian sites in Jerusalem, such as the Church of the Holy Sepulchre. Jerusalem reached a peak in size and population at the end of the Second Temple Period, when the city covered two square kilometers (0.8 sq mi.) and had a population of 200,000. From the days of Constantine until the 7th century, Jews were banned from Jerusalem.

The eastern continuation of the Roman Empire, the Byzantine Empire, maintained control of the city for years. Within the span of a few decades, Jerusalem shifted from Byzantine to Persian rule and returned to Roman-Byzantine dominion once more. Following Sassanid Khosrau II's early 7th century push into Byzantine, advancing through Syria, Sassanid Generals Shahrbaraz and Shahin attacked the Byzantine-controlled city of Jerusalem (Persian: Dej Houdkh). They were aided by the Jews of Palestine, who had risen up against the Byzantines.

In the Siege of Jerusalem (614), after 21 days of relentless siege warfare, Jerusalem was captured. The Byzantine chronicles relate that the Sassanid army and the Jews slaughtered tens of thousands of Christians in the city, an episode which has been the subject of much debate between historians. The conquered city would remain in Sassanid hands for some fifteen years until the Byzantine Emperor Heraclius reconquered it in 629.

Jerusalem is considered Islam's third holiest city after Mecca and Medina. Among Muslims of an earliest era it was referred to as Madinat bayt al-Maqdis "City of the Temple". which was restricted to the Temple Mount. The rest of the city "...was called Iliya, reflecting the Roman name given the city following the destruction of 70 c.e.: Aelia Capitolina". Later the Temple Mount became known as al-Haram al-Sharif, "The Noble Sanctuary", while the city around it became known as Bayt al-Maqdis, and later still, al-Quds al-Sharif "The Noble City". The Islamization of Jerusalem began in the first year A.H. (620 CE), when Muslims were instructed to face the city while performing their daily prostrations and, according to Muslim religious tradition, Muhammad's night journey and ascension to heaven took place. After 16 months, the direction of prayer was changed to Mecca. In 638 the Islamic Caliphate extended its dominion to Jerusalem. With the Arab conquest, Jews were allowed back into the city. The Rashidun caliph Umar ibn al-Khattab signed a treaty with Monophysite Christian Patriarch Sophronius, assuring him that Jerusalem's Christian holy places and population would be protected under Muslim rule. When led to pray at the Church of the Holy Sepulchre, the holiest site for Christians, the caliph Umar refused to pray in the church so that Muslims would not request converting the church to a mosque. He prayed outside the church, where the Mosque of Umar (Omar) stands to this day, opposite the entrance to the Church of the Holy Sepulchre. According to the Gaullic bishop Arculf, who lived in Jerusalem from 679 to 688, the Mosque of Umar was a rectangular wooden structure built over ruins which could accommodate 3,000 worshipers. When the Muslims went to Bayt Al-Maqdes for the first time, They searched for the site of the Far Away Holy Mosque (Al-Masjed Al-Aqsa) that was mentioned in Quran and Hadith according to Islamic beliefs. According to Islamic legend, they found the site full of rubbish, they cleaned it and started using it for prayers thereafter. The Umayyad caliph Abd al-Malik commissioned the construction of the Dome of the Rock in the late 7th century. The 10th century historian al-Muqaddasi writes that Abd al-Malik built the shrine in order to compete in grandeur with Jerusalem's monumental churches. Over the next four hundred years Jerusalem's prominence diminished as Arab powers in the region jockeyed for control.

In 1099, The Fatimid ruler expelled the native Christian population before Jerusalem was conquered by the Crusaders, who massacred most of its Muslim and Jewish inhabitants when they took the solidly defended city by assault, after a period of siege; later the Crusaders created the Kingdom of Jerusalem. By early June 1099 Jerusalem's population had declined from 70,000 to less than 30,000.

In 1187, the city was wrested from the Crusaders by Saladin who permitted Jews and Muslims to return and settle in the city. Under the Ayyubid dynasty of Saladin, a period of huge investment began in the construction of houses, markets, public baths, and pilgrim hostels as well as the establishment of religious endowments. However, for most of the 13th century, Jerusalem declined to the status of a village due to city's fall of strategic value and Ayyubid internecine struggles.

In 1244, Jerusalem was sacked by the Khwarezmian Tartars, who decimated the city's Christian population and drove out the Jews. The Khwarezmian Tartars were driven out by the Ayyubids in 1247. From 1250 to 1517, Jerusalem was ruled by the Mamluks. During this period of time many clashes occurred between the Mamluks on one side and the crusaders and the Mongols on the other side. The area also suffered from many earthquakes and black plague.

In 1517, Jerusalem and environs fell to the Ottoman Turks, who generally remained in control until 1917. Jerusalem enjoyed a prosperous period of renewal and peace under Suleiman the Magnificent - including the rebuilding of magnificent walls around the Old City. Throughout much of Ottoman rule, Jerusalem remained a provincial, if religiously important center, and did not straddle the main trade route between Damascus and Cairo. The English reference book Modern history or the present state of all nations written in 1744 stated that "Jerusalem is still reckoned the capital city of Palestine".

The Ottomans brought many innovations: modern postal systems run by the various consulates; the use of the wheel for modes of transportation; stagecoach and carriage, the wheelbarrow and the cart; and the oil-lantern, among the first signs of modernization in the city. In the mid 19th century, the Ottomans constructed the first paved road from Jaffa to Jerusalem, and by 1892 the railroad had reached the city.

With the annexation of Jerusalem by Muhammad Ali of Egypt in 1831, foreign missions and consulates began to establish a foothold in the city. In 1836, Ibrahim Pasha allowed Jerusalem's Jewish residents to restore four major synagogues, among them the Hurva. In the 1834 Arab revolt in Palestine, Qasim al-Ahmad led his forces from Nablus and attacked Jerusalem, aided by the Abu Ghosh clan, entered the city on May 31, 1834. The Christians and Jews of Jerusalem were subjected to attacks. Ibrahim's Egyptian army routed Qasim's forces in Jerusalem the following month.

Ottoman rule was reinstated in 1840, but many Egyptian Muslims remained in Jerusalem and Jews from Algiers and North Africa began to settle in the city in growing numbers. In the 1840s and 1850s, the international powers began a tug-of-war in Palestine as they sought to extend their protection over the region's religious minorities, a struggle carried out mainly through consular representatives in Jerusalem. According to the Prussian consul, the population in 1845 was 16,410, with 7,120 Jews, 5,000 Muslims, 3,390 Christians, 800

Turkish soldiers and 100 Europeans. The volume of Christian pilgrims increased under the Ottomans, doubling the city's population around Easter time.

In the 1860s, new neighborhoods began to develop outside the Old City walls to house pilgrims and ıelieve the intense overcrowding and poor sanitation inside the city. The Russian Compound and Mishkenot Sha'ananim were founded in 1860. In 1867 an American Missionary reports an estimated population of Jerusalem of 'above' 15,000, with 4,000 to 5,000 Jews and 6,000 Muslims. Every year there were 5,000 to 6,000 Russian Christian Pilgrims.

In 1917 after the Battle of Jerusalem, the British Army, led by General Edmund Allenby, captured the city, and in 1922, the League of Nations at the Conference of Lausanne entrusted the United Kingdom to administer the Mandate for Palestine, the neighbouring mandate of Transjordan to the east across the River Jordan, and the Iraq Mandate beyond it.

From 1922 to 1948 the total population of the city rose from 52,000 to 165,000 with two thirds of Jews and one-third of Arabs (Muslims and Christians). The situation between Arabs and Jews in Palestine was not quiet. In Jerusalem, in particular, riots occurred in 1920 and in 1929. Under the British, new garden suburbs were built in the western and northern parts of the city and institutions of higher learning such as the Hebrew University were founded.

As the British Mandate for Palestine was expiring, the 1947 UN Partition Plan recommended "the creation of a special international regime in the City of Jerusalem, constituting it as a corpus separatum under the administration of the United Nations." The international regime (which also included the city of Bethlehem) was to remain in force for a period of ten years, whereupon a referendum was to be held in which the residents were to decide the future regime of their city. However, this plan was not implemented, as the 1948 war erupted, while the British withdrew from Palestine and Israel declared its independence. The war led to displacement of Arab and Jewish populations in the city. The 1,500 residents of the Jewish Quarter of the Old City were expelled and a few hundred taken prisoner when the Arab Legion captured the quarter on 28 May. The Arab Legion also attacked Western Jerusalem with snipers. Arab residents of Katamon, Talbiya, and the German Colony were driven from their homes.

The war of 1948 resulted in Jerusalem being divided, with the old walled city lying entirely on the Jordanian side of the line. A no-man's land between East and West Jerusalem came into being in November 1948: Moshe Dayan, commander of the Israeli forces in Jerusalem, met with his Jordanian counterpart Abdullah el Tell in a deserted house in Jerusalem's Musrara neighborhood and marked out their respective positions: Israel's position in red and Jordan's in green. This rough map, which was not meant as an official one, became the final line in the 1949 Armistice Agreements, which divided the city and left Mount Scopus as an Israeli exclave inside East Jerusalem. Barbed wire and concrete barriers ran down the center of the city, passing close by Jaffa Gate on the western side of the old walled city, and a crossing point was established at Mandelbaum Gate slightly to the north of the old walled city. Military skirmishes frequently threatened the ceasefire. After the establishment of the State of Israel, Jerusalem was declared its capital. Jordan formally annexed East Jerusalem in 1950, subjecting it to Jordanian law. Only the United Kingdom and Pakistan formally recognized such annexation, which, in regard to Jerusalem, was on a de facto basis. Also, it is dubious if Pakistan recognized Jordan's annexation.

After 1948, since the old walled city in its entirety was to the east of the armistice line, Jordan was able to take control of all the holy places therein, and contrary to the terms of the armistice agreement, Israelis were denied access to Jewish holy sites, many of which were desecrated. 34 of the 35 synagogues in the Old City ,including the Hurva and the Tiferet Yisrael Synagogue, were destroyed over the course of the next 19 years, either razed or used as stables and hen-houses. Many other historic and religiously significant buildings were replaced by modern structures. The Jewish Quarter became known as Harat al-Sharaf and was occupied by refugees from the 1948 war. In 1966 the Jordanian authorities relocated 500 of them to the Shua'fat refugee camp as part of plans to redevelop the area.

Jordan allowed only very limited access to Christian holy sites. During this period, the Dome of the Rock and al-Aqsa Mosque underwent major renovations.

In 1967, the Six-Day War saw hand to hand fighting between Israeli and Jordanian soldiers on the Temple Mount, and it resulted in Israel capturing East Jerusalem. Hence Jewish and Christian access to the holy sites inside the old walled city was restored, while the Temple Mount remained under the jurisdiction of an Islamic waqf. The Moroccan Quarter, which was located adjacent to the Western Wall, was vacated and razed to make way for a plaza for those visiting the wall. Since the war, Israel has expanded the city's boundaries and established a ring of Jewish neighbourhoods on land east of the Green Line. Since 1967, Israel has gone to considerable lengths to make the sections of Jerusalem it captured in the Six Day War more Jewish.

However, the takeover of East Jerusalem was met with international criticism. Following the passing of Israel's Jerusalem Law, which declared Jerusalem, "complete and united", the capital of Israel, the United Nations Security Council passed a resolution that declared the law "a violation of international law" and requested all member states to withdraw all remaining embassies from the city.

The status of the city, and especially its holy places, remains a core issue in the Israeli-Palestinian conflict. The Israeli government has approved building plans in the Muslim Quarter of the Old City in order to expand the Jewish presence in East Jerusalem, while prominent Islamic leaders have made claims that Jews have no historical connection to Jerusalem, alleging that the 2,500-year old Western Wall was constructed as part of a mosque. Palestinians envision East Jerusalem as the capital of a future Palestinian state, and the city's borders have been the subject of bilateral talks. A strong longing for peace is symbolized by the Peace Monument (with farming tools made out of scrap weapons), facing the Old City wall near the former Israeli-Jordanian border and quoting from the book of Isaiah in Arabic and Hebrew.

The airport nearest to Jerusalem is Atarot Airport, which was used for domestic flights until its closure in 2001. Since then it has been under the control of the Israel Defense Forces due to disturbances in Ramallah and the West Bank. All air traffic from Atarot was rerouted to Ben Gurion International Airport, Israel's largest and busiest airport, which serves nine million passengers annually.

Egged Bus Cooperative, the second-largest bus company in the world, handles most of the local and intercity bus service out of the city's Central Bus Station on Jaffa Road near the western entrance to Jerusalem from highway 1. As of 2008, Egged buses, taxicabs and private cars are the only transportation options in Jerusalem. This is expected to change with the completion of the Jerusalem Light Rail, a new rail-based transit system currently under construction. According to plans, the first rail line will be capable of transporting an estimated 200,000 people daily, and will have 24 stops. It is scheduled for completion in 2010.

Another work in progress is a new high-speed rail line from Tel Aviv to Jerusalem, which is scheduled to be completed in 2017. Its terminus will be an underground station (80 m (262.47 ft) deep) serving the International Convention Center and the Central Bus Station, and is planned to be extended eventually to Malha station. Israel Railways operates train services to Malha train station from Tel Aviv via Beit Shemesh.

Begin Expressway is one of Jerusalem's major north-south thoroughfares; it runs on the western side of the city, merging in the north with Route 443, which continues toward Tel Aviv. Route 60 runs through the center of the city near the Green Line between East and West Jerusalem. Construction is progressing on parts of a 35-kilometer (22-mile) ring road around the city, fostering faster connection between the suburbs. The eastern half of the project was conceptualized decades ago, but reaction to the proposed highway is still mixed.

Safed

Safed is a city in the Northern District of Israel. Located at an elevation of 900 metres (2,953 ft), Safed is the highest city in the Galilee and of Israel. Due to its high elevation, Safed experiences warm summers and cold, often snowy, winters. Since the sixteenth century, Safed has been considered one of Judaism's Four Holy Cities, along with Jerusalem, Hebron and Tiberias; since that time, the city has remained a center of Kabbalah, also known as Jewish mysticism.

Due to its beautiful setting surrounded by pine forests and its mild mid-year temperatures, Safed has become a summer holiday resort frequented by Israelis and foreign visitors alike.

Hebron

Hebron is located in the southern West Bank, 30 km (19 mi) south of Jerusalem. Nestled in the Judean Mountains, it lies 930 meters (3,050 ft) above sea level. It is the largest city in the West Bank and home to around 165,000 Palestinians, and over 500 Jewish settlers concentrated in and around the old quarter. The city is most notable for containing the traditional burial site of the biblical Patriarchs and Matriarchs and is therefore considered the second-holiest city in Judaism after Jerusalem. The city is also venerated by Muslims for its association with Abraham and was traditionally viewed as one of the "four holy cities of Islam."

Hebron is a busy hub of West Bank trade, responsible for roughly a third of the area's gross domestic product, largely due to the sale of marble from quarries. It is locally well-known for its grapes, figs, limestone, pottery workshops and glassblowing factories, and is the location of the major dairy product manufacturer, al-Junaidi. The old city of Hebron is characterized by narrow, winding streets, flat-roofed stone houses, and old bazaars. The city is home to Hebron University and the Palestine Polytechnic University.

Tiberias

Tiberias is a city on the western shore of the Sea of Galilee, Lower Galilee, Israel. Established in 20 CE, it was named in honour of the emperor Tiberius.

Tiberias has been venerated in Judaism since the middle of the 2nd-century and since the 16th century, has been considered one of Judaism's Four Holy Cities, along with Jerusalem, Hebron and Safed. In the 2nd-10th centuries, Tiberias was the largest Jewish city in the Galilee, and the political and religious hub of the Jews of Palestine. According to Christian tradition, Jesus performed several miracles in the Tiberias district, making it an important pilgrimage site for devout Christians. Tiberias has historically been known for its hot springs, believed to cure skin and other ailments, for thousands of years.

Tiberias was founded sometime around 20 CE in the Judea Province of Rome by Roman-Jewish client king Herod Antipas, son of Herod the Great, who made it the capital of his realm in Galilee. It had a Jewish majority, living alongside a heterogeneous population. It was named in honor of the Roman Emperor Tiberius. There is a legend that Tiberias was built on the site of the Israelite village of Rakkat, mentioned in the Book of Joshua (Joshua 19:35). A discussion of Tiberias as Rakkat appears in the Talmud. In The Antiquities of the Jews, the Roman Jewish historian Josephus states that Tiberias was near Emmaus. This location is repeated in The Wars of the Jews.

Under the Roman Empire, the city was known by its Greek name an adaptation of the taw-suffixed Semitic form that preserved its feminine grammatical gender.

In the days of Antipas, the more religious (as opposed to Hellenized) Jews refused to settle there; the presence of a cemetery rendered the site ritually unclean. Antipas settled many non-Jews there from rural Galilee and other parts of his domains in order to populate his new capital, and built a palace on the acropolis. The prestige of Tiberias was so great that the sea of Galilee soon came to be named the sea of Tiberias; however, what would now be called Jewish zealots continued to call it 'Yam Ha-Kinerett', its traditional name. The city was governed by a city council of 600 with a committee of 10 until 44 CE when a Roman Procurator was set over the city after the death of Agrippa I. In 61 CE Agrippa II annexed the city to his kingdom whose capital was Caesarea Phillippi. During the First Jewish-Roman War Josephus Flavius took control of the city and destroyed Herod's palace but was able to stop the city from being pillaged by his Jewish army. Where most other cities in Palestine were razed, Tiberias was spared because its inhabitants remained loyal to Rome after Josephus Flavius had surrendered the city to the Roman emperor Vespasian. It became a mixed city after the fall of Jerusalem; with Judea subdued, the southern Jewish population migrated to Galilee.

In 145 CE, Rabbi Shimon bar Yochai "cleansed the city of ritual impurity allowing Jews to settle in the city in numbers." The Sanhedrin, the Jewish court, also fled from Jerusalem during the Great Jewish Revolt against the Roman Empire, and after several moves eventually settled in Tiberias in about 150 CE. It was to be its final meeting place before its disbanding in the early Byzantine period. Following the expulsion of all Jews from Jerusalem after 135, Tiberias and its neighbor Sepphoris became the major Jewish centres. From the time when Yochanan bar Nafcha (d. 279) settled in Tiberias, the city became the focus of Jewish religious scholarship in the land. The Mishnah along with the Jerusalem Talmud, (the written discussions of generations of rabbis in the Land of Israel - primarily in the academies of Tiberias and Caesarea), was probably compiled in Tiberias by Rabbi Judah haNasi in around 200 CE. The 13 synagogues served the spiritual needs of a growing Jewish population.

In the 6th century Tiberias was still the seat of Jewish religious learning. In light of this, Bishop Simeon of Beth Arsham urged the Christians of Palestine to seize the leaders of Judaism in Tiberias, to put them to the rack, and to compel them to command the Jewish king, Dhu Nuwas, to desist from persecuting the Christians in Najran.

In 614, Tiberias was the site where during the final Jewish revolt against the Byzantine Empire, some of the Jewish population supported the Persian invaders; the Christians were massacred and the churches destroyed. In 628 the Byzantium army retook Tiberias and the slaughter of the Christians was then reciprocated with a slaughter of the Jews.

8 Buddhism Religious Tourism Spots

Buddhism is a religion and philosophy encompassing a variety of traditions, beliefs and practices, largely based on teachings attributed to Siddhartha Gautama, commonly known as the Buddha (P?li/Sanskrit "the awakened one"). The Buddha lived and taught in the northeastern Indian subcontinent some time between the 6th and 4th centuries BCE. He is recognized by Buddhists as an awakened or enlightened teacher who shared his insights to help sentient beings end suffering (or dukkha), achieve nirvana, and escape what is seen as a cycle of suffering and rebirth.

Two major branches of Buddhism are recognized: Theravada ("The School of the Elders") and Mahayana ("The Great Vehicle"). Theravada-the oldest surviving branch-has a widespread following in Sri Lanka and Southeast Asia. Mahayana is found throughout East Asia and includes the traditions of Pure Land, Zen, Nichiren Buddhism, Tibetan Buddhism, Shingon, Tendai and Shinnyo-en. In some classifications Vajrayana-a subcategory of Mahayana practiced in Tibet and Mongolia-is recognized as a third branch. While Buddhism remains most popular within Asia, both branches are now found throughout the world. Estimates of Buddhists worldwide vary significantly depending on the way Buddhist adherence is defined. Lower estimates are between 350-500 million.

Buddhist schools vary on the exact nature of the path to liberation, the importance and canonicity of various teachings and scriptures, and especially their respective practices. The foundations of Buddhist tradition and practice are the Three Jewels: the Buddha, the Dharma (the teachings), and the Sangha (the community). Taking "refuge in the triple gem" has traditionally been a declaration and commitment to being on the Buddhist path and in general distinguishes a Buddhist from a non-Buddhist. Other practices may include following ethical precepts, support of the monastic community, renouncing conventional living and becoming a monastic, the development of mindfulness and practice of meditation, cultivation of higher wisdom and discernment, study of scriptures, devotional practices, ceremonies, and in the Mahayana tradition, invocation of buddhas and bodhisattvas.

Mahabodhi Temple

The Mahabodhi Temple is a Buddhist temple in Bodh Gaya, the location where Siddhartha Gautama, the Buddha, attained enlightenment. Bodh Gaya is located about 96 km (60 mi) from Patna, Bihar state, India. Next to the temple, to its western side, is the holy Bodhi tree. In the Pali Canon, the site is called Bodhimanda, and the monastery there the Bodhimanda Vihara. The tallest tower is 55 metres (180 ft) tall.

Traditional accounts say that, around 530 BC, Siddhartha Gautama, a young Indian Prince who saw the suffering of the world and wanted to end it, reached the sylvan banks of Falgu River, near the city of Gaya, India. There he sat in meditation under a peepul tree (Ficus religiosa or Sacred Fig), which later became known as the Bodhi tree. According to Buddhist scriptures, after three days and three nights, Siddharta attained enlightenment and the answers that he had sought. Mahabodhi Temple was built to mark that location.

The Buddha then spent the succeeding seven weeks at seven different spots in the vicinity meditating and considering his experience. Several specific places at the current Mahabodhi Temple relate to the traditions surrounding these seven weeks:

- The first week was spent under the Bodhi tree.
- During the second week, the Buddha remained standing and stared, uninterrupted, at the Bodhi tree. This spot is marked by the Animeshlocha Stupa, that is, the unblinking stupa or shrine, which is located on the north-east of the Mahabodhi Temple complex. There stands a statue of Buddha with his eyes fixed towards the Bodhi tree.
- The Buddha is said to have walked back and forth between the location of the Animeshlocha Stupa and the Bodhi tree. According to legend, lotus flowers sprung up along this route, it is now called

Ratnachakarma or the jewel walk.

In approximately 250 BCE, about 250 years after the Buddha attained Enlightenment, Buddhist Emperor Asoka visited Bodh Gaya with the intention of establishing a monastery and shrine. As part of the temple, he built the diamond throne (called the Vajrasana), attempting to mark the exact spot of the Buddha's enlightenment, was established. Asoka is considered the founder of the Mahabodhi Temple. The present temple dates from the 5th-6th century, although in the words of one scholar it is largely a nineteenth-century British Archaeological Survey of India reconstruction based on what is generally believed to be an approximately fifth-century structure. Prior to that, there seems to have been a pyramidal structure perhaps built in about the second century (Ku???a period). Knowledge of it comes only from a small, circa fourth century terracotta plaque found at modern Patna. It is significant that this version does not have the upper terrace with the small temples in the four corners. These small temples, although not used as such today, probably reflected certain esoteric traditions in Buddhism that were emerging more and more into less esoteric contexts by the late fourth and early fifth century. The pyramidal temple probably replaced an open pavilion that had been constructed around the tree and the Asokan platform . Representations of this early temple arc found at Sanci, on the tora?as of St?pa I, dating from around 25 BC, and on a relief carving from the stupa railing at Bh?hrut (Fig.20), from the early ?u?ga period (c. 185-c. 73 BC).

It is one of the earliest Buddhist temples built entirely in brick that is still standing in India, from the late Gupta period. Buddhism declined when the dynasties patronizing it declined, following White Hun and the early Arab Islamic invasions such as that of Muhammad bin Qasim. A strong revival occurred under the Pala Empire in the northeast of the subcontinent (where the temple is situated). Mahayana Buddhism flourished under the Palas between the 8th and the 12th century. However, after the defeat of the Palas by the Hindu Sena dynasty, Buddhism's position again began to erode and became nearly extinct in India. During the 12th century CE, Bodh Gaya and the nearby regions were invaded by Muslim Turk armies. During this period, the Mahabodhi Temple fell into disrepair and was largely abandoned. Over the following centuries, the monastery's abbot or mahant became the area's primary landholder and claimed ownership of the Mahabodhi Temple grounds.

In the 1880s, the then-British government of India began to restore Mahabodhi Temple under the direction of Sir Alexander Cunningham. A short time later, in 1891, the Sri Lankan Buddhist leader Anagarika Dharmapala started a campaign to return control of the temple to Buddhists, over the objections of the mahant. The campaign was partially successful in 1949, when control passed from the Hindu mahant to the state government of Bihar, which established a temple management committee. The committee has nine members, a majority of whom, including the chairman, must by law be Hindus. Mahabodhi's first head monk under the management committee was Anagarika Munindra, a Bengali man who had been an active member of the Maha Bodhi Society.

Mahabodhi Temple is constructed of brick and is one of the oldest brick structures to have survived in eastern India. It is considered to be a fine example of Indian brickwork, and was highly influential in the development of later architectural traditions. According UNESCO, "the present temple is one of the earliest and most imposing structures built entirely in brick from Gupta period".

Mahabodhi Temple's central tower rises 55 metres (180 ft), and were heavily renovated in the 19th century. The central tower is surrounded by four smaller towers, constructed in the same style.

The Mahabodhi Temple is surrounded on all four sides by stone railings, about two metres high. The railings reveal two distinct types, both in style as well as the materials used. The older ones, made of sandstone, date to about 150 BCE, and the others, constructed from unpolished coarse granite, are believed to be of the Gupta period (300-600 CE). The older railings have scenes such as Lakshmi, the Hindu goddess of wealth, being bathed by elephants; and Surya, the Hindu sun god, riding a chariot drawn by four horses. The newer railings have figures of stupas (reliquary shrines) and garudas (eagles). Images of lotus flowers also appear commonly.

Nalanda

Nalanda is the name of an ancient center of higher learning in Bihar, India. The site of Nalanda is located in the Indian state of Bihar, about 55 miles south east of Patna, and was a Buddhist center of learning from 427 to 1197 CE. It has been called "one of the first great universities in recorded history." Some buildings were constructed by the Mauryan emperor Ashoka the Great (i.e. Raja Asoka: 273-232 BCE) which is an indication of an early establishment of the Buddhist learning center Nalanda. The Gupta

Empire also patronized some monasteries. According to historians, Nalanda flourished between the reign of the Gupta king ?akr?ditya (also known as Kum?ragupta, reigned 415-55) and 1197 CE, supported by patronage from Buddhist emperors like Harsha as well as later emperors from the Pala Empire. The complex was built with red bricks and its ruins occupy an area of 14 hectares. At its peak, the university attracted scholars and students from as far away as China, Greece, and Persia. Nalanda was sacked by Turkic Muslim invaders under Bakhtiyar Khalji in 1193, a milestone in the decline of Buddhism in India. The great library of Nalanda University was so vast that it is reported to have burned for three months after the Mughals set fire to it, sacked and destroyed the monasteries, and drove the monks from the site. In 2006, Singapore, China, India, Japan, and other nations, announced a proposed plan to restore and revive the ancient site as Nalanda International University.

The Buddha is mentioned as having several times stayed at Nalanda. When he visited Nalanda he would usually reside in P?v?rika's mango grove, and while there he had discussions with Up?li-Gahapati and D?ghatapass?, with Kevatta, and also several conversations with Asibandhakaputta.

The Buddha visited Nalanda during his last tour through Magadha, and it was there that Sariputta uttered his "lion's roar," affirming his faith in the Buddha, shortly before his death. The road from Rajagaha to Nalanda passed through Ambalatthik?, and from Nalanda it went on to P?talig?ma. Between Rajagaha and Nalanda was situated the Bahuputta cetiya.

According to the Kevatta Sutta, in the Buddha's time Nalanda was already an influential and prosperous town, thickly populated, though it was not until later that it became the centre of learning for which it afterwards became famous. There is a record in the Samyutta Nikaya, of the town having been the victim of a severe famine during the Buddha's time. S?riputta, the right hand disciple of the Buddha, was born and died in Nalanda.

Nalanda was the residence of Sonnadinn?. Mahavira is several times mentioned as staying at Nalanda, which was evidently a centre of activity of the Jains. Mahavira is believed to have attained Moksha at Pavapuri, which is located in Nalanda (also according to one sect of Jainism he was born in the nearby village called Kundalpur).

King Asoka (250 BC) is said to have built a stupa in the memory of Sariputta. According to Tibetan sources, Nagarjuna taught there.

Historical studies indicate that the University of Nalanda was established during the reign of the Gupta emperor Kumaragupta. Both Xuanzang and Prajñavarman cite him as the founder, as does a seal discovered at the site.

As historian Sukumar Dutt describes it, the history of Nalanda university "falls into two main divisions--first, one of growth, development and fruition from the sixth century to the ninth, when it was dominated by the liberal cultural traditions inherited from the Gupta age; the second, one of gradual decline and final dissolution from the ninth century to the thirteen--a period when the tantric developments of Buddhism became most pronounced in eastern India."

A number of monasteries grew up during the P?la period in ancient Bengal and Magadha. According to Tibetan sources, five great Mahaviharas stood out: Vikramashila, the premier university of the era; Nalanda, past its prime but still illustrious, Somapura, Odantapur?, and Jaggadala. The five monasteries formed a network; "all of them were under state supervision" and there existed "a system of co-ordination among them . . it seems from the evidence that the different seats of Buddhist learning that functioned in eastern India under the Pila were regarded together as forming a network, an interlinked group of institutions," and it was common for great scholars to move easily from position to position among them.

During the Pali period the Nalanda was less singularly outstanding, as other P?la establishments "must have drawn away a number of learned monks from Nalanda when all of them . . came under the aegis of the Palis."

In 1193, the Nalanda University was sacked by the Islamic fanatic Bakhtiyar Khilji, a Turk; this event is seen by scholars as a late milestone in the decline of Buddhism in India. The Persian historian Minhaj-i-Siraj, in his chronicle the Tabaquat-I-Nasiri, reported that thousands of monks were burned alive and thousands beheaded as Khilji tried his best to uproot Buddhism and plant Islam by the sword; the burning of the library continued for several months and "smoke from the burning manuscripts hung for days like a dark pall over the low hills."

The last throne-holder of Nalanda, Shakyashribhadra, fled to Tibet in 1204 CE at the invitation of the Tibetan translator Tropu Lotsawa (Khro-phu Lo-tsa-ba Byams-pa dpal). In Tibet he started an ordination lineage of the Mulasarvastivadin lineage to complement the two existing ones.

When the Tibetan translator Chag Lotsawa (Chag Lo-tsa-ba, 1197-1264) visited the site in 1235, he found it damaged and looted, with a 90-year-old teacher, Rahula Shribhadra, instructing a class of about 70 students. During Chag Lotsawa's time there an incursion by Turkish soldiers caused the remaining students to flee. Despite all this, "remnants of the debilitated Buddhist community continued to struggle on under scarce resources until c. 1400 CE when Chagalaraja was reportedly the last king to have patronized Nalanda."

Ahir considers the destruction of the temples, monasteries, centers of learning at Nalanda and northern India to be responsible for the demise of ancient Indian scientific thought in mathematics, astronomy, alchemy, and anatomy.

According to some Indian historians, increasing pressure was felt on Nalanda from Brahmanical society over the course of the 10th century. According to historian Prakash Buddh, a Yajna a fire sacrifice performed by Hindus resulted in a great conflagration which consumed Ratnabodhi, the nine-storeyed library of Nalanda. In his Social history of India, the historian Sadasivan states, "the enormous manuscript library of the University was set on fire by Trithikas (all sects of Brahmins) with the support of Jainas due to the mounting jealousy they nurtured against the great center of learning."

Rajgir

Rajgir is a city and a notified area in Nalanda district in the Indian state of Bihar. The city of Rajgir (ancient Rajagaha; Pali: Rajagaha) was the first capital of the kingdom of Magadha, a state that would eventually evolve into the Mauryan Empire. Its date of origin is unknown, although ceramics dating to about 1000 BC have been found in the city.

Rajgir is connected to Patna via Bakhtiarpur by rail and road. Bakhtiarpur lies midway between Patna and Mokameh. Road access is byNH 30A to Bakhtiarpur and NH 31 towards south to reach Bihar Sharif. From Mokameh NH 31 to Bihar Sharif. From there, NH 82 will leads to Rajgir. Rajgir is around 100 KM from both Patna and Mokameh. It is located in a green valley surrounded by rocky hills. Indian Railways run trains directly from Rajgir to New Delhi, Shramjeevi Express.

The name Rajgir might come from Sanskrit Rajagaha 'house of the king' or "royal house", or the word rajgir might have its origian in its plain literal meaning, "royal mountain". It was the ancient capital city of the Magadha kings until the 5th century BC when Ajatashatru moved the capital to Pataliputra. In those days, it was called Rajgrih, which translates as 'the home of Royalty'.

The epic Mahabharata calls it Girivraja and recounts the story of its king, Jarasandha, and his battle with the Pandava brothers and their allies Krishna. Jarasandha who hailed from this place had been defeated by Krishna 17 times. The 18th time Krishna left the battlefield without fighting. Because of this Krishna is also called 'ranacora' (one who has left the battlefield). Mahabharata recounts a wrestling match between Bhima, one of the pandavas, and Jarasandha, the then king of Rajgir. Jarasandha was invincible as his body could rejoin any dismembered limbs. According to the legend, Bhim split Jarasandha into two and threw the two halves facing opposite to each other so that they could not join. There is a famous Jarasandha's Akhara(place where martial arts are practiced).

It is also mentioned in Buddhist and Jain scriptures, which give a series of place-names, but without geographical context. The attempt to locate these places is based largely on reference to them and to other locations in the works of Chinese Buddhist pilgrims, particularly Faxian and Xuanzang. It is on the basis of Xuanzang in particular that the site is divided into Old and New Rajgir. The former lies within a valley and is surrounded by low-lying hills. It is defined by an earthen embankment (the Inner Fortification), with which is associated the Outer Fortification, a complex of cyclopean walls that runs (with large breaks) along the crest of the hills. New Rajgir is defined by another, larger, embankment outside the northern entrance of the valley and next to the modern town.

It is sacred to the memory of the founders of both the religions: Buddhism and Jainism and associated with both the historical Buddha and Mahavira.

It was here that Gautama Buddha spent several months meditating, and preaching at Griddhkuta, ('Hill of the Vultures'). He also delivered some of his famous sermons and converted King Bimbisara of Magadha and countless others to his religion.On one of the hills is the Saptparni cave where the First Buddhist Council was held under the leadership of Maha Kassapa. Lord Mahavira spent fourteen years of his life at Rajgir and Nalanda, spending chaturmas (i.e. 4 months of the rainy season) at a single place in Rajgir (Rajgruhi) and the rest in the places in the vicinity. It was the capital of his favourite shishya (follower) king Shrenik. Thus Rajgir is a very important religious place for Jains also.

Rajgir is also famous for its association with Haryanka Kings Bimbisara and Ajatashatru. Ajatashatru kept his father Bimbsara in captivitiy here. The sources do not agree which of the Buddha's royal contemporaries, Bimbisara and Ajatashatru, was responsible for its construction. Ajatashatru is also credited with moving the capital to Pataliputra (modern Patna).

Sanchi

Sanchi is a small village in Raisen District of the state of Madhya Pradesh, India, it is located 46 km north east of Bhopal, and 10 km from Besnagar and Vidisha in the central part of the state of Madhya Pradesh. It is the location of several Buddhist monuments dating from the 3rd century BCE to the 12th century CE and is one of the important places of Buddhist pilgrimage. It is a nagar panchayat in Raisen district in the Indian state of Madhya Pradesh. Toranas surround the Stupa and they each represent love, peace, trust, and courage.

The 'Great Stupa' at Sanchi was originally commissioned by the emperor Ashoka the Great in the 3rd century BCE. Its nucleus was a simple hemispherical brick structure built over the relics of the Buddha. It was crowned by the chatra, a parasol-like structure symbolising high rank, which was intended to honour and shelter the relics.

Dubdi Monasteryte

Dubdi Monastery, occasionally called Yuksom Monastery is a Buddhist monastery of the Nyingma sect of Tibetan Buddhism near Yuksom, in the Geyzing subdivision of West Sikkim district, in northeastern India.

The Chogyar Namgyal established the first monastery known as the Dubdi Monastery in 1701, at Yuksom in Sikkim, which is part of Buddhist religious pilgrimage circuit involving the Norbugang Chorten, Pemayangtse Monastery, the Rabdentse ruins, the Sanga Choeling Monastery, the Khecheopalri Lake, and the Tashiding Monastery.

Established in 1701, it is professed to be the oldest monastery in Sikkim and is located on the top of a hill which is about an hour's walk (3 kilometres (1.9 mi)) from Yuksom. It was also known as the Hermit's Cell after its ascetic founder Lhatsun Namkha Jigme, who along with two other lamas from Tibet met at Norbugang near Yuksom and crowned Phuntsog Namgyal as the first King or Chogyal of Sikkim at Norbugang

Yuksom in 1642. The literal meaning of 'Dubdi' in local language is "the retreat".

Chudamani Vihara

Chudamani Vihara was a Buddhist vihara (monastery) in Nagapattinam, Tamil Nadu, India. Chudamani Vihara was constructed in 1006 CE by the Srivijayan king Sri Vijaya Soolamanivarman with the patronage of Rajaraja Chola. The vihara building survived in dilapidated condition till 1867, when Jesuit missionaries demolished it. Since 1856, about 350 Buddha bronzes have been found at Nagapattinam, dating from the 11th to the 16th century.

Borobudur

Borobudur, or Barabudur, is a 9th-century Mahayana Buddhist monument near Magelang, Central Java, Indonesia. The monument comprises six square platforms topped by three circular platforms, and is decorated with 2,672 relief panels and 504 Buddha statues. A main dome, located at the center of the top platform, is surrounded by 72 Buddha statues seated inside perforated stupa.

The monument is both a shrine to the Lord Buddha and a place for Buddhist pilgrimage. The journey for pilgrims begins at the base of the monument and follows a path circumambulating the monument while ascending to the top through the three levels of Buddhist cosmology, namely K?madh?tu (the world of desire), Rupadhatu (the world of forms) and Arupadhatu (the world of formlessness). During the journey the monument guides the pilgrims through a system of stairways and corridors with 1,460 narrative relief panels on the wall and the balustrades.

Evidence suggests Borobudur was abandoned following the 14th-century decline of Buddhist and Hindu kingdoms in Java, and the Javanese conversion to Islam. Worldwide knowledge of its existence was sparked in 1814 by Sir Thomas Stamford Raffles, then the British ruler of Java, who was advised of its location by native Indonesians. Borobudur has since been preserved through several restorations. The largest restoration project was undertaken between 1975 and 1982 by the Indonesian government and UNESCO, following which the monument was listed as a UNESCO World Heritage Site. Borobudur is still used for pilgrimage; once a year Buddhists in Indonesia celebrate Vesak at the monument, and Borobudur is Indonesia's single most visited tourist attraction.

Candi Surawana

Candi Surawana (sometimes called Candi Surowono) is a small temple, of the Majapahit Kingdom, located in the Canggu Village of the Kediri (near Pare) district in Java, Indonesia. It was believed to have been built in 1390 AD as a memorial to Wijayarajasa, the Prince of Wengker. As of today the temple is not fully intact. Only the base of the temple has been restored to its original form and many more bricks are waiting around the structure to be reassembled.

Atamasthana

These are 8 main places of worship in the Ancient Sacred city of Anuradhapura, Sri Lanka. These places are valued for their artistic, historical and archaeological value.

1. Sri Maha bodhiya
2. Ruwanwelisaya
3. Thuparamaya
4. Lovamahapaya
5. Abhayagiri Dagaba
6. Jetavanarama
7. Mirisaveti Stupa
8. Lankarama

Blue Cliff Monastery

Blue Cliff Monastery is a 80-acre (0.32 km2) Buddhist monastery located in Pine Bush, New York. It was founded in May 2007 by monastic and lay practitioners from Plum Village in France.

The monastery is under the direction of Thich Nhat Hanh's Order of Interbeing in the Vietnamese Zen tradition. Blue Cliff Monastery follows the same practices and daily schedules as its root monastery Plum Village and its sister monasteries Deer Park Monastery in Escondido, California and Magnolia Grove Monastery in Batesville, Mississippi.

Blue Cliff Monastery was created when the monastics moved from Maple Forest Monastery and the Green Mountain Dharma Center. In 1997 Maple Forest Monastery was founded in Woodstock, Vermont and a year latter Green Mountain Dharma Center was founded in Hartland, Vermont. Maple Forest was the monks residence and Green Mountain was the nuns residence. On May 2007 both centers moved to Blue Cliff Monastery.

The Monastery is located in the lush green Hudson Valley of New York (one hour and 30 minutes away from NYC). Inside the property there are two ponds and a creek, and out of its 80 acres 65 are forest. Visitors are welcome to practice mindfulness with the fourfold community of monks, nuns, laymen and laywomen. Typically days of mindfulness are held twice a week (Thursdays and Sundays). Retreats are held frequently throughout the year.

9 Zoroastrianism Religious Tourism Spots

Zoroastrianism is a religion and philosophy based on the teachings of prophet Zoroaster (also known as Zarathustra, in Avestan) and was formerly among the world's largest religions. It was probably founded some time before the 6th century BCE in Persia (Iran). The term Zoroastrianism is, in general usage, essentially synonymous with Mazdaism (the worship of Ahura Mazda, exalted by Zoroaster as the supreme divine authority).

In Zoroastrianism, the Creator Ahura Mazda is all good, and no evil originates from Him. Thus, in Zoroastrianism good and evil have distinct sources, with evil (druj) trying to destroy the creation of Mazda (asha), and good trying to sustain it. Mazda is not immanent in the world, and His creation is represented by the Amesha Spentas and the host of other Yazatas, through whom the works of God are evident to humanity, and through whom worship of Mazda is ultimately directed. The most important texts of the religion are those of the Avesta, of which a significant portion has been lost, and mostly only the liturgies of which have survived. The lost portions are known of only through references and brief quotations in the later works, primarily from the 9th to 11th centuries.

In some form, it served as the national- or state religion of a significant portion of the Iranian people for many centuries. It first dwindled when the Achaemenid Empire was invaded by Alexander III of Macedon, after which it collapsed and disintegrated and it was further gradually marginalized by Islam from the 7th century onwards with the decline of the Sassanid Empire. The political power of the pre-Islamic Iranian dynasties lent Zoroastrianism immense prestige in ancient times, and some of its leading doctrines were adopted by other religious systems. It has no major theological divisions (the only significant schism is based on calendar differences), but it is not uniform. Modern-era influences have a significant impact on individual and local beliefs, practices, values and vocabulary, sometimes complementing tradition and enriching it, but sometimes also displacing tradition entirely.

Zoroastrians believe that there is one universal and transcendent God, Ahura Mazda. He is said to be the one uncreated Creator to whom all worship is ultimately directed. Ahura Mazda's creation-evident as asha, truth and order-is the antithesis of chaos, which is evident as druj, falsehood and disorder. The resulting conflict involves the entire universe, including humanity, which has an active role to play in the conflict.

The religion states that active participation in life through good thoughts, good words, and good deeds is necessary to ensure happiness and to keep chaos at bay. This active participation is a central element in Zoroaster's concept of free will, and Zoroastrianism rejects all forms of monasticism. Ahura Mazda will ultimately prevail over the evil Angra Mainyu or Ahriman, at which point the universe will undergo a cosmic renovation and time will end. In the final renovation, all of creation-even the souls of the dead that were initially banished to "darkness"-will be reunited in Ahura Mazda, returning to life in the undead form. At the end of time, a savior-figure (a Saoshyant) will bring about a final renovation of the world (frasho.kereti), in which the dead will be revived.

In Zoroastrian tradition, the malevolent is represented by Angra Mainyu (also referred to as "Ahriman"), the "Destructive Principle", while the benevolent is represented through Ahura Mazda's Spenta Mainyu, the instrument or "Bounteous Principle" of the act of creation. It is through Spenta Mainyu that transcendental Ahura Mazda is immanent in humankind, and through which the Creator interacts with the world. According to Zoroastrian cosmology, in articulating the Ahuna Vairya formula, Ahura Mazda made His ultimate triumph evident to Angra Mainyu. As expressions and aspects of Creation, Ahura Mazda emanated the Amesha Spentas ("Bounteous Immortals"), that are each the hypostasis and representative of one aspect of that Creation. These Amesha Spenta are in turn assisted by a league of lesser principles, the Yazatas, each "Worthy of Worship" and each again a hypostasis of a moral or physical aspect of creation.

In Zoroastrianism, water (apo, aban) and fire (atar, adar) are agents of ritual purity, and the associated purification ceremonies are considered the basis of ritual life. In Zoroastrian cosmogony, water and fire are respectively the second and last primordial elements to have been created, and scripture considers fire to have its origin in the waters. Both water and fire are considered life-sustaining, and both water and fire are represented within the precinct of a fire temple. Zoroastrians usually pray in the presence of some form of fire (which can be considered evident in any source of light), and the culminating rite of the principle act of worship constitutes a "strengthening of the waters". Fire is considered a medium through which spiritual insight and wisdom is gained, and water is considered the source of that wisdom.

While the Parsees in India have traditionally been opposed to proselytizing, probably for historical reasons, and even considered it a crime for which the culprit may face expulsion, Iranian Zoroastrians have never been opposed to conversion, and the practice has been endorsed by the Council of Mobeds of Tehran. While the Iranian authorities do not permit proselytizing within Iran, Iranian Zoroastrians in exile have actively encouraged missionary activities, with The Zarathushtrian Assembly in Los Angeles and the International Zoroastrian Centre in Paris as two prominent centres.

As in many other faiths, Zoroastrians are strongly encouraged to marry others of the same faith, but this is not a requirement of the religion itself. Rather, it is a creation of those in India. Some members of the Indian Zoroastrian community (the Parsis) contend that a child must have a Parsi father to be eligible for introduction into the faith, but this assertion is considered by most to be a violation of the Zoroastrian tenets of gender equality, and may be a remnant of an old Indian legal definition (since overruled) of Parsi. This issue is a matter of debate within the Parsi community, but with the increasingly global nature of modern society and the dwindling number of Zoroastrians, such opinions are less vociferous than they were previously.

In Zoroastrian tradition, life is a temporary state in which a mortal is expected to actively participate in the continuing battle between truth and falsehood. Prior to being born, the soul (urvan) of an individual is still united with its fravashi, of which there are very many, and which have existed since Mazda created the universe. During life, the fravashi acts as a guardian and protector. On the fourth day after death, the soul is reunited with its fravashi, in which the experiences of life in the material world are collected for the continuing battle in the spiritual world. For the most part, Zoroastrianism does not have a notion of reincarnation, at least not until the final renovation of the world. Despite this, followers of

Ilm-e-Kshnoom in India believe in reincarnation and practice vegetarianism, two principles unknown to Orthodox Zoroastrianism.

In Zoroastrian scripture and tradition, a corpse is a host for decay, i.e., of druj. Consequently, scripture enjoins the "safe" disposal of the dead in a manner such that a corpse does not pollute the "good" creation. These injunctions are the doctrinal basis of the fast-fading traditional practice of "ritual exposure", most commonly identified with the so-called "Towers of Silence" for which there is no standard technical term in either scripture or tradition. The practice of ritual exposure is only practised by Zoroastrian communities of the Indian subcontinent, where it is not illegal, but where alternative disposal methods are desperately sought after diclofenac poisoning has led to the virtual extinction of scavenger birds. Other Zoroastrian communities either cremate their dead, or bury them in graves that are cased with lime mortar.

Zoroastrian Sacred Sites

The primary religion in Iran today is the Shia sect of Islam but the far older faith of the prophet Zoroaster is still openly practiced, particularly in the central and northwestern regions of the country. Zoroaster's name in its original form is found in the sacred scripture the Avesta as Zarathushtra. It is not possible to say exactly when he lived but contemporary scholarship has mostly agreed upon the dates of 660-583 BC, with his birthplace being in the region of northwestern Iran now known as Azerbaijan. Similar to other great sages of archaic times, Zoroaster's life is part history and part legend. Tales are told of signs in the sky announcing his coming, of marvels and omens attending his birth, and of acts of power that he performed as a young boy. Around the age of twenty he withdrew from the world to seek the divine through study, wandering and solitary meditation in remote mountain areas. At the age of thirty he experienced the first of seven mystical visions from which he developed his spiritual philosophy and initiated his ministry. In these visions, an angelic entity by the name of Vohu Manah appeared to Zoroaster and escorted him to the throne of the Creator, Ahura Mazda. The wisdom teachings he received from Ahura Mazda are given in the form of seventeen hymns, the Gathas, contained in the Avesta scripture. The Zoroastrian religion has three central commands of Good Thoughts, Good Words, and Good Deeds.

Zoroaster was born in an age of agriculturalists and his religion is therefore deeply associated with the natural world. Besides its emphasis on the eternal conflict of good and bad, Zoroastrianism is also characterized by nature worship, by deification of the sun, moon and stars, and by scrupulously followed injunctions regarding the protection of the earth. In the Zoroastrian faith, reverence is shown to the Creator Ahura Mazda both directly and through the veneration of his various creations and their supernatural guardians. Fire is believed to pervade the other six principal creations and is always present at Zoroastrian ceremonies. During their prayers, believers face towards a fire, or else towards the sun or the moon, which are regarded as heavenly fires and as Ahura Mazda himself. Fire is, however, not regarded as a symbol but as a holy being that comes to man's assistance in return for nourishment and worship. The veneration of fire is also equated with the invocation of truth in the mind and heart of the believer.

The practice of Zoroastrian pilgrimage in contemporary Iran is similar to that of pre-Islamic Persia, though practiced on a vastly reduced scale. In the early period of the religion, it seems that the hearth-fire of each family dwelling was used for worship but that around the 4th century BC communal temples began to be constructed. Fire temples were built in villages and cities, and at remote places in the high mountains sacred rocks, caves and holy springs were venerated. Mythological and archaeological evidence indicates that these mountain sites had been pagan sacred places well before the development of Zoroastrianism. The Greek historian Herodotus, writing in the 5th century BC, made the comment about the early Zoroastrian use of their mountain shrines, "It is not their custom to make and set up statues and temples and altars but they offer sacrifices on the highest peaks of the mountains." Over the centuries of use, however, these natural sacred sites were elaborated and simple temples were built. These mountain shrines, more so than the fire temples of the cities and villages, became the focus of the Zoroastrian pilgrimage tradition.

With the coming of Islam in the 7th century AD, Zoroastrianism lost its position as the dominant religion, large numbers of Zoroastrians converted to Islam, and many remote shrines were abandoned and forgotten. The mountainous region of central Iran around the city of Yazd became a stronghold of Zoroastrianism and today remains the only significant area where shrine pilgrimage is still practiced according to the ancient traditions. There are six holy shrines (called pirs or pirangah) in the Yazd region and the yearly pilgrimages to them are an occasion for the gathering of members of different villages. Although each village has its own fire temple where initiations, agricultural festivals and funeral ceremonies are held, the annual pilgrimages to Pir-e Sabz and the other five mountain shrines are the most important religious periods of the year. Pilgrims may visit any of the shrines throughout the year but the religious benefit is considered greatest when an individual participates in the communal yearly pilgrimages. Pilgrimage ceremonies at the shrines generally last for five days and the pilgrimages themselves are referred to by the Muslim term hajj. Pilgrimage is simultaneously an undertaking of spiritual significance as well as an opportunity for feasting, music and dancing.

Writing on the founding legends of the six major shrines in the Yazd region, Michael Fischer comments that their "mythical origin is a variant of the Bibi Shahbanu legend, namely, that at the time of the Arab invasion a daughter or son or member of the court of Yazdegird III fled before an Arab army towards Khorassan, came to a point of exhaustion near Yazd, called upon God, and was taken into the mountain, rock, well, or cave before the bewildered Arab eyes. The second part of the legend concerns a process of rediscovery. That is to say, the location of these sites of ascension to the next world was lost. Then, in relatively recent times, they were rediscovered by a shepherd, child, or other person in need, to whom a spirit or saint (pir) appeared in a vision or a dream. This spirit aids the human protagonist by solving the mystery of lost sheep, lost path, and so on, requesting in return that a shrine be built." This legend, commonly used by devout Zoroastrians in order to sanctify their mountain shrines, is however, known to date from an historical period demonstrably more recent than the shrines themselves. The Zoroastrian mountain shrines of the Yazd region were used as holy places long before the birth of Islam and therefore predate any legends associated with that religion. The six shrines are:

- Pir-e Sabz (Chak-Chak); 72 kilometers from Yazd, near Ardakan; pilgrimage period June 14-18.
- Seti Pir; east of Yazd, pilgrimage period June 14-18, often visited on the way to the shrine of Pir-e Sabz.
- Pir-e Narestuneh (Narestan); Kharuna mountains, six miles east of Yazd; pilgrimage period: later part of June, after Pir-e Sabz.
- Pir-e Banu-Pars; near Sharifabad; pilgrimage period in early July.
- Pir-e Naraki; at the foot of Mt. Nareke, south of Yazd; pilgrimage period in mid-August.
- Pir-e Herisht; near Sharifabad.

The shrine of Shekaft-e Yazdan (the 'Cleft of God') in the Tutgin valley near the village of Zardju is sometimes visited after the pilgrimage to the shrine of Pir-e Banu-Pars. (Another sacred site in the Yazd region is the Muslim shrine of Haji Khezr, in the town of Kuhbanan.)

Pir-e-Sabz Shrine

For Iranian Zoroastrians, summer begins with the pilgrimage to Pir-e-Sabz. This remote site is the holiest and most visited of the Zoroastrian mountain shrines. Shrine legends tell of a conquering Arab army that had pursued Nikbanoo, the daughter of the Sassanian Emperor Yazdgird III, to this region. Fearing capture, she prayed to Ahura Mazda to protect her from the enemy. In the nick of time the mountain miraculously opened up and gave her protection. This legendary site, where a holy spring issues from the towering cliff, is also called Chak-Chak, which means 'drop-drop' in Persian. Growing beside the source of the holy spring is an immense and ancient tree which legends says used to be Nikbanoo's cane, and the waters of the spring are believed to be tears of grief shed by the mountain for Lady Nikbanoo. The shrine enclosure, a man-made cave, is floored with marble and its walls are darkened by soot from the fires kept eternally burning in the sanctuary. Each year from June 14 to 18, many thousands of Zoroastrians from Iran, India and other countries flock to the temple of Pir-e Sabz. One of the pilgrim trails to Chak-Chak is a dirt road starting near the village of Elabad, north of Yazd. It is a time-honored tradition for pilgrims to stop the moment they see the sight of the shrine and continue the rest of their journey by foot. Several roofed pavilions have been constructed on the cliffs below the shrine and throughout the day and night these are tightly packed with pilgrims.

Zoroastrian Sacred Mountains

Sources of information on Zoroastrian sacred mountains are found in parts of Zoroastrian Avesta literature known as Zamyad Yasht and the Pahlavi Bundahishn.

Mt. Ushi-darena (translated as 'Support of Divine Consciousness' or 'Sustainer of Divine Wisdom') is the mountain where Zoroaster attained illumination and received the revealed knowledge of the supreme god, Ahura Mazda. Another Zoroastrian saint mentioned in the Avestan Yasht literature, Asmo-Khanvant, also attained spiritual illumination upon Ushi-

Darena. This mountain appears to be situated in the Mt. Alborz range near Azerbaijan, Zarathustra's traditional birthplace. The Bundahishn, however, places it in Seistan (or Sajestan), east of Iran in the region referred to in the Avesta (Vendidad I, 9-10) as Vaekereta, the ancient name of Kabul (or Sajestan). The Greeks called in Dranjiana and in the Pahlavi writings it is known as Hushdastar.

Mt. Asnavant, now known as Mt. Ushenai in the Azerbaijan region near the sacred lake of Chaechasta (also known as Urumiah). Asnavant is another mountain where Zarathustra lived for a number of years practicing solitary meditation. In the Bundahishn, Mt. Asnavant is referred to as the seat of Adar Gushasp, the Sacred Fire. It is on this mountain where Zarathustra is believed to have gained the power and energy to go out into the world as a great spiritual teacher, while it was on Mt. Ushi-Darena that he achieved the realization of that which he later taught. The legends of Mt. Asnavant indicate that it has a power that dispels ignorance and develops purity.

Mt. Hara-Berezaiti, identified as Mt. Alborz. The Bundahishn mentions as existing at this mountain a "Bridge of Judgement" or "Bridge of Moral Discrimination" which is a pathway leading to the Otherworld. This bridge or pathway is supposed to run between two mountains, Chakad-e-Daitik and the Arezur ridge of Mt. Alborz. The Zoroastrian scriptures tell of a saintly king, Yima Vivanghvant, who received the power of prophecy from Ahura Mazda upon this mountain.

Yazd Tourist Attractions

It is important to consider the heat while you are in Yazd. The sights in open air are better to be visited in cooler time of the day. Also, those attractions that are exposed to the sunshine should be visited during certain times of the day. I don't recommend to go against the lifestyle of local people specially when it comes to important points. Sometimes, it really gets hot and you will jeopardize your health if you do not follow their recommendations. So, make sure you visit Yazd in the order shown below:

Towers of Silence

These are two hills at the South West of the city where until almost 60 years ago, Zoroastrians, the followers of an ancient Iranian religion, exposed corpse of the deceased ones to the vultures. It will be nice to ascend one of them and see inside it for yourself.

Varahram Fire Temple

As long as you are in the mood of this ancient religion and probably hear from your local guide about the beliefs of Zoroastrians, it will be a good idea to go to the most famous fire temple of the world where the oldest fire is burning since 15 centuries ago. Many of the followers of Zoroastrianism come to Yazd every year to pay a visit to this temple.

Yazd Friday Mosque

Because of its ivan being located at the South of the courtyard, like any other mosques in Iran, it is better to get there fairly soon in the morning when there's enough light to see the details of the mosque and enjoy the beauty of its glazed ceramics and bricks.

Fahadan Quarter

When you visit Yazd, you have a great opportunity to explore this unique community of people who are living in a settlement existing there from lots of centuries ago. At least, this Yazd tourist attraction has been here from 900 years ago when the city walls were built around it. It is full of mud-made walls, narrow lanes and indigenous architecture.

12-Imam Shrine

Inside Fahadan, you see lots of examples of vernacular architecture like wind catchers (badgirs) and water reservoirs. Also, there are monuments like 12-Imam Shrine that was built in 11th century in honor of 12 Imams of Shiites. Nobody is buried there, but the calligraphy in this building is one of two unique stylized scripts found in the entire country.

Alexander's Prison

Some call this structure Haroon's prison too. It actually had been a traditional school called Zia'eh School built in 14th century. Its dome has been beautifully built and decorated with plain bricks. Because of a deep octagonal pit in the courtyard that has got only one entrance and exit, such name is attributed to this building.

After visiting this sight, you can continue on foot to the Northern part of Fahadan quarter. This is where you see the remnants of the ancient city walls and watch towers. Then, you can take some time for lunch and a bit of siesta like local people or go to the another Yazd tourist attraction:

Water Museum

When you visit Yazd, this is the best opportunity you have to get familiar with water supplement system in Iran and how some of the most amazing methods invented by Iranians have helped the survival of millions of people in several continents throughout centuries.

Also, when it is very hot outside in early afternoon, this can be a cool place where you learn a lot and spend some time in this interesting museum.

Yazd Bazaar

Later in the afternoon when the bazaar stores reopen, you can stroll a bit more in the shady cool passageways of the bazaar and learn about the traditional businesses and guilds like brocade producers and sellers in this interesting place.

Mir Chaqmaq Tekieh

Quite close to the bazaar, there's an interesting structure stretched from North to the South with its face toward West called Mir Chaqmaq Tekieh with two high minarets. During Moharam month when Shiites commemorate the martyrdom of their third Imam, people gather in this building and in front of it to see the religious passion play and procession. You can go to the top of the minarets and have a look at the entire city.

Mir Chaqmaq Mosque

This is a 4-minarets mosque with a small courtyard making it possible to have lots of shade inside for the worshippers. Sometimes it is allowed for tourists to visit the mosque and in some years it is not due to the change in the decisions, but you can have a look at it from the minarets of Mir Chaqmaq Tekieh. It is located near the Tekieh.

Ateshgah of Baku

The Baku Ateshgah or "Fire Temple" is a castle-like religious structure in Surakhani, a suburb of greater Baku, Azerbaijan. "Atash" is the Persian word for fire.

The pentagonal complex, which has a courtyard surrounded by cells for monks and a tetrapillar-altar in the middle, was built during the 17th and 18th centuries. It was abandoned after 1883 when oil and gas plants were established in the vicinity. The complex was turned into a museum in 1975 and now receives 15,000 visitors a year. It was nominated for World Heritage Site status in 1998 and was declared a state historical-architectural reserve by decree of the Azeri President on 19 December 2007.

The toponym Ateshgah/Atashgah (Persian and Azerbaijani pronunciation) or Ateshgyakh/Atashgyakh (Russian pronunciation) literally means "home of fire." The Persian-origin term atesh means fire, and is present in several languages as a Persian loan-word including in Azerbaijani and Hindustani. Gah derives from Middle Persian and means "throne" or "bed". The name refers to the fact that the site is situated atop a now-exhausted natural gas field, which once caused natural fires to spontaneously burn there as the gas emerged from seven natural surface vents. Today, the fires in the complex are fed by gas piped in from Baku, and are only turned on for the benefit of visitors.

Local legend associates the temple at Surakhany with the Fire temples of Zoroastrianism, but this is presumably based on the general identification of any "home of fire" (the common meaning of atashgah) as a Zoroastrian place of worship. While the word exists in Zoroastrian vocabulary, it denotes the altar-like repository for a sacred wood-fire or the sanctum sanctorum where the fire altar stands, but not the greater building around it.

Surakhani, the name of the town where the Ateshgah is located, likely means "a region of holes" but might perhaps be a reference to the fire glow as well. A historic alternative name for Azerbaijan as a whole has been Odlar Yurdu, Azeri for land of fires.

Bahram Fire Temple

Bahram Fire temple, Mil Hill or Rey Fire temple is one of the historical religious places in Rey, Iran which has stood since the Sassanid Empire. Mil Hill is assumed to be Bahram V Fire temple.

Udvada

Udvada is a town in Gujarat, renowned for its Zoroastrian Atash Behram. This place of worship is the oldest still-functioning example of its kind, and has established Udvada as a pilgrimage center for Zoroastrians the world over.

Udvada is a coastal town 200 km north of Mumbai, around 8 km off the national highway, NH8. Trains ply from Mumbai to Udvada, including the Gujarat Express, the Ferozepur Janta Express and Saurashtra Express. Udvada means the 'grazing ground of camels', which it was before it became a fishing village.

The importance of Udvada in Parsi (Indian Zoroastrian) history and religion centres around the Atash Behram (from Middle Persian Atash Warharan for "Victorious Fire", the highest grade of ritual fire of the Zoroastrians) housed in the fire temple there.

The Udvada Atash Behram is the most sacred of the Zoroastrian fire temples in India and the oldest continuously burning fire-temple fire in the world. The Udvada Atash Behram is one of nine Atash Behrams worldwide, eight of which are in western India (four in Mumbai, two in Surat, one in Navsari, and the one in Udvada), and one of which is in Yazd, in central Iran.

Following the Muslim conquest of most of Greater Iran in the 7th century, Zoroastrians gradually became a marginalized community, and by about the 10th century, the formerly Zoroastrian-held territories had become largely Islamic. One group of Zoroastrians fled from Greater Khorasan to the west coast of India in order to preserve their religious customs and beliefs. Upon landing, the refugees founded the settlement of Sanjan, which lies about 30km south of Udvada.

According to the same legend, on their journey the Zoroastrians had carried ash from a sacred fire (according to a latter-day embellishment of the story, they had carried a fire itself), which a priest is said to have then used for the bed of the Sanjan fire when it was consecrated. A related legend recounts that this fire was consecrated as Atash Bahram fires traditionally are, that is, out of 16 fires, including that of a funeral pyre, a shepherd's hearth, a goldsmith's hearth, a potter's kiln and from a fire caused by lightning.

Some centuries after their arrival (probably in the late 14th century), Sanjan was attacked by troops of the Delhi Sultanate (possibly those of Muhammad bin Tughluq) and the Parsis fled again, into caves in the nearby Barhot hills, 14 km south of Sanjan. The sacred fire went with them. Several years later it was installed in Navsari. In the 18th century, a decision was made to return the flame to Sanjan, but along the way, the priests preferred to remain in Udvada, where the fire temple was consecrated in 1742.

The first recorded use of the name in reference to the fire there appears in a 1905 work by Jivanji Modi, who made several allusions to the "Iranshah Fire" within the space of two pages. In 1920, when Shahpurshah Hodivala published his English language translation of the Qissa-i Sanjan, he assumed that this was the original name of the fire. It had been so called because it was consecrated to be the earthly representative of Yazdegerd III, the last Zoroastrian king of Iran, this explanation is accepted by almost all devout Parsis, and even the few skeptics among them tend to refer to the fire as the Iranshah.

In the Present-day

Ceremonial anniversary celebrations are held at the Atash Behram on the day of its founding. The ceremonies in Udvada are held on the ninth day of the ninth month in the Shahenshahi (imperial) version of the Zoroastrian calendar (which, in 2006, was on 25 April). Pilgrims from all over the world visit the temple on that day. Special ceremonies are also held on the 20th day of each month. In the Zoroastrian calendar, that day is dedicated to the divinity Verethragna (Avestan, Middle Persian Waharam, hence Behram), hypostasis of victory.

According to tradition and later as a result of legal verdict, nine priestly families of Sanjan and their heirs are the sole lawful guardians of the fire and its temple. They alone have the right to enjoy its income. The position of high priest passes in turn from the head of one family to the head of another.

Udvada is also the religious centre of the Ilm-e-Kshnoom, a very small Zoroastrian sect based on a mystic and esoteric interpretation of religious texts.

Founded in the early 20th century, this sect found a following among the prominent Unvala family of Udvada (after whom adherents of the Ilm-e-Kshnoom are also called the 'Unvala sect'), who then attempted to establish new standards of worship at the Atash Behram. The Unvalas eventually took the caretakers of the Atash Behram to court (which led to the nine families also gaining a legal footing), and when in 1936 two priests of the Atash Behram died, the Unvalas refused to accept their nominated successors. Maneckji Nusserwanji Dhalla, a highly respected theologian of the time, was called upon to intervene, and the issue was settled after over 25 years of discord. Dhalla had barely returned to his home town when the Ilm-e-Kshnoom sought to establish their priest as another 'high' priest.

Udvada also hosts a Zoroastrian heritage museum, sponsored by the Government of Gujarat.

The town, and its ambience, is under threat from the advancing sea (and consequent salinity) and commercialization. The Mumbai based Save Udvada Committee, supported by the Indian and Gujarat state governments, is engaged in combating sea-driven erosion. There have also been attempts to get Udvada declared a World Heritage Site, to protect the ancient residences and the fire temple. The typical Parsi homes here with their high ceilings, sloped roofs with ornamental skirting, and double otlas (porches) are over a century old, and considered worth preserving.

10 Islam Religious Tourism Spots

Islam is the monotheistic religion articulated by the Qur'an, a text considered by its adherents to be the verbatim word of God, and the teachings and normative example (called the Sunnah and Hadith) of Muhammad, considered the last Prophet of Islam by most Muslims. The word Islam means 'submission to God', and an adherent of Islam is called a Muslim.

Muslims believe that God is one and incomparable. Muslims also believe that Islam is the complete and universal version of a primordial faith that was revealed at many times and places before, including through the prophets Abraham, Moses and Jesus. Muslims maintain that previous messages and revelations have been partially changed or corrupted over time, but consider the Qur'an to be both unaltered and the final revelation from God. Religious concepts and practices include the five pillars of Islam, which are basic concepts and obligatory acts of worship, and following Islamic law, which touches on virtually every aspect of life and society, encompassing everything from banking and welfare, to warfare and the environment.

Most Muslims belong to one of two denominations; with 80-90% being Sunni and 10-20% being Shia. About 13% of Muslims live in Indonesia, the largest Muslim country, 25% in South Asia, 20% in the Middle East, 2% in Central Asia, 4% in the remaining South East Asian countries, and 15% in Sub-saharan Africa. Sizable communities are also found in China and Russia, and parts of the Caribbean. Converts and immigrant communities are found in almost every part of the world. With about 1.41-1.57 billion Muslims, comprising about 21-23% of the world's population (see Islam by country), Islam is the second-largest religion and one of the fastest-growing religions in the world.

The word islam is a verbal noun originating from the triliteral root s-l-m, and is derived from the Arabic verb 'áslama, which means "to give up, to desert, to surrender (to God)." Another word derived from the same root is salaam (????) which means 'Peace'. Muslim, the word for an adherent of Islam, is the active participle of the same verb of which Isl?m is the infinitive. Believers demonstrate submission to God by worshipping Him, following His commands, and avoiding polytheism. The word sometimes has distinct connotations in its various occurrences in the Qur'an. In some verses (ayat), there is stress on the quality of Islam as an internal conviction: "Whomsoever God desires to guide, He expands his breast to Islam." Other verses connect isl?m and d?n (usually translated as "religion"): "Today, I have perfected your religion (d?n) for you; I have completed My blessing upon you; I have approved Islam for your religion." Still others describe Islam as an action of returning to God-more than just a verbal affirmation of faith. Another technical meaning in Islamic thought is as one part of a triad of islam, im?n (faith), and ihs?n (excellence) where it represents acts of worship (`ib?dah) and Islamic law (sharia).

Bali

The tourism industry is primarily focused in the south, while significant in the other parts of the island as well. The main tourist locations are the town of Kuta (with its beach), and its outer suburbs of Legian and Seminyak (which were once independent townships), the east coast town of Sanur (once the only tourist hub), in the center of the island Ubud, to the south of the Ngurah Rai International Airport, Jimbaran, and the newer development of Nusa Dua and Pecatu.

The American government lifted its travel warnings in 2008. As of 2009, the Australian government still rates it at a 4 danger level (the same as several countries in central Africa) on a scale of 5.

An offshoot of tourism is the growing real estate industry. Bali real estate has been rapidly developing in the main tourist areas of Kuta, Legian, Seminyak and Oberoi. Most recently, high-end 5 star projects are under development on the Bukit peninsula, on the south side of the island. Million dollar villas are being developed along the cliff sides of south Bali, commanding panoramic ocean views. Foreign and domestic (many Jakarta individuals and companies are fairly active) investment into other areas of the island also continues to grow. Land prices, despite the worldwide economic crisis, have remained stable.

In the last half of 2008, Indonesia's currency had dropped approximately 30% against the US dollar, providing many overseas visitors value for their currencies. Visitor arrivals for 2009 were forecast to drop 8% (which would be higher than 2007 levels), due to the worldwide economic crisis which has also affected the global tourist industry, but not due to any travel warnings.

Bali's tourism economy survived the terrorist bombings of 2002 and 2005, and the tourism industry has in fact slowly recovered and surpassed its pre-terrorist bombing levels; the longterm trend has been a steady increase of visitor arrivals. At 2010, Bali received 2.57 million foreign tourists. It is surpassed the target of 2.0-2.3 million tourists. The average occupancy of starred hotels achieved 65 percent (last year 60.8 percent), so still capable for accommodates tourists for next some years without any addition of new rooms/hotels, although at the peak season some of them are fully booked.

Bali received the Best Island award from Travel and Leisure in 2010. The award was presented in the show "World's Best Awards 2010" in New York, on 21 July. Hotel Four Seasons Resort Bali at Jimbaran also received an award in the category of "World Best Hotel Spas in Asia 2010". The award was based on a survey of travel magazine Travel + Leisure readers between 15 December 2009 through 31 March 2010, and was judged on several criteria. The Ayana Resort received the designation; #1 Spa in the world by Conde Naste's Traveller Magazine for 2010 by their readers poll . The island of Bali won because of its attractive surroundings (both mountain and coastal areas), diverse tourist attractions, excellent international and local restaurants, and the friendliness of the local people.

The Ngurah Rai International Airport is located near Jimbaran, on the isthmus at the southernmost part of the island. Lt.Col. Wisnu Airfield is found in north-west Bali.

A coastal road surrounds the island, and three major two-lane arteries cross the central mountains at passes reaching to 1,750m in height (at Penelokan). The Ngurah Rai Bypass is a four-lane expressway that partly encircles Denpasar and enables cars to travel quickly in the heavily populated south. Bali has no railway lines.

December 2010: Government of Indonesia has invited investors to build Tanah Ampo Cruise Terminal at Karangasem, Bali amounted $30 million.

A Memorandum of Understanding has been signed by 2 ministers, Bali's Governor and Indonesian Train Company to build 565 kilometers railway along the coast around the island. It will be operated since 2015.

Cairo

On September 17, five Islamic monuments were officially inaugurated in the Al-Darb Al-Ahmar area of Cairo. The Al-Imam mosque, the Al-Laythmosque, the Al-Set Meska mosque, the Ali Labib house and the well zone of Youssef at the Salah El-Din Citadel have all been undergoing restoration work, which cost around LE 9.5 million. These monuments including the first phase construction of the new lighting system of the Salah El-Din Citadel were inaugurated at the ceremony. The ceremony took place at the Salah El-Din Citadel.

Dr. Zahi Hawass, the Secretary General of the Supreme Council of Antiquities (SCA), Dr. Hamdi Zaqzouq, the Minister of Endowment, and Cairo Governor Abdel Azim Waziri inaugurated the special ceremony along with top governmental officials.

The restoration of these important historical edifices is a part of the Supreme Council of Antiquities' dedication to preserve Egypt's Islamic heritage.

The most outstanding restoration-conversion attraction, amid the decrepit villages of the Egyptian capital unfamiliar to visitors, one extremely ambitious project has been undertaken with the creation of a vast, green open space in a once run-down area of Cairo. Interestingly since the project was started, another dimension has been added -a rehabilitation of the surrounding residential district called Darb Al Ahmar, so impoverished it needed the Aga Khan to give it a facelift.

For years, tourists have long been kept off the area by the virtually unofficial wasteland or rubbish dump lying alongside the derelict eastern rim of old Cairo's medieval city walls. From its early beginnings as the massive wastebasket to a gigantic mountain pile of dirt, it ended up obscuring residents' views of the fortress wall and pretty minarets nearby through the years. It has become, in a sense, irreverent that it lies beside the walled old cemetery known as the City Of the Dead, where scores of homeless Cairenes have found shelter in tombs housing urns of the more-privileged.

In 2004, on the metropolis shared by the living and the dead, where dust, debris and garbage have collected through the millennium, arose a $45 million project the Aga Khan Development Network designed to complete in 7 years to uplift the destitute.

Four years after unexplained shoveling, digging and earth-moving the contractors were doing much to the perplexity of locals, the project finally took shape. Out of the barren 30-hectare Darassa Hills came a lush, green park overlooking Cairo's Islamic city. It would bring hundreds of jobs, a place for the busy Cairenes to de-stress, open views of the Citadel never there before; notwithstanding, give people hope in a hometown that had never produced them profits.

Opened to the public end on a trial basis, it welcomed the first guests. Once the city built in ancient times by the Fatimids and named Al Quahire or the victorious, the previous 20 percent devoted to open space now had tourists flocking to it. From Easter till end of September, for about 5 and a half weeks, the park construction concentrated on the finer details of what would become an interesting rehab site inaugurated September 17 during a special event at the Citadel.

Istanbul

The city consists of three separate elements - the old Turkish town (Eminönöü, Aksaray, Fatih), in the form of an almost equilateral triangle, which extends from the right bank of the Golden Horn to the Sea of Marmara; linked with the old town by the Galata and Atatürk Bridges, the district of Beyoglu with its suburbs of Galata and

Harbiye, largely inhabited by foreigners, on the slopes between the Golden Horn and the Bosporus; and the district of Üsküdar, with its suburbs, on the Asiatic side of the Bosporus. Istanbul is a unique and unforgettable sight with its towers and its palaces and the numerous domes and minarets of the 35 large and over a hundred smaller mosques rising above the water. Little is left of the colorful Oriental life of the old capital of the Sultans, and the people now wear European dress. Street names and shop signs are in the Latin alphabet; and the old rows of brown timber houses with red roofs and latticed kafes (bow-windows) have given place in the central areas to stone and reinforced-concrete blocks.

The climate of Istanbul is marked by sharp contrasts. In the evening it is frequently cool, even in summer. Among the city's numerous birds visitors will be impressed particularly by the black kites and, on the Bosporus, the black cormorants. Dolphins are a frequent sight in the Bosporus and the Sea of Marmara.

About 660 B.C. Dorian Greeks founded on what is now Seraglio Point the city of Byzantion (in Latin Byzantium), which controlled access to the Black Sea at the entrance to the Bosporus. In 513 B.C. the town was captured by the Persian King Darius I. During the sixth and fifth century it was a member of the first and second Attic Leagues. In 148 B.C. the free city of Byzantion entered into an alliance with Rome, and thereafter it several times lost and then regained its freedom. In A.D. 196 the city was captured and harshly treated by Septimius Severus, but soon recovered. In 324, after his victory over Licinius, Constantine I (306-37) resolved to make a second capital of the Empire.

In the autumn of 326 a beginning was made with the construction of a line of town walls taking in an area which extended far to the west, and on May 11th 330 the new city was solemnly inaugurated, under the name of Nova Roma or New Rome, soon to be changed to Constantinopolis. Like Rome the new city was divided into fourteen regions, and even had its seven hills. After the division of the Empire in 395 Constantinople became the capital of the Eastern Roman Empire. In the reign of Justinian (527-65) who rebuilt the city in greater magnificence after much of it had been reduced to ashes during the Nika Insurrection, it enjoyed its period of greatest splendor. Late Greek and Roman culture developed into the distinctive Byzantine culture, which found expression in the Greek language.

Soon afterwards, however, the Empire was torn by domestic and external conflicts. The city was harried by the Avars and Persians (627) and by the Arabs under the Omayyad caliphs; in 813 and again in 924 it was besieged by the Bulgars; and in 907 and 1048 Russian fleets appeared off Constantinople. Finally came the catastrophe of 1204, when, following disputes over the succession to the Imperial throne, the Crusaders captured the city and founded a Latin Empire.

After the Ottoman conquest of Asia Minor in the 13th century and the transfer of the capital from Bursa to Edirne (Adrianople) Constantinople was increasingly encircled by Turks. In 1453 Mehmet II Fatih (the Conqueror) took the city, which now became the Ottoman capital under the name of Istanbul. There was a great wave of building by the Sultans and Turkish grandees, particularly by Selim I (1512-20) and Süleiman the Magnificent (1520-66). Many major buildings were also erected in the 17th and 18th century During the 19th century Western influences began to make themselves felt in the city's architecture.

After the First World War, in which Turkey had been allied with the Central Powers, Istanbul was occupied by the Allies. In 1922, following Turkey's victory in the War of Independence, Turkish troops re-entered the city. In 1923 the Sultanate and Caliphate were abolished and Turkey became a Republic and its first President, Mustafa Kemal Atatürk, moved the capital to Ankara. In a drastic program of reform Atatürk banned the fez, the wearing of veils by women, the Order of Dervishes and polygamy and introduced the Latin alphabet, the metric system and regular surnames. The aspect of Istanbul has since then been increasingly Europeanized by the driving of wide modern streets through the old town, the pulling down of the old wooden houses and their replacement by new blocks of flats and offices, the establishment of a new commercial and business center north of Taksim Square and the development of whole new districts of the city.

Istanbul made a bid to host the 27th Summer Olympic Games in the year 2000.

Copt (Coptic) Spots

A Copt (Coptic) is a native Egyptian Christian. Copts form a major ethno-religious group that has ancient origins. Copts are Egyptians whose ancestors embraced Christianity in the first centuries after Christ. The word "Coptic" was originally used to refer to Egyptians in general (see etymology section), but it has undergone a semantic shift over the centuries to mean more specifically Egyptian Christian. This semantic shift dates back to the time when Christians became an Egyptian minority, after the Muslim conquest of Egypt in the 7th century.

Egypt's Coptic Church is one of Christianity's earliest, brought here by Mark, writer of the oldest New Testament gospel. The liturgy closely resembles those seen in other Eastern Orthodox churches, though the Copts' leader, or pope, has always been based in Egypt. This church was actually built in the 1990s, a tribute to its ancient heritage, modern engineering, and the affluence of some in Egypt's Coptic minority. But that wealth is in small pockets of Egypt's upper class and a Copt diaspora in rich countries.

The Coptic Church developed separately from other Eastern churches. The Coptic Church's clerical hierarchy had evolved by the sixth century. A patriarch, referred to as the pope, heads the church. A synod or council of senior priests (people who have attained the status of bishops) is responsible for electing or removing popes. Members of the Coptic Church worldwide (about 1 million Copts lived outside of Egypt as of 1990) recognize the pope as their spiritual leader. The pope, traditionally based in Alexandria, also serves as the chief administrator of the church. The administrator's functionaries includes hundreds of priests serving urban and rural parishes, friars in monasteries, and nuns in convents.

The main language in the eastern part of the Roman Empire was Greek, also used by the Egyptian Christians (Copts). Some Egyptians had started to write their own language using Greek letters (old Coptic) before the advent of Christianity; Coptic later became the principal script and language of Christian Egypt below the official Greek (then Arabic) level, and it remains alive today in the Coptic Church, for liturgical use. Greek was the state language used for administration and education, until replaced by Arabic at the end of the 7th century. In the first century after the Moslem annexation of Egypt, documents might be produced in three languages, Greek, Coptic and Arabic. Coptic enjoyed a revival under Islam: most of the Coptic books in collections today date to the Islamic Period. Contrary to the common perception that Coptic was only used for liturgy, there are many Coptic texts in medicine, mathematics, and alchemy. From the 11th century onwards, Arabic was used to write Christian material often side by side with Coptic, producing bilingual texts which were instrumental in the process of the European decipherment of Egyptian language by Kircher and successors such as Champollion.

Following Islam's spread through Egypt, Muslims alternately tolerated and persecuted the Copts. Heavy taxation of Christians encouraged mass conversions to Islam, and within two centuries, Copts had become a distinct minority. By the tenth century, Arabic had replaced Coptic as the primary spoken language, and Coptic was relegated to a liturgical language.

Historic Egyptian Copt (Coptic) Spots

St.Catherine's Monastery Sinai

The oldest Christian monastery still in existence in the world and houses also the richest collection of icons and precious manuscripts. St Cathrine's basilica is through a massive 12th- century entry door, in the Fatimid style: this door opens directly onto the narthex where, under thick protective glass, is displayed a marvelous collection of icons dating from the 5th to 7th centuries

Coptic Museum

Founded in 1910, it contains the finest extant collection of Coptic art: the collections belonged to Marcos Smaika Pasha . The Museum consists of two pavilions and a square court: the older one contains ornamental latticework (the "musharabiya") and wooden ceilings from the oldest Coptic palaces, as well as fountains, windows in stucco and mosaics, marble and stone columns . The Museum has thirty rooms containing frescoes, wooden sheathing, worked metals, vases, objects in glass, tapestries, papyrus scrolls, manuscripts, icons and ivory sculpture. There is also a library with seven thousand books and manuscripts, mostly in the Coptic language.

The Holy Family's Journey to Egypt

The advent of the Holy Family to Egypt, seeking refuge, is an event of the utmost significance in our dear country's long, long history. The tortuous trails they followed in their passage across Sinai, and their subsequent travels within Egypt After their short, but all-too-felt, stay in Old Cairo, the Holy Family moved in a southerly direction, reaching Cairo suburb of Maadi which, in earliest Pharaonic times was an outlying district of Memphis, the capital of Egypt then they boarded El Sorian Monastery "Wadi El Natroun"In the earliest decades of Christianity, the desert expanses of Wadi el-Natroun became the site of anchoretic settlement and, later, of many monasteries, in spiritual commemoration of the Holy Family's passage through the Valley. Virgen Mary Church "Zeitoun"is one of the Holy Family's remarkable stops along Egypt.

The Hanging Church

Built at the close of the Century and beginning of the 5th Century. So called because it was built on the southern tower of the Babylon Castle, headquarters of the Byzantine army in Misr al Qadima (Old Cairo). It is built in the Basilica style.

Larnaca, Cyprus

Though Larnaca is part of Cyprus and an important port for the country at that, it would appear that the city belongs to all mankind, preserving our collective inheritance as residents of this planet. It is said that the city was built by Noah's grandson, and the important

Neolithic settlement in the area and the migratory birds from distant lands that grace the Salt Lake, combine to give telling credence to this. Christianity and Islam both have deep imprints on the city and tourists can combine a vacation with deep religious experiences in Larnaca's monumental Churches and the shrine built to honor the Aunt of the Prophet himself. Situated as it is at the confluence of Europe and Asia, the city gives every visitor a truly remarkable experience.

Larnaca provides a unique expose to history. It is a delight for those who relish the past but can also kindle a spark in the most hardened modernist. It is fascinating to walk through the city, as rarely can one be transported in such realistic manner back several centuries, in the midst of a modern urban center with cafes and other trappings of spots that all vacationers love. The combination of a calm atmosphere and a warm people will calm the most stressed nerves as will a day on the pristine sands of the Mackenzie beach. There are many cities by the sea but few have kept them with as much love and spirit as you find in Larnaca. You can spend quality time just strolling along the palm fringed avenue, stopping to savor the scene over some beverage at a café.

An important landmark of Larnaca is the Stavrovouni Monastry. It was founded in the 4th century, reportedly with a fragment of the Holy Cross. It has a majestic location on the top of a rocky hill with a commanding view of the countryside. The monks have a rich tradition of icon painting. Women and photography are prohibited and men must be properly dressed if they wish to visit.

Larnaca has many well kept records of its past from the 8th to the 10th century. The Agia Phaneromeni Church is a fine piece of architecture from this period. The Ayios Lazarus is a 9th century Church built on the tomb of St. Lazarus, Larnaca's first Bishop, after his resurrection by Lord Jesus. The architectural highlight of this splendid structure is the decoration of icons on the main doors of entrance. The Church is also worth a visit for its rare museum collection of art, apart from its imposing bell tower. The latter, though of relatively recent origin, is still 150 years old. The Kition archeological site is another experience without which no tourist should return to the city's modern airport! The site has temples and settlements from the 10th century.

Reasons that only accomplished historians can explain, make one jump from the 10th to the 17th century, in the journey along Larnaca's past. The Larnaca Castle, used as a prison by the British, has splendid views and an absorbing collection in its museum. The city does have a range of museums as one might expect, and it is possible to spend days on end browsing amongst rare treasures and still leave much unseen. The 18th century Kamares aqueduct is worth a visit for its imposing and characteristic sweep of the landscape.

A visit to the Lefkara village sets a suitable tone for the end of a Larnaca visit. It is known for lace and silver, and while the handicrafts can be sourced from one's hotel shopping mall or an up-market boutique, purchases from the friendly craftspeople leaves lasting fragrance on your souvenirs.

Saudi Arabia

Saudi Arabia, although many would not think so, actually has a thriving tourism industry and there is a lot to see in this very historic country full of culture and intrest to many.

Mecca

This is the most holy place to all Muslims and pilgrims are always present here all year round. This is also a popular tourist spot in Saudi Arabia for non-Muslims where they got to witness the different events and festivals held in Mecca. There are also the Mountain of Light, the Holy Mosque, and the Grand Mosque where you could truly appreciate the wonderful Islam religion.

Al Masjid Al Nabawi

A major tourist spot in Saudi Arabia and considered by the Muslims as the second holiest mosque in the world. The place was once the residence of Prophet Muhammad and now has become the focal point for religious instructions. This is an important landmark in the rich heritage of the country of Saudi Arabia.

Masjid al Qiblatain

A top tourist spot in Saudi Arabia that displays the rich architecture of the country. The mosque is among the list of the world's oldest mosques that was once a small building and now renovated to receive 2,000 people all at once. This mosque plays an important role in the history of Islam religion.

Quba Mosque

Quba Mosque is the holiest of all the mosques found in Madina and is also the world's oldest mosque. This ancient mosque is part of the most famous tourist spot in Saudi Arabia. It is a belief that the first stones of the edifice were put in place personally by the Prophet himself. The architectural design of the mosque is also very interesting.

Jawatha Mosque

This tourist spot in Saudi Arabia is among the oldest religious mosques within the country. It was built during the seventh century by the Bani Abdul Qais tribe and was believed to be the first of all the mosques within the eastern section of Saudi Arabia. Within its ruins, you will be able to view the past glorious days of the mosque.

Dumat al Jundal

A tourist spot in Saudi Arabia that will let you encounter romance within its ancient ruins. This mystical city of Dumat al Jundal will take you back to the time of the tenth century B.C. and lets you discover the interesting history of Saudi Arabia. The place is located within a beautiful oasis on the northern part of the Great Nafud Desert.

Tayma

Don't miss out this fascinating tourist spot in Saudi Arabia where a very prosperous settlement of the Jews once inhabit the area. You need to spend enough time in order to thoroughly seek the wondrous scattered in the area and learn the interesting history that comes with them.

Medain Saleh

A tourist spot in Saudi Arabia that is not just beautiful but also important in the history of the country. Scattered within the area are about 131 tombs and the total land area of the place is estimated to be 13.4 kilometers. Aside from the tombs, there are also towers, walls, houses, and other kinds of ruined structures.

Rock Carving Site

There are a number of rock carving sites in Saudi Arabia and the most notable of them all is Jubbah. Travel through time as you learn the ancient art of the primeval folks and understand the way of their life during the prehistoric era. These arts in the ancient rocks are truly intriguing and fascinating.

Al Ula

An interesting tourist spot in Saudi Arabia that was once an active site of the commerce and trade activities. The place has been the heart of the Saudi Arabian Civilization until the first century B.C. Surrounding Al Ula are wonderful carved tombs and other ancient structures.

Brunei

Brunei can be deceiving in all its riches available for tourists. Don't be fooled and know what awaits the gambling tourist who is looking for a new and exciting place to visit. So here are the top ten tourist spots for Brunei which all should visit if traveling in this historic country.

Jame'Asr Hassanil Bolkiah Mosque

Brunei has a lot of cultural and religious tourist attractions. That should be expected due to the 600 year rule of sultans in the country. A lot of these religious sites have become historic as the years have gone by. The Jame'Asr Hassanil Bolkiah Mosque is by far the most splendid one of them all. It is also one of the most important religious sites in the country.

It is located in Kampong Kiarong, which is quite close to the nation's capital. Though it is mainly a place of worship among Muslims, it is open to visits by those not of the faith during Thursdays. You'll definitely enjoy the architectural masterpieces to be witnessed here.

Royal Regalia Museum

A tour of the many tourist attractions of Brunei will give you various glimpses into the royal buildings and cultural centers. Not only do they speak of the architectural prowess of the country, they also speak volumes regarding the people's history.

The Royal Regalia Museum is one of the most culturally significant places to visit if you want to understand the people's culture and history. The collections you will find here portray the regal life of the royal dynasties that ruled the land, which also reflects the political aspects of the nation.

Brunei History Center

600 years worth of history is preserved in the Brunei History Center. Historical edifices are preserved here for the perusal and appreciation of generations to come. It was built in 1982 under the consent of the reigning sultan of the time. If you want to take a crash course into the country's history then this History Center place will give you quite a comprehensive introduction.

Kampong Ayer

Kampong Ayer is locally dubbed as the Venice of the East. It is one of the tourist attractions in the country that you shouldn't miss. This place is sometimes called the 'water village'. It is quite interesting that the moniker 'Venice of the East' wasn't coined by one of the locals but was given by a foreign visitor.

Omar Ali Saifuddin Mosque

One of the important mosques in the country is the Omar Ali Saifuddin Mosque. This mosque is quite picturesque being situated on an artificial lagoon near the Brunei River. This religious site has become quite popular in South East Asia being known for it transient beauty. Incidentally, this mosque was named after the country's 28th sultan.

Istana Nurul Iman

The residence of the nation's sultan, Istana Nurul Iman, is a spectacular place to visit. In fact, it is the biggest palace in the whole country. The palace was designed by the Philippines' national artist for architecture, Leandro V. Locsin. Unfortunately, the palace itself isn't usually open to visitors. You can only adore the lavish residence during the annual Hari Raya Puasa Festival.

Jerudong Theme Park

This is one of the most popular tourist attractions in the country. It is often frequented by a lot of visitors all year round. It is open to the public and visitors are not required to purchase any ticket to gain entry. It's a great place to have a picnic or just spend a relaxing afternoon. There are rides for visitors and food kiosks in case you get hungry.

Drottningholm

This tourist attraction is actually where the country's royal family resides. The very first palace built in this site was constructed in the 16th century. However, it was destroyed in 1961 and a new palace was constructed the following year. The place is quite charming and reflects the country's glory.

Religious Pilgrimage

The main religion of this nation is Islam. And as such, one of the highlights to any visit here would be a religious pilgrimage. People come here not only to admire the beautifully crafted mosques but also to worship. The architecture of these religious buildings is already a welcome treat to any visitor.

Visiting the Royal Residences

One of the big attractions of Brunei is the lavishly decorated and designed royal residences. The members of the sultanate's royalty live in regal homes that are wonderfully decorated and fashioned. Some of these places are also historic sites as well.

Yemen

For those looking for something new, the tourist spots in Yemen will appeal to your sense of exploration and adventure. That they're not as famous and crowded as the tourist sights in other countries makes them all the more appealing.

Aden

Situated by the Arabian Sea, it is filled with numerous fortresses and tunnels. Two of the most vital historical landmarks are the Water Reservoirs of Al-Taweelah and the Fort of Jabal 'Aly. Most of the monuments are situated in the Old city of Aden and the surrounding area.

Crater

This ancient city is famous for its ancient mosques, most notably the Mosque of Abban. The Lighthouse in Crater is another major sightseeing spot. The city is also famous for its markets, including the Al-Taweel,

Za'afaran and the Buhara Market.

Taiz City

One of the upcoming tourist spots in Yemen, the city is 256 km from Sana. The most distinguishable landmarks are the Al Ma'tabiyyah dome and the Al Muzaffar mosque. There is also a museum housing artifacts and relics.

Tomb of Sheikh Ahmad

One of the most famous tombs in the country is that of Sheikh Ahmad Bin Alwan, a Sufist who lived c. 1300 AD. His tomb is located just to the southwest of Taiz. The tomb is under a mosque and draws scores of visitors annually.

Al Mocha

The city is west to Taiz (approximately 94 km). The most conspicuous landmark here is the Shazli mosque. Dating back 500 years, it is one of the most remarkable tourist spots in Yemen. Other sightseeing spots include the Malik Beach, Yakhtal Beach and the many palm trees in the area.

Al Janad

It was here the first mosque in Yemen was built in 630 AD. Landmarks include the ancient mosque set at the mountains. There are also water canals by the mountain. Also part of the attraction is the Weekly Souks or markets.

Hudedah

The main attractions in this city are the beaches along the western end, ideal for swimming or fishing. There are also several valleys here including the Wadi Surdud and the Wadi Zabid valleys. Bura Mountain is the tallest in the vicinity at 2,400 m. Rass Mountain reaches a height of 2,000 m above sea level.

Mukalla City

The fishing center of the country, the city is one of the most beautiful tourist spots in Yemen due to the sultan palace. This was built by Omar bin Awad Al-Qu'aity. The Al-Ghuweizy Castle, the public markets and museum are other attractions.

Al Shehir City

The olden part of the city is filled with ancient landmarks including old walls and gates. The newer section is renowned for the white stones used on the buildings. The city is also known for its jewelry shops, boats and markets.

The Hadramout Valley

At 160 km, it is the longest in the entire Arabian Peninsula. It goes all the way to Thamoud up to the Masila Valley. In some areas there are palm trees and plants surrounding it. The tourist spots in Yemen are both remarkable and distinctive. What the sites may lack in popularity is made up for by their notable appearance.

Bahrain

The tourist spots in Bahrain constitute some of the finest sightseeing locations in the Middle East. Today, people from all over the world are coming to Bahrain to get a glimpse of Arab culture and architecture.

Al Fateh Mosque

Set near King Faisal Highway, the Al Fateh Mosque is one of the biggest mosques in the world, with room for 7,000 worshippers. The 60 ton dome is made entirely of fiberglass and draws tourists and religious devotees by the thousands.

Al Khamis Mosque

This mosque is regarded as one of the most ancient in all of Islam. The foundation was set down in 692 AD during the time of Caliph Umar II. Its most distinguishing traits are the twin minarets.

Arad Fort

No list of the tourist spots in Bahrain would be complete without mentioning the Arad Fort. Built sometime in the 15th century, very little is known of its past. Today however, it is one of the visually striking sights in Bahrain, especially at night.

Bab Al Bahrain

Situated at Manama's business district, it is the site of the Bahrain financial harbor. The monument has been renovated and now sports

Islamic inspired designs. In the vicinity are the Gold City shopping mall and a handicraft shop.

Bahrain Fort

A UNESCO World Heritage site, the fort is composed of mounds made by the primitive peoples in 2300 BC. It is one of the most highly regarded tourist spots in Bahrain, as it used to be the seat of the Dilmun civilization. The name actually means Bahrain Castle.

The Bahrain National Museum

Located near King Faisal Highway, it is the largest museum in Bahrain. The $30 million complex encompasses 6,000 years of the land's history. Apart from historical artifacts, other halls focus on Bahrain culture and life. Exhibits of flora and fauna are also to be found there.

The Dilmun Burial Mounds

This burial ground dates back to the time of the Dilmun civilization. The mounds come in a variety of sizes but most of them are 15 by 30 ft (4.5 by 9 m). Because the bodies were buried with some items, it has proven to be a valuable archaeological resource.

Riffa Fort

This tourist spot in Bahrain offers some of the finest views of Hunanaiya valley. During the 1860s, the fort was the seat of power in the area. Today the structure offers glimpses of royal life and architecture in the 19th century.

The Barbar Temple

The temple is an archaeological site in the village of Barbar. To date, three of these temples have been unearthed, the oldest going back to 3000 BC. Tools and assorted weapons have been found along the site too.

Tree of Life

This tree can be found 2 km from the Jebel Dukhan, the highest peak in Bahrain. It is a 100 year old tree and stands alone. What makes it fascinating is the entire area is free of water.

The tourist spots in Bahrain are not just fine examples of Arab architecture and history. It also offers first time visitors the chance to understand a different culture.

Kosovo

Discovering the best tourist areas in Kosovo is the easiest and best way to experience this grand and ancient country which is quickly becoming a great place for tourism.

Prishtina

The capital city of the country is also a great tourist spot in Kosovo. Take a walking tour of the city as you visit one building to another like museums, mosques, monuments, and government buildings. It is also quite interesting to have a visit to the offices of Kosovo's important international organizations.

Drini River Waterfall

This tourist spot in Kosovo is a fantastic place during the summer months. The waterfall is located behind the village of Berdynaj in the northern part of Pec. The road going to the river is already amazing aside from the great view of the waterfall.

The Pec Patriarchy

Located about two kilometers away from the center of Pec City in the northwest direction. This is where the foundation of the Serbian Orthodox Church Patriarchy is located since 1302. This tourist spot in Kosovo is a gorgeous monastery full of amazing paintings.

The Rugova Gorge

Driving further from the Pec Patriarchy is the Rugova Gorge. A tourist spot in Kosovo that is a canyon composed of very steep walls. The highest reach of the walls of the gorge is about 300 meters.

The Gjakova Old Bazaar

This tourist spot in Kosovo is an ancient and very attractive shopping center that dates back to 17th century. The place has been reconstructed after it was damaged by fire during the battle in 1999. An ancient mosque that was constructed during the 15th century is found at the center of the shopping center.

The Mitrovica Bridge

This tourist spot in Kosovo is a fascinating representation of the division between the populace of the country. The bridge serves as a dividing path between Albanians and Serbs in Mitrovica. Approaching and taking a good look at the bridge is always safe except when political situation becomes worse.

Prizren

Of all the cities in Kosovo, Prizren is the most historical since it has lots of lovely Islamic architecture. This tourist spot in Kosovo is a home of monasteries and mosques that dates back to the fourteenth century. Tour around the city and admire the wonderful mosques spread across the city and the most notable of them is the Mosque of Sinan Pasha.

Brod

A very spectacular village in the country of the Balkans and the place is inhabited by the Gorani people. Walking around the village is very ideal to really see the uniqueness of the place. Their houses are made of mountain rocks and other materials from their immediate area. A horse ride going to the mountains is a wonderful opportunity to see the beauty of nature in this part of the world.

Novo Brdo

A tourist spot in Kosovo that was a metropolis during the year 1326 according to historical documents. The place has a large medieval fortress that was constructed on the peak of the cone of an extinct volcano. Taking a visit to the ruins of the fortress will give you a good experience to cherish.

Ulpiana

A tourist spot in Kosovo that was once an ancient city of the Romans. Located in Lipljan, the remains of this once great city are significant for the history of the country. Mosaics, basilica, and tombstones were unearthed from the area including ceramics, coins, jewelry, and weapons.

Afghanistan

One of the countries in South-Central Asia, Afghanistan has an improving tourism. The tourism industry is an important contributor to the country's economic growth. To enjoy the tourists' vacations in the country, they should spend time visiting the top 10 tourist spots in Afghanistan.

Masjet-e-Jam

Also known as the Friday Mosque, the Masjet-e-Jam in Heart is one of the finest and most popular Islamic sites in the world. Inside the mosque, tourists can see a big bronze cauldron as well as a Sherbet receptacle. Moreover, the place features Sultan Ghiyas-ud-din's tomb.

Gardens of Babur

The Gardens of Babur in Kabul features several plant species. The tourist destination is also the place where the remains Moghul Emperor Babur were buried. In the gardens, people can find a small but attractive mosque.

Bot-e-Bambiyan

The Bot-e-Bambiyan features popular Buddha statues from the 3rd century and the 5th century. The heights of the statues are 36 meters and 53 meters. This place is considered as one of the major archaeological places in Afghanistan.

The Mausoleum of Ahmed Shah Durrani

Found in Kandahar, the Mausoleum of Ahmed Shah Durrani is one of the significant historical monuments in the place. Ahmed Shah Durrani played an essential role in the history of the country because he led numerous territorieal campaigns from 1747 to 1772.

Sultan Masood Palace

The Sultan Masood Palace in Ghazni was constructed in 112 A.D. Inside the palace, people can find antique furnishings. The palace has soldiers' quarters, government offices and a throne room. It also features several small but beautiful gardens.

The Museum of Islamic Art

The Museum of Islamic Art in Ghazni became open to the public in 1966. This tourist spot displays the Timurid architecture. Numerous collections of artifacts and antique items are stored and featured at the site such as bronzes and ceramic tiles. The remains of Sultan Abdul Razaq were buried in the museum.

The Shrine of Baba Wali

Located in Heart, the Shrine of Baba Wali provides a relaxing view of the Arghandab River. Near the shrine, tourists can find other attractive tourist spots including the Elephant Mountain. The site is open to public seven days a week.

Shahr-e-Gholgola

Also called as the Town of Noise, Shahr-e-Gholgola in Bamiyan features the ruins of a wealthy city that existed in the 5th century and 7th century. One of the nice attractions at the town is the historic citadel where the massacre of the residents in the place led by Genghis Khan started.

Mousallah Complex

The Mousallah Complex in Heart features the ruins of the ancient madrassa. At the site, people can find 12 minarets. In addition, this tourist destination is also the place where Gaur Shad's mausoleum were constructed.

Kabul Bala Hisar

The Kabul Bala Hisar is a historic town that has a very strong and complex defensive system. One of the interesting places in the town is the fortress, which was used as a military college since 1939. Within the premises of the town, people can find the residences of popular emperors and Afghan rulers.

Afghanistan features numerous historic and archaeological sites. To have a notable travel to the country, it is beneficial if foreigners visit these tourist destinations.

11 Hindu Religious Tourism Spots

Hinduism is the predominant and indigenous religious tradition of South Asia. Hinduism is often referred to as Sanatana Dharma (a Sanskrit phrase meaning "the eternal law") by its adherents. Generic "types" of Hinduism that attempt to accommodate a variety of complex views span folk and Vedic Hinduism to bhakti tradition, as in Vaishnavism. Hinduism also includes yogic traditions and a wide spectrum of "daily morality" based on the notion of karma and societal norms such as Hindu marriage customs.

Hinduism is formed of diverse traditions and has no single founder. Among its roots is the historical Vedic religion of Iron Age India, and as such Hinduism is often called the "oldest living religion" or the "oldest living major religion".

Demographically, Hinduism is the world's third largest religion, after Christianity and Islam, with more than a billion adherents, of whom approximately 1 billion live in India. Other significant populations are found in Nepal (23 million), Bangladesh (14 million) and the Indonesian island of Bali (3.3 million).

A large body of texts is classified as Hindu, divided into ?ruti ("revealed") and Smriti ("remembered") texts. These texts discuss theology, philosophy and mythology, and provide information on the practice of dharma (religious living). Among these texts, the Vedas are the foremost in authority, importance and antiquity. Other major scriptures include the Upanishads, Puranas and the epics Mahabharata and Ramayana. The Bhagavad Gita, a treatise from the Mahabharata, spoken by Krishna, is of special importance.

The word Hindu is derived from the Sanskrit word Sindhu, the historic local appellation for the Indus River in the northwestern part of the Indian subcontinent. and is first mentioned in the Rig Veda The usage of the word Hindu was further popularized by the Arabic term al-Hind referring to the land of the people who live across river Indus. and the Persian term Hind? referring to all Indians. By the 13th century, Hindustan emerged as a popular alternative name of India, meaning the "land of Hindus".

Originally, Hindu was a secular term which was used to describe all inhabitants of the Indian subcontinent (or Hindustan) irrespective of their religious affiliation. It occurs sporadically in Sanskrit texts such as the later Rajataranginis of Kashmir (Hinduka, c. 1450), some 16th-18th century Bengali Gaudiya Vaishnava texts, including Chaitanya Charitamrita and Chaitanya Bhagavata, usually to contrast Hindus with Yavanas or Mlecchas. It was only towards the end of the 18th century that the European merchants and colonists referred collectively to the followers of Indian religions as Hindus. Eventually, it came to define a precisely religious identity that includes any person of Indian origin who neither practiced Abrahamic religions nor non-Vedic Indian religions, such as Jainism, Buddhism, Sikhism, or tribal (Adivasi) religions, thereby encompassing a wide range of religious beliefs and practices related to Sanatana Dharma.

The term Hinduism was introduced into the English language in the 19th century to denote the religious, philosophical, and cultural traditions native to India.

Dhakeshwari Temple

Dhakeshwari National Temple is a famous Hindu temple in Dhaka, Bangladesh and is state-owned, giving it the distinction of Bangladesh's "National Temple". The name "Dhakeshwari" means "Goddess of Dhaka". The temple is located southwest of the Salimullah Hall of Dhaka University. Since the destruction of Ramna Kali Mandir in 1971 by the Pakistan Army during the Bangladesh Liberation War, the Dhakeshwari Temple has assumed status as the most important Hindu place of worship in Bangladesh.

Kantajew Temple

Kantajew Temple is a late medieval Hindu temple in Dinajpur, Bangladesh. Built by Maharaja Pran Nath, its construction started in

1702 C.E. and ended in 1752 C.E. , during the reign of his son Maharaja Ramnath. It boasts one of the greatest examples on Terracotta architecture in Bangladesh and once had nine spires, but all were destroyed in an earthquake that took place in 1897 .

Jeshoreshwari Kali Temple

Jeshoreshwari Kali Temple is a famous Hindu temple in Bangladesh, dedicated to the goddess Kali. The temple is located in Ishwaripur, a village in Shyamnagar upazilla of Satkhira. The name "Jeshoreshwari" means "Goddess of Jeshore".

Ramna Kali Mandir

The Ramna Kali Mandir also known as the Ramna Kalibari (house of the Hindu Goddess Kali) was one of the most famous Hindu temples of the Indian subcontinent. It was believed to be over a thousand years old and was situated in Dhaka (capital of present day Bangladesh on the outskirts of the Ramna Park (now renamed as Suhrawardy Udyan). The temple was bulldozed by the Pakistan Army on 27 March 1971 as it commenced its genocide during the Bangladesh Liberation War.

International Society for Krishna Consciousness

The International Society for Krishna Consciousness (ISKCON), also known as the Hare Krishna movement, is a Hindu Gaudiya Vaishnava religious organization. It was founded in 1966 in New York City by A.C. Bhaktivedanta Swami Prabhupada. Its core beliefs are based on traditional Hindu scriptures such as the ?r?mad Bh?gavatam and the Bhagavad-g?t?, both of which, according to the traditional Hindu view, date back more than 5,000 years. The distinctive appearance of the movement and its culture come from the Gaudiya Vaishnava tradition, which has had adherents in India since the late 15th century and Western converts since the early 1930s.

Non-sectarian in its ideals, ISKCON was formed to spread the practice of bhakti yoga (devotion to God), in which aspirant devotees (bhaktas) dedicate their thoughts and actions towards pleasing the Supreme Lord, Krishna (God). ISKCON today is a worldwide confederation of more than 400 centres, including 60 farm communities, some aiming for self-sufficiency, 50 schools and 90 restaurants. In recent decades the movement's most rapid expansions in terms of numbers of membership have been within Eastern Europe (especially since the collapse of the Soviet Union) and India.

Angkor Wat

Angkor Wat is a temple complex at Angkor, Cambodia, built for the king Suryavarman II in the early 12th century as his state temple and capital city. As the best-preserved temple at the site, it is the only one to have remained a significant religious centre since its foundation - first Hindu, dedicated to the god Vishnu, then Buddhist. It is the world's largest religious building. The temple is at the top of the high classical style of Khmer architecture. It has become a symbol of Cambodia, appearing on its national flag, and it is the country's prime attraction for visitors. Angkor Wat combines two basic plans of Khmer temple architecture: the temple mountain and the later galleried temple, based on early South Indian Hindu architecture, with key features such as the Jagati. It is designed to represent Mount Meru, home of the devas in Hindu mythology: within a moat and an outer wall 3.6 kilometres (2.2 mi) long are three rectangular galleries, each raised above the next. At the centre of the temple stands a quincunx of towers. Unlike most Angkorian temples, Angkor Wat is oriented to the west; scholars are divided as to the significance of this. The temple is admired for the grandeur and harmony of the architecture, its extensive bas-reliefs and for the numerous devatas (guardian spirits) adorning its walls.

The modern name, Angkor Wat, means "City Temple"; Angkor is a vernacular form of the word ??? nokor which comes from the Sanskrit word ??? nagara meaning capital or city. Wat is the Khmer word for temple. Prior to this time the temple was known as Preah Pisnulok, after the posthumous title of its founder, Suryavarman II.

Phimeanakas

Phimeanakas or Vimeanakas at Angkor, Cambodia, is a Hindu temple in the Khleang style, built at the end of the 10th century, during the reign of Rajendravarman (from 941-968), then rebuilt by Suryavarman II in the shape of a three tier pyramid as a Hindu temple. On top of the pyramid there was a tower.

According to legend, the king spent the first watch of every night with a woman thought to represent a N?ga in the tower, during that time, not even the queen was permitted to intrude. Only in the second watch the king returned to his palace with the queen. If the naga who was the supreme land owner of Khmer land did not show up for a night, the king's day would be numbered, if the king did not show up, calamity would strike his land.

Preah Khan

Preah Khan sometimes transliterated as Prah Khan, is a temple at Angkor, Cambodia, built in the 12th century for King Jayavarman VII. It is located northeast of Angkor Thom and just west of the Jayatataka baray, with which it was associated. It was the centre of a substantial organisation, with almost 100,000 officials and servants. The temple is flat in design, with a basic plan of successive rectangular galleries around a Buddhist sanctuary complicated by Hindu satellite temples and numerous later additions. Like the nearby Ta Prohm, Preah Khan has been left largely unrestored, with numerous trees and other vegetation growing among the ruins.

Hare Krishna Danmark

Krishnabevægelsen (ISKCON) er et usekterisk åndeligt samfund med rødder i Indiens bhakti-tradition (hengivelse til en almægtig Gud). Krishna er et navn på Gud. Alle vi levende sjæle er evige dele af Gud/Krishna. Bhakti-yoga er metoden for at genoplive bevidstheden om dette kærlige lyksalige forhold, som er alle evige væseners oprindelige tilstand.

På disse sider finder De nyheder, information og svar på de mest almindelige spørgsmål om os. Krishnabevægelsen er et internationalt samfund (ISKCON - International Society for Krishna Conscoiusness) grundlagt i 1966 af A. C. Bhaktivedanta Swami Prabhupada.

Krishnabevægelsens formål er at formidle viden om den Højeste Person Krishna som Han beskrives i den vediske litteratur, samt kundskab om alle væseners evige forhold til Ham. Vi følger en historisk set gammel tradition og filosofi som efterleves af vore medlemmer, hjemme eller i templet.

Vor ambition er at give dybere kundskab til samfundet som helhed. Dette gør vi blandt andet gennem litteratur, foredrag, offentlige arrangementer, radio etc. Der er også mulighed for et studiebesøg hos os. God fornøjelse!

Hanseswari Temple

Hanseswari Temple is situated at Bansberia, which is 47 km north of Kolkata in West Bengal. It was built in the beginning of 19th century. The main deity is the blue neem-wood idol of the four-armed goddess Hanseswari, a manifestation of Goddess Kali.

The temple is 21 m high and has 13 towers. The peak of each tower is shaped as a lotus flower. Built according to Tantric principles, this five-storey shrine follows the structure of a human body - Ira, Pingala, Bajraksha, Sushumna and Chitrini.

Vasudeva Temple and Swanbhaba Kali Temple are nearby. Bansberia Railway Station on the Howrah-Katwa main line is the nearest railway station.

Kalighat Kali Temple

Kalighat Kali Temple is a Hindu temple dedicated to the Hindu goddess Maa Kali. It is one of the 51 Shakti Peethas.

Kalighat was a Ghat (landing stage) sacred to Kali on the old course of the Hooghly river (Bhagirathi) in the city of Calcutta. The name Calcutta is said to have been derived from the word Kalighat. The river over a period of time has moved away from the temple. The temple is now on the banks of a small canal called Adi Ganga which connects to the Hoogly. The Adi Ganga was the original course of the river Hoogly (Ganga). Hence the name Adi (original) Ganga.

Dakshineswar Kali Temple

The Dakshineswar Kali Temple is a Hindu temple located in Dakshineswar near Kolkata. Situated on the eastern bank of the Hooghly River, the presiding deity of the temple is Bhavatarini, an aspect of Kali, literally meaning, 'She who takes Her devotees across the ocean of existence'. The temple was built by Rani Rashmoni, a philanthropist and a devotee of Kali in 1855. The temple is famous for its association with Ramakrishna a mystic of 19th Century Bengal.

The temple compound, apart from the nine-spired main temple, contains a large courtyard surrounding the temple, with rooms along the boundary walls. There are twelve shrines dedicated to Shiva-Kali's companion-along the riverfront, a temple to Radha-Krishna, a bathing ghat on the river, a shrine dedicated to Rani Rashmoni. The chamber in the northwestern corner just beyond the last of the Shiva temples, is where Ramakrishna spent a considerable part of his life.

Padmanabhaswamy Temple

The Padmanabhaswamy temple, also known as the Sri Padmanabhaswamy temple, is a famous Hindu temple of Lord Vishnu, located inside the Fort in the city of Thiruvananthapuram, Kerala, India. The temple is one of the 108 divya desam, the holiest abodes of Lord Vishnu. The main deity, Padmanabhaswamy, is a form of Vishnu in Ananthasayanam posture (in eternal sleep of yognidra). This is an ancient temple and the city of Thiruvananthapuram derives its name from the name of the presiding deity enshrined in the temple.Lord Shripadmanabhaswamy is known as Ananthapadmanabhan. Ananthapadmanabhan was the commander in chief of Anizhom Thirunal Marthanda Varma.Present Chempil Arayan Ananthapadmanabhan Valiya Arayan.This history neglected on communal grounds.

Chettikulangara Devi Temple

Chettikulangara Sree Bhagavathi temple is one of the most renowned temples in Kerala. The temple is located at Chettikulangara in Mavelikkara taluk of Alappuzha district in the south Indian state of Kerala. The temple is situated about 4 km west of Mavelikkara, 7 km north of Kayamkulam on SH6 (Kayamkulam - Thiruvalla Highway)

Kodungallur

Kodungallur is a municipal town in the Thrissur District, in the state of Kerala, India. It was known in ancient times as Mahodayapuram or Shinkli. Muziris (Muchiri or Muyirikkodu or Vanchi), the world famous and prosperous seaport at the mouth of the Periyar River (also known as Choorni Nadi) was very near to

Kodungallur. Kodungallur was also the capital of Kulasekhara dynasty (Second Cheras), who ruled Kerala and some parts of Tamil Nadu from 9th century to 12th century AD.

Kodungallur is also the entry point to the Greater Cochin from the North Western parts of Kerala. The Corporation of Cochin has drafted a Master Plan that aims to develop Kodungallur as the satellite township around the Kochi city.

Guruvayur Temple

The Guruvayur Sree Krishna Temple is a famous Krishna temple located in the town of Guruvayur in the Thrissur district of Kerala. It is one of the most important places of worship for Hindus and is often referred to as "Bhooloka Vaikuntam" which translates to the holy abode of Vishnu on Earth. The divine idol installed here represents the enchanting form of Sree Krishna endowed with the four lustrous arms carrying the conch Panchajanya, the discus Sudarshana Chakra, the mace Kaumodaki and the lotus. Adorned with the divine Tulasi garland the idol represents the majestic form of Maha Vishnu as revealed to Vasudeva and Devaki at the time of Krishna avatar; Hence it is also known as Dwaraka of the south (of India). Shri Krishna is popularly known here by different names such as Kannan, Unni-Kannan (Baby Krishnan), Unni-Krishnan, Balakrishnan, and Guruvayoorappan.

The presiding deity in the sanctum-sanctorum is Mahavishnu. He faces east (the direction of the rising sun) and his idol is 4 ft tall. Even though this is not a much small idol, devotees consider him as Little Krishna. He is angry form, standing on a stool. He has 4 hands : The upper right hand holding chakra, lower right hand holding lotus, upper left hand holding shankha and lower left hand holding gada. He stabs gada on the basement. He is worshipped according to the pooja routines laid down by Adi Sankaracharya and later written formally in the Tantric way by Chennas Narayanan Namboodiri (born in 1427). The Chennas Namboodiris are the hereditary Tantris of the Guruvayur temple. The temple/pooja routines are strictly followed without any compromise. The Tantri is available full time at the Temple to ensure this. The Melsanti (Chief Priest) enters the Sri Kovil (sanctum sanctorum) at 2:30 AM and does not drink even a glass of water up to the completion of noon poojas at 12:30 PM. The vedic traditions being followed here with absolute perfection and sincerity is the hallmark of the Guruvayur temple. It is important to note here that, even though the shrine is considered to be one of the holiest spots for Vaishnavites, the temple is not a part of the 108 Divya Desams.

Sabarimala

Sabarimala is a Hindu pilgrimage center located in the Western Ghat mountain ranges of Pathanamthitta District in Kerala. Sabarimala is believed to be the place where the Hindu God Ayyappan meditated after killing the powerful demoness, Mahishi. Ayyappan's temple is situated here amidst 18 hills. The temple is situated on a hilltop at an altitude of 468 m above mean sea level, and is surrounded by mountains and dense forests. Temples exist in each of the hills surrounding Sabarimala. While functional and intact temples exist at many places in the surrounding areas like Nilackal, Kalaketi, and Karimala, remnants of old temples survive to this day on remaining hills.

Sabarimala is linked to Hindu pilgrimage, predominantly for men of all ages; Ayyappan Devotees must go at least once in their lifetime and it is the largest annual pilgrimage in the world with an estimated 45-50 million devotees visiting every year. Women between the ages of 10 and 50 are not allowed to enter the temple, since the story attributed to Ayyappa prohibits the entry of the women in the menstrual age group. This is because Ayyappan is a Bramachari (Celibate). The temple is open for worship only during the days of Mandalapooja (approximately November 15 to December 26), Makaravilakku (January 14- "Makara Sankranti") and Vishu (April 14), and the first six days of each Malayalam month.

Naina Devi

Naina Devi is a town and a municipal council in Bilaspur district in the Indian state of Himachal Pradesh. The Temple of Shri Naina Devi Ji is situated on a hilltop in the Bilaspur Distt. of Himachal Pradesh in India.It was built by a Gurjar Shepherd. The temple is connected with National Highway No. 21. The temple at the top of the hill can be reached via road (that curves round the hill up to a certain point) and then by concrete steps (that finally reach the top). There is also a cable car facility that moves pilgrims from the base of the hill all the way to the top. The hills of Naina Devi overlook the Gobind Sagar lake. The lake was created by the Bhakra-Nangal Dam.

Badrinath Temple

Badrinath temple, sometimes called Badrinarayan temple, is situated along the Alaknanda river, in the hill town of Badrinath in Uttarakhand state in India. It is widely considered to be one of the holiest Hindu temples, and is dedicated to god Vishnu. The temple and town are one of the four Char Dham and Chota Char Dham pilgrimage sites. It is also one of the 108 Divya Desams, holy shrines for Vaishnavites. The temple is open only six months every year (between the end of April and the beginning of November), due to extreme weather conditions in the Himalayan region.

Several murtis are worshipped in the temple. The most important is a one meter tall statue of Vishnu as Lord Badrinarayan, made of black Saligram stone. The statue is considered by many Hindus to be one of eight swayam vyakta keshtras, or self-manifested statues of Vishnu. The murti depicts Vishnu sitting in meditative posture, rather than His far more typical reclining pose. In November each year, when the town of Badrinath is closed, the image is moved to nearby Jyotirmath.

Meenakshi Amman Temple

Meenakshi Sundareswarar Temple or Meenakshi Amman Temple is a historic Hindu temple located in the holy city of Madurai in India. It is dedicated to Lord Shiva - who is known here as Sundareswarar or Beautiful Lord- and his consort, Parvati who is known as Meenakshi. The temple forms the heart and lifeline of the 2500 year old city of Madurai. The complex houses 14 magnificent Gopurams or towers including two golden Gopurams for the main deities, that are elaborately sculptured and painted. The temple is a significant symbol for the Tamil people, and has been mentioned since antiquity in Tamil literature, though the present structure is believed to have been built in 1600. The tallest temple tower is 51.9 metres (170 ft) high.

Rameswaram

Rameswaram is a town in Ramanathapuram district in the Indian state of Tamil Nadu. It is located on Pamban Island separated from mainland India by the Pamban channel and is about 50 kilometres from Mannar Island, Sri Lanka. Pamban Island, also known as Rameswaram Island, is connected to mainland India by the Pamban Bridge. Rameswaram is the terminus of the railway line from Chennai and Madurai. Together with Kashi, it is considered to be one of the holiest places in India to Hindus, and part of the Char Dham pilgrimages. Hence, it is a bustling pilgrim centre.

It is situated in the Gulf of Mannar at the very tip of the Indian peninsula. According to legend, this is the place from where Lord Rama built a bridge Ram Setu (also known as Adam's Bridge) across the sea to Lanka to rescue his consort Sita from her abductor Ravana. Both the Vaishnavites and Shaivites visit this pilgrimage centre which is known as the Varanasi of the south.

Ex-president of India, Dr. A.P.J. Abdul Kalam, hails from a fishing hamlet called Dhanushkodi situated on this island.

Mahabalipuram

Mahabalipuram, derived from 'Mamallapuram' is a town in Kancheepuram district in the Indian state of Tamil Nadu. It has an average elevation of 12 metres (39 feet).

Mahabalipuram was a 7th century port city of the South Indian dynasty of the Pallavas around 60 km south from the city of Chennai in Tamil Nadu. The name Mamallapuram is believed to have been given after the Pallava king Narasimhavarman I, who took on the epithet Maha-malla (great wrestler), as the favourite sport of the Pallavas was wrestling. It has various historic monuments built largely between the 7th and the 9th centuries, and has been classified as a UNESCO World Heritage Site.

Chidambaram Temple

Chidambaram Temple is a Hindu temple dedicated to Lord Shiva located in the heart of the temple town of Chidambaram, 78 km south of Pondicherry and 60 km north of Karaikal in Cuddalore District, the east-central part of the Tamil Nadu state of southeastern India. The Sangam classics refer to Viduvelvidugu Perumtaccan, respected clan of traditional Vishwakarmas, as being the chief architect of the temple renovation. There have been several renovations in its history, particularly during the days of Pallava/Chola emperors in ancient and pre-medieval periods.

In Hindu literature, Chidambaram is one of the five holiest Shiva temples, each representing one of the five natural elements; Chidambaram represents akasha (aether). The other four temples in this category are:

Thiruvanaikaval Jambukeswara (water), Kanchi Ekambareswara (earth), Thiruvannamalai Arunachaleswara (fire) and Kalahasti Nathar (wind).

Konark Sun Temple

Konark Sun Temple is a 13th-century Sun Temple (also known as the Black Pagoda), at Konark, in Odisha. It was constructed from oxidizing and weathered ferruginous sandstone by King Narasimhadeva I (1236-1264 CE) of the Eastern Ganga Dynasty. The temple is one of the most well renowned temples in India and is a World Heritage Site. It is one of the Seven Wonders of India (as per the poll collected by NDTV).

Kailash Temple

Kailash Temple, also Kailasa Temple is one of the 34 monasteries and temples, extending over more than 2 km, that were dug side by side in the wall of a high basalt cliff in the complex located at Ellora, Maharashtra, India. Of these 34 monasteries and temples, the Kailasa (cave 16) is a remarkable example of Indian rock-cut architecture on account of its striking proportion; elaborate workmanship architectural content and sculptural ornamentation.. It is designed to recall Mount Kailash, the abode of Lord Shiva. While it exhibits typical Dravidian features, it was carved out of one single rock. It was built in the 8th century by the Rashtrakuta king Krishna I.

The Kailash Temple is notable for its vertical excavation-carvers started at the top of the original rock, and excavated downward, exhuming the temple out of the existing rock. The traditional methods were rigidly followed by the master architect which could not have been achieved by excavating from the front. The architects found to design this temple were from the southern Pallava kingdom.

It is estimated that about 200,000 tons of rocks was scooped out over hundreds of years to construct this monolithic structure. From the chisel marks on walls of this temple, archeologists could conclude that three types of chisels were used to carve this temple.

All the carvings are done in more than one level. A two-storeyed gateway opens to reveal a U-shaped courtyard. The courtyard is edged by a columned arcade three stories high. The arcades are punctuated by huge sculpted panels, and alcoves containing enormous sculptures of a variety of deities. Originally flying bridges of stone connected these galleries to central temple structures, but these have fallen.

Within the courtyard are two structures. As is traditional in Shiva temples, an image of the sacred bull Nandi fronts the central temple housing the lingam. In Cave 16, the Nandi Mandap and main Shiva temple are each about 7 meters high, and built on two stories. The lower stories of the Nandi Mandap are both solid structures, decorated with elaborate illustrative carvings. The base of the temple has been carved to suggest that elephants are holding the structure aloft.

A living rock bridge connects the Nandi Mandap to the porch of the temple. The temple itself is tall pyramidic structure reminiscent of a South Indian temple. The shrine - complete with pillars, windows, inner and outer rooms, gathering halls, and an enormous lingam at its heart - carved from stone, is carved with niches, plasters, windows as well as images of deities, mithunas (erotic male and female figures) and other figures. Most of the deities at the left of the entrance are Shaivaite (followers of Lord Shiva) while on the right hand side the deities are Vaishnavaites (followers of Lord Vishnu).

There are two Dhvajastambhas (pillars with the flagstaff) in the courtyard. The grand sculpture of Ravana attempting to lift Mount Kailasa, the abode of Lord Shiva, with his full might is a landmark in Indian art.

Vaishno Devi

Vaishno Devi Mandir is one of the holiest Hindu temples dedicated to Shakti, located in the hills of Vaishno Devi, Jammu and Kashmir, India. In Hinduism, Vaishno Devi, also known as Mata Rani and Vaishnavi, is a manifestation of the Mother Goddess.

The temple is near the town of Katra, in the Reasi district in the state of Jammu and Kashmir. It is one of the most revered places of worship in Northern India. The shrine is at an altitude of 5200 feet and a distance of approximately 14 kilometres (8.4 miles) from Katra. Approximately 8 million pilgrims (yatris) visit the temple every year and it is the second most visited religious shrine in India, after Tirumala Venkateswara Temple. The Shri Mata Vaishno Devi Shrine Board maintains the shrine. A rail link from Udhampur to Katra is being built to facilitate pilgrimage. The nearest airport is Jammu Airport which has very high flight frequency. All leading domestic airlines have their services to Jammu Airport.

Somnath

The Somnath Temple located in the Prabhas Kshetra near Veraval in Saurashtra, on the western coast of Gujarat, India, is one of the twelve

Jyotirlinga shrines of the God Shiva. Somnath means "The Protector of (the) Moon God". The Somnath Temple is known as "the Shrine Eternal", having been destroyed six times and rebuilt six times. Most recently it was rebuilt in November 1947, when Sardar Vallabhbhai Patel visited the area for the integration of Junagadh and mooted a plan for restoration. After Patel's death, the rebuilding continued under K. M. Munshi, another minister of the Government of India.

Amarnath Temple

Located in the Indian state of Jammu and Kashmir and situated on Mount Amarnath, the Amarnath caves are one of the most famous shrines in Hinduism. Dedicated to the god Shiva, the shrine is said to be over 5,000 years old. The shrine forms an important part of Hindu mythology..

Inside the main Amarnath cave lies an ice stalagmite resembling the Shiva Linga, which waxes during May to August and gradually wanes thereafter. This lingam is said to grow and shrink with the phases of the moon, reaching its height during the summer festival. According to Hindu mythology, this is the cave where Shiva explained the secret of life and eternity to his divine consort Parvati. Two other ice formations represent Parvati and Shiva's son, Ganesha.

The cave is situated at an altitude of 3,888 m (12,756 ft), about 141 km (88 mi) from Srinagar, the capital of Jammu and Kashmir. The Central Reserve Police Force, Indian Army and Indian Paramilitary Forces maintain a strong presence in the region due to security concerns.

Akshardham (Delhi)

Akshardham is a Hindu temple complex in Delhi, India. Also referred to as Delhi Akshardham or Swaminarayan Akshardham, the complex displays millennia of traditional Indian and Hindu culture, spirituality, and architecture. The building was inspired and moderated by Pramukh Swami Maharaj, the spiritual head of the Bochasanwasi Shri Akshar Purushottam Swaminarayan Sanstha, whose 3,000 volunteers helped 7,000 artisans construct Akshardham.

The temple, which attracts approximately 70 percent of all tourists who visit Delhi, was officially opened on 6 November 2005. It sits on the banks of the Yamuna adjacent to the 2010 Commonwealth Games village. The monument, at the center of the complex, was built off of the Vastu

Shastra and Pancharatra Shastra. The complex features a large central monument crafted entirely of stone, exhibitions on incidents from the life of Swaminarayan and the history of India, an IMAX feature, a musical fountain, and large landscaped gardens. The temple is named after a belief in Swaminarayan Hinduism.

Tirumala Venkateswara Temple

Tirumala Venkateswara Temple is a famous Hindu temple of Lord Vishnu in the form of Lord Venkateswara located in the hill town Tirumala, near Tirupati in the Chittoor district of Andhra Pradesh, India. It is located 580 kilometres (360 mi) south of state capital, Hyderabad , about 200 kilometers from Bangalore, about 120 kilometers from Vellore, Tamilnadu, and 157 kilometres (98 mi) north west of Chennai. The temple is situated on Venkatadri, one of the seven hills of Tirumala, and hence is also known as the Temple of Seven Hills. The presiding deity of the temple, Lord Venkateswara, is also known by other names - Balaji, Vishnu, Govinda and Srinivasa.

The temple is reportedly the richest and the most visited place of worship in the world. The temple is visited by about 50,000 to 100,000 pilgrims daily (3 to 4 crore people annually on an average), while on special occasions and festivals, like the annual Brahmotsavam, the number of pilgrims shoots up to 500,000, making it the most visited holy place in the world.

According to legend, the temple has a murti (deity) of Lord Venkateswara, believed to have resided there for the entire Kali Yuga. In Sri Vaishnava tradition, the temple is considered one of the 108 Divya Desams.

Haridwar

Haridwar pronunciation is an important pilgrimage city and municipality in the Haridwar district of Uttarakhand, India. The River Ganges, after flowing for 253 kilometres (157 mi) from its source at Gaumukh at the edge of the Gangotri Glacier, enters the Indo-Gangetic Plains of North India for the first time at Haridwar, which gave the city its ancient name, Gangadwára.

Haridwar is regarded as one of the seven holiest places to Hindus. According to the Samudra manthan, Haridwar along with Ujjain, Nasik and Allahabad is one of four sites where drops of Amrit, the elixir of immortality, accidentally spilled over from the pitcher while being carried by the celestial bird Garuda. This is manifested in the Kumbha Mela being celebrated every 3 years in one of the 4 places, and thus every 12 years in Haridwar. Amidst the Kumbha Mela, millions of pilgrims, devotees, and tourists congregate in Haridwar to perform ritualistic bathing on the banks of the river Ganges to wash away their sins to attain Moksha. Brahma Kund, the spot where the Amrit fell, is located at Har ki Pauri (literally, "footsteps of the Lord") and is considered to be the most sacred ghat of Haridwar.

Haridwar is the headquarters and the largest city of the district. Today, the city is developing beyond its religious importance, with the fast developing industrial estate of State Infrastructure and Industrial Development Corporation (SIDCUL), and the close by township of Bharat Heavy Electricals Limited in Ranipur, Uttarakhand as well as its affiliated ancillaries.

12 Religious Tourist Attractions

There are many definitions for the term "religion" in common usage. On this web site, we define it very broadly, in order to include the greatest number of belief systems: "Religion is any specific system of belief about deity, often involving rituals, a code of ethics, and a philosophy of life." Thus we include here all of the great monotheistic religions, Eastern religions; Neopagan religions; a wide range of other faith groups, spiritual paths, and ethical systems; and beliefs about the existence of God(s) and Goddess(es). We recognize that most people define "religion" in a much more exclusive manner.

Religion is a cultural system that creates powerful and long-lasting meaning, by establishing symbols that relate humanity to beliefs and values. Many religions have narratives, symbols, traditions and sacred histories that are intended to give meaning to life or to explain the origin of life or the universe. They tend to derive morality, ethics, religious laws or a preferred lifestyle from their ideas about the cosmos and human nature.

The word religion is sometimes used interchangeably with faith or belief system, but religion differs from private belief in that it has a public aspect. Most religions have organized behaviors, including clerical hierarchies, a definition of what constitutes adherence or membership, congregations of laity, regular meetings or services for the purposes of veneration of a deity or for prayer, holy places (either natural or architectural), and/or scriptures. The practice of a religion may also include sermons, commemoration of the activities of a god or gods, sacrifices, festivals, feasts, trance, initiations, funerary services, matrimonial services, meditation, music, art, dance, public service, or other aspects of human culture.

The development of religion has taken different forms in different cultures. Some religions place an emphasis on belief, while others emphasize practice. Some religions focus on the subjective experience of the religious individual, while others consider the activities of the religious community to be most important. Some religions claim to be universal, believing their laws and cosmology to be binding for everyone, while others are intended to be practiced only by a closely defined or localized group. In many places religion has been associated with public institutions such as education, hospitals, the family, government, and political hierarchies.

Some academics studying the subject have divided religions into three broad categories: world religions, a term which refers to transcultural, international faiths; indigenous religions, which refers to smaller, culture-specific or nation-specific religious groups; and new religious movements, which refers to recently developed faiths. One modern academic theory of religion, social constructionism, says that religion is a modern concept that suggests all spiritual practice and worship follows a model similar to Christianity, and thus religion, as a concept, has been applied inappropriately to non-Western cultures.

Religious Tourism Attraction in Beneath

Beneath the heavens above, there is enough space for all the spires of church buildings of the various denominations - Catholics, Lutherans, The Russian Orthodox, Old Believers, Jewish, Baptists, Seventh-day Adventists, Armenian Apostolic ...This country is home to people of many different faiths, thus even in a small town one sometimes finds the churches or houses of worship of three or four denominations - buildings which have become amazing tourist sights as a result of Latvia's complex history and the creative spirit of its people.

Throughout history, and with the support of once current ruling powers, each one of the largest Christian denominations (Catholic, Lutheran, and Russian Orthodox) was once dominant in Latvia, and therefore in Riga, majestic cathedrals rise next to small churches and humble houses of worship. On their vaults and stained glass windows, culture history experts will be able to reveal the "footprint" of nearly all of the great art and architectural styles known to Europe. The "pearl fishers" of sacral art will find it exciting to visit not only the capital city of Latvia with its Dome, the St. Peter's Church, and the Nativity of Christ Cathedral, but also smaller towns and villages. For instance, if one goes to ?audona in the Madona District, the three congregations - Catholic, Lutheran and Orthodox, have now found a common home in an Orthodox Church building, which was built and consecrated in 1863. During World War II, the building was damaged in a fire, but during the Soviet era it was utilised for the needs of a library.

Catholics and Old Believers in Latgale

Almost all of those interested in pilgrimage and religious tourism are often surprised about a self-evident co-existencc of two branches of Christianity - Western (Catholicism and Protestantism) and Eastern (Orthodox and Old Believers). Unforgettable sites and objects of religious art are to be found in Latgale, the stronghold of Catholicism in Latvia, where crucifixes are evident in public space and a sacred site of international renown at Aglona bears witness to the strong faith of the region's people. Latgale, however, is home also to a number of Orthodox Church buildings harbouring outstanding pieces of sacred art, for instance, a national scale monument of architecture, the Š?eltova Orthodox church in the Aglona District is the only one built back in 1836 that has preserved its original Empire style; the miniature wooden church with white columns is located by the roadside, amidst a cemetery surrounded by a birch grove.

Still, one of the biggest surprises in Latgale is its small and mysterious Old Believers churches - built of stone or brick in the towns, or of brightly painted timber - in the villages. The Old Believers' community is a secluded one; therefore one should not be too optimistic that the doors of all of these churches will be wide open. However, when the visit has been arranged in advance, those small houses of God reveal a centuries old tradition and gems of sacred art to the well-wishing visitor.

Churches in Kurzeme

Kurzeme, the heart of the Duchy of Courland, for its part, has fostered to these very days not only the stately Catholic and Lutheran churches, the benches of which still carry the touch of mediaeval worshipers, but also the small, quiet coastal churches, traditionally without a steeple (so as not to lead seafarers astray), and with models of sailing ships attached to the roof beams.

Kurzeme also offers a particular surprise to its visitors with its amazing Baroque and Rococo woodcarvings and painted ceilings done by local artisans who most often as not did not even have a surname. Take note of the name of the Apri?i Lutheran church in the Aizpute District - this small structure built in the 17th century as a private chapel for a local landowner is one of the most splendid examples of the Baroque and Rococo style in the Baltics.

Pipe Organs

Still, the sacred art scene of Latvia would not be complete without music. There are about 300 of the so-called historical organs in this country, namely, musical instruments built before 1945, and several of which have been listed among the treasures of the world heritage. For instance, the organ in the Holy Trinity Lutheran Cathedral of Liepaja is the only remaining original, unreconstructed pipe organ in the world that can still be played.

The organ of the Riga Dome Cathedral and the central panel of its façade have been preserved since 1601. Pipe organ experts consider that Riga may be considered a metropolis not only of Art Nouveau, but also of the Romantic period organs. Whether you have decided to undertake a journey along Latgale's sacred pilgrimage routes or just to visit the largest churches of Old Riga, in each of these you will encounter the true spirit of the Latvian people and find time for prayer in contemplation on the Almighty.

Bogota tourist attractions

Aside from being tourist icons and an indication of the importance of Catholicism, the temples in which it is practiced, and the history that precedes them, the sanctuaries of Guadalupe and Monserrate, atop Bogotá's highest mountain peaks, represent the Christian faith that drives hundreds of people.

This happens daily there, as well as in over 200 churches and parishes spread throughout the city.

Following the Spanish conquest, Bogotá grew architecturally in the Spanish style. Churches, plazas, and parks were gradually built around the church, which was always the main axis and meeting point for the whole community.

This feature may be appreciated in the vast majority of Bogotá's sections, where these buildings preserve a growing interest, not only for the religious ceremonies that take place, but by the historic and cultural value that led to the construction of many of them.

Visiting several of the most traditional churches is a plan that consolidates Bogotá also as a religious destination. Aside from pilgrimages and solemn celebrations, there are fascinating stories and legends on why the temples were erected - temples with a superb architecture and astonishing ornaments inside. Any moment - not just Sundays and Holy Week - is ideal for delving into the architecture and history of the city's most emblematic churches and their surroundings.

Religious Tourism in Italy

The religious Tours represent an important phenomenon that involves the Tourism industry. Nowadays all over the world there are 40 million people spending 4 billion dollars that love to visit the places of worship . They are driven by the wish to discover the roots of Christianity and to be moved by those holy places. This great business is particularly flourishing in Italy where there are a lot of significant, beautiful and charming destination and the Christian culture deeply radicated. The itinerary that we propose here ties many important Italian religious destinations:

Venezia, Padova, Torino, Firenze, Loreto, Assisi, Lanciano, Roma, Montecassino, Pompei, San Giovanni Rotondo.

Pampanga Religious Tourist Attractions

Sta. Catalina Church (Arayat, Pampanga)

Built in honor of St. Catherine of Alexandra, it is one of the oldest churches in the province and is known for its classical architecture.

San Guillermo Parish Church (Bacolor, Pampanga)

One of Pampanga's oldest churches. It features fascinating works of architecture, such as its classic altar in antique carved design and décor blending with religious frescos reminiscent of neoclassical works of European art.

Apu Chapel (Angeles City, Pampanga)

This is the shrine of the Our Lord of the Holy Sepulchre (Apung Mamacalulu). Devotees from all over Pampanga flock to this shrine every Friday to venerate the supposedly miraculous image of Jesus Christ lying in the sepulcher. It is also every Friday when people buy household items, clothing including audio-video equipment in a makeshift market called "tiangge" at bargain prices.

Holy Rosary Cathedral (Angeles City, Pampanga)

Located at the intersection of Sto. Rosario and Sto. Entierro Streets, the Holy Rosary Church was constructed from 1877 to 1896 by the townspeople of Angeles by forced labor system known as "polos y servicios" imposed by the Spanish colonial government. From 1899 to 1900 the church was used by the US Army as a military hospital. In 1896 - 1898, the backyard of the church became the execution grounds to the Spanish forces in shooting down Filipino rebels and suspects. It has a beautiful transient and measures 70m. long, 20m. wide and 12m. high. The dominant element of façade is the symmetry created by recessed arched windows which are in harmony with the segmented ones.

Apalit Parochial Church (Apalit, Pampanga)

Located at the town plaza, it was built in the year 1629 - 1630 and designed in Baroque architecture. The painting on the ceilings and dome are filled with beautiful paintings and are worth studying. The style of the façade is reminiscent of European neo-classic churches. It was rebuilt by Father Antonio Redondo between the years 1876 - 1880. Its towers were finished in 1896 by the Rev. Toribio Fanjul, who purposely made them low to minimize the effects of earthquakes.

St. Catherine Parish Church (Arayat, Pampanga)

One of the oldest churches in Pampanga and known for its classical architectures. No records on builder and date of construction of present church. The church measures 70m. long, 16m. wide and 12m. high. The presbytery, ceiling and the main altar have been recently renovated. The original stone of the façade has been covered with cement and painted white.

San Guillermo Parish Church (Bacolor, Pampanga)

It is one of the oldest and largest churches in Pampanga. It was constructed by the Augustinian friars in 1576 on the lot of Don Guillermo Manabat, a rich landlord believed to be the founder of Bacolor. The church was restored by Fr. Manuel Diaz in 1897. The church measured 56m. long, 15m. wide and 12m. high. It has a central nave and an ample and well-lighted transept with windows. The main retablo, side retablos and pulpit are gilded with gold leaf. The richness of the decoration of Bacolor is indicative of the advanced stage of its baroque style. In spite of the 1991 eruption of Mt. Pinatubo which half-buried the church on Oct. 1, 1995, masses are still held every Sunday morning.

St. Andrew Parish Church (Candaba, Pampanga)

The simplicity of line and scarcity of ornamentation are the main traits of the façade of this church, the triangular pediment with its protruding center helps maintain the simplicity of line. A new feature of the façade is the depressed three-centered arches of the windows on the second level. The second level is separated by a cornice decorated with geometric designs.

St. Joseph Parish Church (Florida Blanca, Pampanga)

Pseudo-Gothic elements blend subtly along the classic design of the structure. The flame-like arch of the main entrance and lateral doors provide contrast to the triangular pediment. The structures are simple and the large voids lend drama to an otherwise bare design.

Betis Catholic Church (Guagua, Pampanga)

The jewel in the crown is the Betis Church (Santiago de Galicia Parish), built in the early 1700s and repaired continually throughout the 1800s. The unadorned exterior does not prepare the visitor for what he's about to witness inside: the main altar (retablo) with ornate carvings and saints peering out of their niches like ancient dolls, and the paintings on the ceiling that attract comparison with the Sistine Chapel. NCCA declared this church a National Treasure, one of only ten churches in the country bestowed that honor. The main attraction is the original ceiling mural done by the famous painter Simon Flores (1839-1904). Not to be missed are the original Simon Flores painting of the Holy Family, the artesian well (dug in

Church of Lubao (Lubao, Pampanga)

Built in 1572, by Architect Fr. Antonio Herrera, the Augustinian mission constructed this church in 1614-1630 out of locally made bricks and sand mixed in egg albumin. The church was occupied in 1898 by the revolutionary forces, used as hospital in 1899 by the American forces, and was destroyed in 1942 by the Japanese shelling. It was then repaired in 1949-1952 under the direction of Fr. Melencio Garcia. It measures 82.45m.

long, 21.12m. wide and 10.50m. high. The walls are 2.46m thick. It has one nave originally painted by Italian artists, Dibella and Alberoni. The five story belfry 15.31m. high remains unrestored.

St. Nicholas of Tolentino Parish Church (Macabebe, Pampanga)

It was founded in 1575 under the advocation of San Nicolas de Tolentino. The church measures 70m. long, 17m. wide and 11m. high. The façade of the church has scantly ornamentation and its architectural symmetry is lost amid and the various forms assumed the windows and the main entrance. Simple neo-classic lines of the façade.

Church of Magalang (Magalang, Pampanga)

San Bartolome Church - Established by the Augustinians in 1605, it was the scene of the encounter between the followers of Andres Malong led by Melchor de Vera and the Spanish troops in 1660. Moved to San Bartolome in 1734, the church was swept by Parua river in the flood of 1863. It was re-established in Barrio San Pedro on December 13, 1863. The 3-aisle church is made of stone and wood. It is 55m. long, 21m. wide and 7m. high. Interplay of arches, as seen on the main entrance, doors and niches, pediments and fenestrations, including those of the bellowers and adjacent convent suggest a touch of baroque.

St. Michael Archangel Parish Church (Masantol, Pampanga)

The church was built by the parish priest of Macabebe who attended to the spiritual needs of Masantol. The center bell tower is of renaissance influence. The cemented façade contrasts with natural texture and color of the original stones at the sides.

Minalin Church

The Minalin Church (Sta. Monica Parish), located on the town's highest ground called burul (the town had moved to its present site due to flooding, hence 'minalis,' later corrupted to minalin) but despite its elevation, silt from the river has already invaded its beautiful church. The peeled palitada reveals the original red brick walls, giving the church its unique old-rose touches. The ancient mural paintings in the adjoining convent, one of which is a primitive-looking map with details of trees, ducks, crows, a boat, a hunter and a crocodile. A detail not to be missed are the corbels and beams in the convent and high up in the church's ceiling, with carvings that some say depict pre-Hispanic pagan deities like naga (serpent), dapu (crocodile) and galura (eagle), but Siuala ding Meangubie believes they depict only one creature, bulig (mudfish).

Sta. Rita of Casia Parish Church (Sta. Rita)

Building of the church had to be delayed until late 19th century due to economic adjuristicial conditions. The single-nave church is 55m long, 13m wide and 10m high. It has a large and well lit transept. The solid brass façade has baroque characteristics and the single columns are relatively slender.

St. Catherine Alexandra Church (Porac)

The original structure is very much intact but slight revisions have been made to the inside. Quite remote, the church underwent restoration in the 1980's. The church is 52m long, 12m wide and 9m high.

Metropolitan Cathedral of San Fernando

(City of San Fernando) - The present church may have been built by the end of the 18th century, constructed most probably by Fr. Sebastian Moreno, its parish priest in 1756, and was restored in 1808. The church measures 70m. long, 13m. wide and 11m. high. The round majestic dome rising from the rotanda of the transept is reminiscent of the baroque style with some renaissance touch. It is the seat of the Archdiocese of the City of San Fernando, Pampanga. President Emilio F. Aguinaldo and his cabinet viewed the Phillippine Revolutionary Army from the windows of the convento on October 9, 1898. The church and the convento were burned by the Philippine Revolutionary Army on orders of Gen. Antonio Luna on May 4, 1899. It was again destroyed by fire in 1939, and later restored by Architect Fernando H. Ocampo.

San Luis Church

(San Luis, Pampanga) is located in a place that used to be called Cabagsac, referring to the proliferation of fruit bats. In fact, today, a fishnet is permanently installed high above the altar precisely to catch thousands of bats that are roosting inside the church. The interior is dark, has an ambience of antiquity and mystery and overpowering odor of bat urine. The main attraction is the three-tower facade, perhaps one of its kind in the country. Not to be missed is the ancient cemetery located in a hidden corner at the back of the church, with some tombstones dating back to the 1800s and bearing the names of the town's prominent families, including Taruc.

Sta. Lucia Parish Church

(Sasmoan, Pampanga) The church is 45m long and 11m wide and 6m high. An author described it as "very beautiful and of very good condition." When looking at the complex of church and convent, one is stuck by the impression that the round and rectangular openings are capriciously aligned. This makes the façade both interesting and unique. Attracts devotees from all over the provinces to honor Sta. Lucia and ask their petitions. She is believed to be a miraculous saint.

St. Anne Parish Church

(Sta. Ana, Pampanga) The church is 58m long, 14m wide and 13 m high. The recently applied coat of red and white paint has turned this centuries old church into a gaudy 20th century anomaly. The massive hexagonal four-storey bellower has blind and open recesses, keeping with the symmetry of the façade. It ends in a balustrade dome topped by a cross.

13 Religious Tourism in Asia

Asia is the world's largest and most populous continent, located primarily in the eastern and northern hemispheres. It covers 8.6% of the Earth's total surface area (or 29.9% of its land area) and with approximately 4 billion people, it hosts 60% of the world's current human population. During the 20th century Asia's population nearly quadrupled.

Asia is traditionally defined as part of the landmass of Eurasia-with the western portion of the latter occupied by Europe-located to the east of the Suez Canal, east of the Ural Mountains and south of the Caucasus Mountains (or the Kuma-Manych Depression) and the Caspian and Black Seas. It is bounded on the east by the Pacific Ocean, on the south by the Indian Ocean and on the north by the Arctic Ocean. Given its size and diversity, Asia-a toponym dating back to classical antiquity-is more a cultural concept incorporating a number of regions and peoples than a homogeneous physical entity (see Subregions of Asia, Asian people). The wealth of Asia differs very widely among and within its regions, due to its vast size and huge range of different cultures, environments, historical ties and government systems.

Asia has been the historical birthplace of all major world religions.

Asian mythology is complex and diverse. The story of the Great Flood for example, as presented to Christians in the Old Testament, is first found in Mesopotamian mythology, in the Epic of Gilgamesh. Hindu mythology tells about an avatar of the God Vishnu in the form of a fish who warned Manu of a terrible flood. In ancient Chinese mythology, Shan Hai Jing, the Chinese ruler Da Yu, had to spend 10 years to control a deluge which swept out most of ancient China and was aided by the goddess Nüwa who literally fixed the broken sky through which huge rains were pouring.

Almost all Asian religions have philosophical character and Asian philosophical traditions cover a large spectrum of philosophical thoughts and writings. Indian philosophy includes Hindu philosophy and Buddhist philosophy. They include elements of nonmaterial pursuits, whereas another school of thought from India, C?rv?ka, preached the enjoyment of material world. Christianity is also present in most Asian countries.

The Abrahamic religions of Judaism, Christianity, Islam and Baha'i Faith originated in West Asia. Judaism, the oldest of the Abrahamic faiths, is practiced primarily in Israel (which has the world's largest Jewish population), though small communities exist in other countries, such as the Bene Israel in India. In the Philippines and East Timor, Roman Catholicism is the predominant religion; it was introduced by the Spaniards and the Portuguese, respectively. In Armenia, Cyprus, Georgia and Russia, Eastern Orthodoxy is the predominant religion. Various Christian denominations have adherents in portions of the Middle East, as well as China and India. The world's largest Muslim community (within the bounds of one nation) is in Indonesia. South Asia (mainly Pakistan, India and Bangladesh) holds 30% of Muslims. There are also significant Muslim populations in China, Iran, Malaysia, southern Philippines (Mindanao), Russia and most of West Asia and Central Asia. The Bahá'í Faith originated in Asia, in Iran (Persia), and spread from there to the Ottoman Empire, Central Asia, India, and Burma during the lifetime of Bahá'u'lláh. Since the middle of the 20th Century, growth has particularly occurred in other Asian countries, because the Bahá'í Faith's activities in many Muslim countries has been severely suppressed by authorities.

The religions of Hinduism, Buddhism, Jainism and Sikhism originated in India, South Asia. In East Asia, particularly in China and Japan, Confucianism, Taoism and Zen Buddhism took shape.

Over 80% of the populations of both India and Nepal adhere to Hinduism, alongside significant communities in Bangladesh, Pakistan, Bhutan, Sri Lanka and Bali. Many overseas Indians in countries such as Burma, Singapore and Malaysia also adhere to Hinduism.

Buddhism has a great following in mainland Southeast Asia and East Asia. Buddhism is the religion of the majority of the populations of Cambodia (98%), Thailand (95%), Burma (89%), Japan (84-96%), Bhutan (75%), Sri Lanka (69%),Laos (67%-98%) and Mongolia (50%). Large Buddhist populations also exist in Singapore (42.5%), Taiwan (35.1%-93%), South Korea (23.2%), Malaysia(19.2%), Nepal(10.7%), Vietnam (9.3-

80%), China(8-80%), North Korea (4.5%-60%), Indonesia (<2%); and small communities in India and Bangladesh. In many Chinese communities, Mahayana Buddhism is easily syncretized with Taoism, thus exact religious statistics is difficult to obtain and may be understated or overstated. The Communist-governed countries of China, Vietnam and North Korea are officially atheist, thus the number of Buddhists and other religious adherents may be under-reported.

Jainism is found mainly in India and in oversea Indian communities such as India and Malaysia. Sikhism is found in Northern India and amongst overseas Indian communities in other parts of Asia, especially Southeast Asia. Confucianism is found predominantly in Mainland China, South Korea, Taiwan and in overseas Chinese populations. Taoism is found mainly in Mainland China, Taiwan, Malaysia and Singapore. Taoism is easily syncretized with Mahayana Buddhism for many Chinese, thus exact religious statistics is difficult to obtain and may be understated or overstated.

Religious places in Asia

Bangladesh Golden Stupa

In mainly Muslim Bangladesh you will not come across many Buddhist temples, but this one is among the few. It stands a baby taxi (tuk-tuk) ride from Bandarban and is quite beautiful and shiny. Not much seems to be going on here, but the views over the valley and Sangu river are magnificent.

Hindu Temple

This tiny Hindu tower would normally not have made the list, if it was not for the fact that it lies in Bangladesh, and not neighboring India. The official name is Khodla Math temple and it lies forgotten in a suburban neighborhood outside Bagerhat. The hollow inner does not contain many surprises, but can be accessed by asking the neighbor for the key to the iron doors.

Historical Mosque

The Bagerhat area flourished under a local hero named Khan Jahan Ali in the 15th century. Islam was taught and mosques were build. To this day some of these old buildings still stand and attract a small crowd of local pilgrims and the odd traveller. They are all very simple and humbled looking. Shait Gumbad mosque is the biggest. It is also called the 60 domes mosque, which is a bit strange considering it actually has 77 of them. Other mosques in the area worth exploring are Singar mosque, Bibi Begni mosque and Dargah mosque. The old mosques of Bagerhat is one of the few World Heritage Sites in Bangladesh.

Bangladesh, Khan Jahan Ali Mausoleum

In the mid 15th century Khan Jahan Ali, a Turkish Muslim saint, arrived to where Bagerhat lies today. He apparently liked the place so much that he founded a beautiful town which artificial ponds, palaces and impressive mosques otherwise unknown to the area. According to inscriptions on his tomb he died in 1459 leaving behind a thriving Islamic culture along with some of the finest architecture in Bangladesh, with some of the mosques still standing today. His mausoleum is still considered a pilgrimage site where people come to pray and pay respect. In the pond in front of the shrine, there are crocodiles which is believed to give good luck if touched (we kid you not).

Brunei, Omar Ali Saifuddien Mosque

A tasteful and modest piece of architecture that shows what oil money can buy. Build in 1958 with the finest material from all over the world; marble from Italy, stained-glass and chandeliers from England, granite from China, carpets from Saudi Arabia and a golden dome. In the artificial lake stands a replica of a royal boat. It's clearly the city's proud landmark and is considered among the most beautiful mosques in the world.

Cambodia, Phnom Chhnork and Phnom Sidaoun

Phnom Chhnork is limestone mountain which rises above the flat plateau outside charming Kampot town. A 203 steps stairway leads up to a cave with a pre-Angkor (7th-century) temple inside. It is build in bricks and dedicated to Shiva with a stalagmite inside acting as a phallic altar. Phnom Sidaoun, whih lies on the same dirt road but a bit before Phnom Chhnork, is a small cave complex next to a working stone quarry. There is a recent image of Buddha and some cave passages. Local kids are happy to act as your local guide. Outside numbing stone beating is going on, which is all done by hand by skinny elders - it is depressing to watch but is unfortunately part of life in poor Cambodia.

Cambodia, Phnom Sorsia

Phnom Sorsia is a small mountian rising from the flat farmland outside Kampot. There is a monastery at the foot and a small colorful temple on the top along with stupas. The mountain also have some cool caves passages where you can see bats. The great thing about this place compared to Phnom Sidaoun, Phnom Chhnork and Wat Kiri Sela is that it is a working monastery, so there will be young novice monks hanging around. As with the other places you will very likely be greeted by some young kid who will tack along as your guide - whether you like or not. But they do know the caves so it might not be such a bad idea.

Cambodia, Wat Kiri Sela Cave Temple

Hidden inside a hollow mountain this cave temple is half tourist attraction and half sacred place. You enter the temple through the "dragon's mouth", a cave passage that will take you to the "dragon's stomach", a hidden valley with tall trees. Self-announced local guides will tack along and energetic point out different rock formations. There are a small pond and some newer Buddha statues, including a reclining Buddha which is a remake of the original one the Khmer Rouge destroyed. In the back of one of the caves a stalagmite is acting as a Buddhas statue and considered equally divine.

China 50,000 Buddhas

The ancient capital of China holds a treasure of more than 51,000 stone Buddha reliefs and figures. Carved into the mountain wall, they range from thumb-size to 17 meters colossuses. The variations are dazzling: sitting, standing, dancing, colourful, worn and smiling Buddhas, Originally all covered, the sandstone has washed away in places leaving the huge Buddha in the blazing sun. These are the oldest stone carvings in China. Monks have carved the many figures as part of meditation in the secluded caves. Here you may come to terms with the concept of the "thousand Buddhas", symbolizing the Buddha's omnipresence through time and space. The surrounding area is covered in coal-dust, true mining-China.

China Debating Monks

Time spent traveling in Tibet guarantees you will emerge with interesting insights into the rituals of Buddhism. Some of them can be quite confronting such as the prostrating pilgrims you'll see along the roads, who may be years into their pilgrimage. While others, like the monks at the Sera monastery seem a lot more positive. At first you'll be unsure of exactly what they are doing! Are they acting? Are they fighting? Are they dancing? Well, apparently they're debating. However, I'm not exactly sure how a discussion about Buddhist scriptures benefits from all the wild hand slapping and gesticulating that goes on in Tibet's Sera Monastery. Regardless of why, it makes for an entertaining way to spend an afternoon.

China

Giant Buddha

When you come to Leshan and see the Giant Buddha, you do not doubt the fact that it is the tallest Buddha in the world. 71m tall he sits, carved out of the rock face where the Dadu river meets the Min river. The construction started 713 AD and it took more than 90 years to finish him. So if you come to Chengdu, swing by for a visit, for it is one of those sights that fully live up to its reputation. Just do not come on a holiday, where half of Chengdu seems to be out here.

Sumtseling Monastery

A Tibetan monastery initiated for more than 300 hundreds years ago by the fifth Dalai Lama. Today it's a massive Buddhism complex, where more than 600 monks live and study. In the morning you can sometimes catch the debating lessons outside on the square, where the novices in lotus position are tested in their ability to answer philosophical questions delivered in a clapping manner by their friends. It's not in the province of Tibet (TAR), so no special permission is need to go here.

Tibetan Monastery Town

Serxu monastery (Serxu Gompa) lies 30km outside the drab town of Serxu (Serxu Xian), in the most nortwestern part of Sichuan. It is a big Tibetan monastery surrounded by rows of prayer wheels and a maze of adobe houses for the red cloaked monks, who count to more than a thousand. Across the river a small cluster of dusty shops makes out the rest of the monastery town. Here weather beaten Tibetans with gold teeth swag down the street (for there is only one street) in wide brim hats and homemade sunglasses. It is a fascinating place full of character and edge.

Tibetan Printing Monastery

In Dege, the last town before Tibet province, lies the red-walled printing monastery. It is a sacred place where pilgrims supposedly circle the outer walls a thousands times. Inside Tibetan scriptures are printed by hand and put to dry, as they have been done for centuries. The store rooms are filled from floor to ceiling with almost 300,000 engraved woodblocks with Tibetan texts. You can watch the printing process in the printing hall, where printers in almost trance turn out pages at an incredible speed. The majority of the Tibetan monasteries still get their textbooks from this printing monastery, and it is considered as one of the most important cultural center for Tibetans along with Potala Palads and Sakya monastery, both in Tibet.

Indonesia

Borobudur

Borobudur is a massive temple on the outskirts of Jogyakarta. The temple is a 9th century Buddhist temple that was abandoned at some point during the 14th century during the decline of Buddhism in Indonesia. It is an enormous complex that is an amazing site to see. The walls are cover with over 1,400 narrative panels that have been methodically carved into the stones. 504 buddhas sit atop the Borobudur complex. But many of the heads have been taken by robbers throughout the years. Wake up early to catch sunrise from atop the temple. It is an amazing view, as the sun comes up over the active volcano.

Pura Batu Bolong Temple

A small Hindu temple in Balinese style build on a rocky outcrop between two bays. The black temple faces Bali and legend tells that virgins were once sacrificed to the sea from the outermost slap of rock. Beside the full and dark moons ceremonies, the only drama today is the crashing waves that can easily cover the whole temple in a mist of sticky sea water. Pura Batu Bolong can easily be reached from Sengigi.

Ulu Watu Hindu Temple

Bali, the land of many different things. The beauty of Bali is so vibrant, you can still see it through the vast toursim industry that engulfs this small island. Known for beautiful culture, amazing surf, and drunk tourists, you need to get out of the main cities to really appreciate the

Balinese culture. Ulu Watu is on the southern tip and is an amazing setting for a temple, sitting high on the ocean cliffs. Keep in mind that it is a very touristic place, so you will not be the only person absorbing the beauty of Ulu Watu. Regardless, it is worth it to watch the sun drop into the ocean. Temples, a famous surf spot sits below and on a good day, can be very impressive to watch.

Laos

Monks and Golden Temples

Where the Mekong River meets the Nam Khan river lies one of the most charming cities in Asia. The old town of Luang Prabang is an ancient capital packed with golden temples, old French colonial houses, and even a royal palace. Though it is fast becoming a mandatory stop on the Southeast Asian trail, it is still tranquil and fairly unspoiled with quiet backstreets and hidden temples just a block away from the French bakeries and cafes on the main street. In the evening the friendly monks overcome their shyness to practice English with the passing travellers, and at dawn they sway down the streets in long orange rows to collect alms from local the Buddhists. It is almost too easy to fall in love with Luang Prabang.

Pak Ou Caves

The sacred Buddha caves at Pak Ou consist of two caves, where Buddhists for centuries have come to pray and place Buddha sculptures in hope for merits. They sit in a steep limestone cliff face right above where the Mekong River meets the Nam Ou river. The upper cave is dark and almost empty, since the old Buddha statues there have been eaten by termites. The lower cave is open and is the famous one. Every surface is littered with big and small Buddha statues. It has been estimated that the cave have once contained more than 6000 statues, though the number is probably closer to 100 today thanks to souvenirs hunters and thoughtless tourists.

Pha Pa Buddha Cave

In 2004 a local guy found a cave up on a steep cliff face. When he crawled through the narrow cave entrance, there were more than just stalagmites inside the cave. 229 Buddha statues in various sizes were looking at him. Nobody knows for sure when and why they were placed, which just add to the magic. Today the cave is a popular pilgrim place for local and monks alike. They come to pray, splash water, banging the gong and to do other quirky rituals. The drive from Tha Khaek goes through picturesque rice paddy fields with nice views of the limestone mountain range in the distance.

Pha That Luang

Beside being the national symbol, the Pha That Luang is the biggest, most holy and shiny stupa in all of Laos. The story goes that in the 3rd century BC a stupa was erected here which contained a bit of Buddha's ribs. Whether that is true is doubtful, but a stupa has for sure been standing here since mid 16th century. Since then, it has many times been reconstructed due to invasions and fires, and the one that stands today is the result of two French reconstruction from 1900 and 1930s. The layout follows, of course, a Buddhist numerological design where every level or feature have some symbolic meaning. But you can easily enjoy it without knowing all the details.

Sikhottabong Stupa

Laos is showered in stupas and pagodas, but some are apparently more important than others. The golden stupa at the Sikhottabong monastery is one of the important ones. Though not as grand, nor as shiny, as Pha That Luang in Vientiane, it is still worth the small trip from Tha Khaek - if nothing else then to chat up some friendly monks. The classic Lao-style temple, next to the stupa, has a big Buddha inside along with the usual buddhist knickknacks that always leave us non-Buddhists in wonder and awe.

Wat Phu Champasak

An ancient Khmer temple complex build in Angkor style a bit earlier (11th century) than Angkor Wat in Cambodia (12th century). Bits and pieces were later added, so the similarities in design with its sister temple of Angkor are big, though it does not have any bas-reliefs. Wat Phu is build at the base of a hill, which due to its slightly penis shape was considered as a representation of Shiva, and therefor holy. Furthermore, a spring drips from the rock ceiling and, since the rock is Shiva's phallus, the water is therefor holy. So Wat Phu is a water temple in honour of Shiva and the only of its kind in the Angkor world. Additional fascinating things can be found on the site, like the crocodile rock and heaps of later added Buddha statues.

Mongolia

Erdene Zuu Monastery

You shouldn't think so, but Mongolia is a great place to experience Tibetan Buddhism. This monastery was Mongolia's first and built in 1586 with stones from the once mighty capitol, Karakorum, of the Mongolian kingdom. Destroyed and abandoned several times, latest under the power of the Stalinist dictator Choibalsan in the 1930's, today the temples are again buzzing with the monk's prayers. A mandatory stop on every Mongolian trip.

Myanmar

Golden Rock

The Golden Rock at Kyaiktiyo Pagoda is one the most holy places in Myanmar. The gold leaf covered rock is natural balancing right on the edge at the top of Mt Kyaiktiyo (1100m). Buddhist believe the rock is perched on a hair of Buddha, given some explanation why this gravity-defying boulder isn't rolling off its base and straight into the valley deep below. At the top there are also other pagodas, Buddhist shrines, and viewing platforms. To get here, you can either take the bus-truck up to the parking lot and then walk the last bit through the cluster of Buddhist kiosks, natural remedies shops and even a guest house, or you can do as many pilgrims, walk all the way from Kinpun village at the base. The trek is a beautiful 16km up-hill walk that have magnificent views over the Kelasa Hills and. There are small kiosks, to rest your feet and get a drink, all the way up.

The Golden Rock was unfortunately behind scaffold being cleaned when this picture was taken.

Shwedagon Gold Pagoda

This amazing gold covered stupa stands 98 meters high and has become the iconic national symbol of Myanmar. It enshrines, among other things, eight hairs of the Buddha, and contains more than 1100 diamonds, where the top one is of 76-carat, and more than 1300 other stones. So it's no surprise that this is the most sacred Buddhist site in the country. At the base there are many smaller stupas, temples, and statues and you can easily spend hours just watching the local pilgrims doing rituals like the symbolic broom sweeping.

Snake Pagoda

The Hmwe Paya pagoda near the ancient cities (Amarapura, Inwa, and Sagaing) could be just one among many in temple-packed Myanmar if it wasn't for the unusual hosts. In 1974 three pythons zigzagged into the temple and curled up around the Buddha statue. Ever since they have been considered holy and are treated as sacred snakes with all that involves of bathing, feeding, and the occasional photo session with locals pilgrims. You hardly notice them when you first arrive to the temple, but after a while you figure out that the curled up things next to the statue are the snakes.

Nepal

Boudhanath Stupa

The Boudhanath Stupa is one of the largest Buddhist stupas (shrines) in the world. This ancient stupa is found in Kathmandu city center, where it is surrounded by small shops and street vendors. You must enter through a small side street and suddenly it is towering up in front of you. There are a lot of visiting Buddhist monks, small temples with distinctive Buddhist prayer wheels, and you can walk on the stupa. There are not really any good restaurants here, but it is recommended to find one of the restaurants that have a roof terrace, so you can sit and have lunch overlooking the enormous stupa.

Hindu Cremation

Just outside Kathmandu city center is Pashupatinath, where Hindu cremations take place along the river. Pashupatinath is composed of a large area with a lot of temples and so-called holy men in orange robes, who sit and meditate. You can take pictures of the latter - but only against payment. As a tourist it is the most appropriate to be on the opposite side of the river and observe the cremation at a distance. For Westerners, it may be an overwhelming experience to see the locals burn their fellow man in public - but even more strange is it to see people swim and children play 30-50 meters further down the same river, where ash and body remains are dumped.

Swayanabath - Monkey Temple

Just outside Kathmandu city center you will find Swayanabath Stupa - also known as The Monkey Temple. There are plenty of sacred monkeys everywhere, and the temple complex is located on a high (about 150 steps) overlooking the capital. There are colorful prayer flags hanging from the treetops to the temple tops and street vendors, who sell fruit and souvenirs. The area itself consists of a strange mix of different types of temples and shrines, and in one of the temples you can see praying / meditating monks who sit and chants. Between the temples lie sleeping dogs and Buddhists come here to sacrifice various foods to Buddha by burning them.

Asia Transportation

There are more than 30 countries in Asia today. Many have changed their names or forms of government since World War II. Some, like Israel, did not even exist before the war. People in United States and Europe are able to travel quickly from one place to another, even when the places are hundreds of miles apart. Transportation is abundant and there are many good roads, railroads, and airlines to choose from.

In Asia transportation and travel is very different. Asia has extremes of surface and climate, so that overland travel is often difficult. High mountains, plateaus, deserts, and jungles make it almost impossible to build roads and railroads in many places.

Few railroads go directly from one country to another. Many people in Asia have never seen or traveled on a railroad. In fact most of them have never traveled more than a few miles from the tiny villages where they were born.

Some countries do have good railroads. India's railway lines were built by the British. Japan, too, as many fine railroads. Highways are even fewer than railroads in Asia. Southwest Asia has no paved roads leading to southern Asia. There are some trails leading north from India through the mountains of Tibet or China but they are not suitable for modern vehicles. Only one surfaced road, built recently by the Chinese, connects Nepal with Tibet.

Fortunately, in recent years there has been rapid growth in air transportation in Asia. Several major airlines not connect countries of Southern Asia with Europe and the United States. Airlines make regular stops at Manila, Hong Kong, Tokyo, Bombay, Taipei, and Beijing. But the central part of Asia has little air service, just as it has few roads or railroads.

14 Religious Tourism Centers in Europe

Europe is one of the world's seven continents. Comprising the westernmost peninsula of Eurasia, Europe is generally divided from Asia to its east by the water divide of the Ural Mountains, the Ural River, the Caspian Sea, the Caucasus region (specification of borders) and the Black Sea to the southeast. Europe is bordered by the Arctic Ocean and other bodies of water to the north, the Atlantic Ocean to the west, the Mediterranean Sea to the south, and the Black Sea and connected waterways to the southeast. Yet the borders for Europe-a concept dating back to classical antiquity-are somewhat arbitrary, as the term continent can refer to a cultural and political distinction or a physiographic one.

Europe is the world's second-smallest continent by surface area, covering about 10,180,000 square kilometres (3,930,000 sq mi) or 2% of the Earth's surface and about 6.8% of its land area. Of Europe's approximately 50 states, Russia is the largest by both area and population (although the country has territory in both Europe and Asia), while the Vatican City is the smallest. Europe is the third-most populous continent after Asia and Africa, with a population of 731 million or about 11% of the world's population.

Europe, in particular Ancient Greece, is the birthplace of Western culture. It played a predominant role in global affairs from the 16th century onwards, especially after the beginning of colonialism. Between the 16th and 20th centuries, European nations controlled at various times the Americas, most of Africa, Oceania, and large portions of Asia. Both World Wars were largely focused upon Europe, greatly contributing to a decline in Western European dominance in world affairs by the mid-20th century as the United States and Soviet Union took prominence. During the Cold

War, Europe was divided along the Iron Curtain between NATO in the west and the Warsaw Pact in the east. European integration led to the formation of the Council of Europe and the European Union in Western Europe, both of which have been expanding eastward since the fall of the Soviet Union in 1991.

Europe lies mainly in the temperate climate zones, being subjected to prevailing westerlies.

The climate is milder in comparison to other areas of the same latitude around the globe due to the influence of the Gulf Stream. The Gulf Stream is nicknamed "Europe's central heating", because it makes Europe's climate warmer and wetter than it would otherwise be. The Gulf Stream not only carries warm water to Europe's coast but also warms up the prevailing westerly winds that blow across the continent from the Atlantic Ocean.

Therefore the average temperature throughout the year of Naples is 16 °C (60.8 °F), while it is only 12 °C (53.6 °F) in New York City which is almost on the same latitude. Berlin, Germany; Calgary, Canada; and Irkutsk, in the Asian part of Russia, lie on around the same latitude; January temperatures in Berlin average around 8 °C (15 °F) higher than those in Calgary, and they are almost 22 °C (40 °F) higher than average temperatures in Irkutsk.

The Geology of Europe is hugely varied and complex, and gives rise to the wide variety of landscapes found across the continent, from the Scottish Highlands to the rolling plains of Hungary.

Europe's most significant feature is the dichotomy between highland and mountainous Southern Europe and a vast, partially underwater, northern plain ranging from Ireland in the west to the Ural Mountains in the east. These two halves are separated by the mountain chains of the Pyrenees and Alps/Carpathians. The northern plains are delimited in the west by the Scandinavian Mountains and the mountainous parts of the British Isles. Major shallow water bodies submerging parts of the northern plains are the Celtic Sea, the North Sea, the Baltic Sea complex and Barents Sea.

The northern plain contains the old geological continent of Baltica, and so may be regarded geologically as the "main continent", while peripheral highlands and mountainous regions in the south and west constitute fragments from various other geological continents. Most of the older geology of Western Europe existed as part of the ancient microcontinent Avalonia.

Historically, religion in Europe has been a major influence on European art, culture, philosophy and law. The largest religion in Europe is Christianity as practiced by Catholic, Eastern Orthodox and Protestant Churches. Following these is Islam concentrated mainly in the south east (Bosnia and Herzegovina, Albania, Kosovo, Kazakhstan, North Cyprus, Turkey and Azerbaijan), and Tibetan Buddhism, found in Kalmykia. Other religions including Judaism and Hinduism are minority religions. Europe is a relatively secular continent and has an increasing number and proportion of irreligious, agnostic and atheistic people, actually the largest in the Western world, with a particularly high number of self-described non-religious people in the Czech Republic, Estonia, Sweden, Germany (East), and France.

Religion in Europe

Religion in Europe has been a major influence on art, culture, philosophy and law. The largest religion in Europe for at least a millennium and a half has been Christianity. Three countries in Southeastern Europe and one country in Eastern Europe have Muslim majorities. Smaller religions include Judaism, Buddhism, Sikhism, and Hinduism which are found in their largest groups in Britain and France.

Little is known about the prehistoric religion of Neolithic Europe. Bronze and Iron Age religion in Europe as elsewhere was predominantly polytheistic (Ancient Greek religion, Ancient Roman religion, Finnish paganism, Celtic polytheism, Germanic paganism, etc.). The Roman Empire officially adopted Christianity in AD 380. During the Early Middle Ages, most of Europe underwent Christianization, a process essentially complete with the Christianization of Scandinavia in the High Middle Ages. The emergence of the notion of "Europe" or "Western World" is intimately connected with the idea of "Christendom", especially since Christianity in the Middle East was marginalized by the rise of Islam from the 8th century, a constellation that led to the Crusades, which although unsuccessful militarily were an important step in the emergence of a religious identity of Europe. At all times, traditions of folk religion existed largely independent from official denomination or dogmatic theology.

The Great Schism of the 11th and Reformation of the 16th century were to tear apart "Christendom" into hostile factions, and following the Age of Enlightenment of the 18th century, atheism and agnosticism became widespread in Western Europe. 19th century Orientalism contributed to a certain popularity of Buddhism, and the 20th century brought increasing syncretism, New Age and various new religious movements divorcing spirituality from inherited traditions for many Europeans. The latest history brought increased secularisation, and religious pluralism.

Christianity

The vast majority of theist Europeans describe themselves as Christians, divided into a large number of denominations. Christian denominations are usually classed in three categories: Catholicism, Eastern Christianity (comprising Eastern Orthodox and Oriental Orthodox churches) and Protestantism (a diverse group including Lutheranism-Zwinglianism, Calvinism-Presbyterianism and Anglicanism as well as numerous minor denominations, including Baptism, Methodism, Evangelicalism, Pentecostalism, etc.).

Catholicism

Roman Catholicism is the largest denomination with adherents mostly existing in Latin Europe (which includes France, Italy, Spain, Southern [Wallon] Belgium, and Portugal), Ireland, Lithuania, Poland, Hungary, Slovakia, Slovenia, Croatia, and the Czech Republic, but also the southern parts of Germanic Europe (which includes Austria, Luxembourg, Northern [Flemish] Belgium, Southern and Western Germany, and Liechtenstein).

Eastern Christianity

- Eastern Orthodoxy (the churches are in full communion, i.e. they see each other as local churches, members of a single religious body)
    - Ecumenical Patriarchate of Constantinople
    - Russian Orthodox Church
    - Serbian Orthodox Church
    - Church of Greece
    - Cypriot Orthodox Church
    - Romanian Orthodox Church
    - Albanian Orthodox Church
    - Bulgarian Orthodox Church
    - Georgian Orthodox Church
- Oriental Orthodoxy

- o Armenian Orthodox Church

Protestantism

- Protestantism (see list of Reformed churches, Porvoo Communion)
  - o Lutheranism-Zwinglianism
- Independent Evangelical-Lutheran Church
- Danish National Church
- Estonian Evangelical Lutheran Church
- Evangelical Lutheran Church-Synod of France and Belgium
- Evangelical Church in Germany
- Reformed Church in Hungary
- Church of Sweden
- Swiss Reformed Church
  - o Anglicanism
- Church of England
- Church of Ireland
- Scottish Episcopal Church
- Church in Wales
- Lusitanian Catholic Apostolic Evangelical Church
- Spanish Reformed Episcopal Church
  - o Calvinism-Presbyterianism
- United Reformed Church
- Evangelical Presbyterian Church in England and Wales
- Church of Scotland
- Presbyterian Church in Ireland
- Methodist Church of Great Britain
- Protestant Church in the Netherlands (Neo-Calvinism)

Free churches

- o Anabaptism-Baptism
- Baptist Union of Great Britain
- Baptist Union of Sweden

- Bruderhof Communities
- Seventh-day Adventist Church

There are numerous minor Protestant movements, including various Evangelical congregations, Jehovah's Witnesses and others.

Judaism

The Jews were dispersed within the Roman Empire from the 2nd century. At one time Judaism was practiced widely throughout the European continent; throughout the Middle Ages, Jews were frequently accused of ritual murder and faced pogroms and legal discrimination. The Holocaust perpetrated by Nazi Germany decimated Jewish population, and today, France is the home of largest Jewish community in Europe with 1% of the total population. Other European countries with notable Jewish populations include Germany, the United Kingdom, Russia and Italy.

Islam

Islam came to parts of European islands and coasts on the Mediterranean during the 7th century Muslim conquests. In the Iberian Peninsula various Muslim states existed before the Reconquista. During the Ottoman expansion Islam was spread into the Balkans and southeastern Europe. Muslim have also been historically present in Russia. In recent years, Muslims have migrated to Europe as residents and temporary workers.

Muslims account for about 9% of the population in France, 5.8% in the Netherlands, 5% in Denmark, just over 4% in Switzerland and Austria, and almost 3% in the United Kingdom. Muslims make up over 95% in Turkey, 38-70% in Albania, 40% in Bosnia and Herzegovina, 33.3% in Macedonia, about 20% in Montenegro, 12% in Bulgaria, between 10 and 15% of the population of Russia., and 90% in Kosovo. Islam has been a factor in the cultural development of the Balkans and parts of Russia.

Other Religions

Numerous minor religious communities are found in Europe, partly non-European religions practiced in diaspora communities, partly new religious movements; among the larger communities are:

- Buddhism thinly spread throughout Europe and growing rapidly in recent years, about 3 million. In Kalmykia, Tibetan Buddhism is prevalent.

- Hinduism mainly among Indian immigrants in the United Kingdom. In 1998 there were an estimated 1.4 million Hindu adherents in Europe.
- Sikhism, nearly 1 million adherents of Sikhism in Europe. Most of the community live in United Kingdom (750,000) and Italy (70,000). Around 10,000 in Belgium and France. Netherlands and Germany have a Sikh population of 12,000. All other countries have less than or 5,000 Sikhs.
- Jainism, small membership rolls, mainly among Indian immigrants in the United Kingdom.
- The Bahá'í Faith, upwards of 60,000, with populations of several thousand in Russia, Switzerland, Italy, France, Spain, Albania, et al.
- various Neopagan movements, taken together accounting for an estimated 40,000 adherents in the UK, besides smaller numbers in other European countries.

Major Tourism Centers in Europe

Sultan Ahmed Mosque

The Sultan Ahmed Mosque (Turkish: Sultanahmet Camii) is a historical mosque in Istanbul, the largest city in Turkey and the capital of the Ottoman Empire (from 1453 to 1923). The mosque is popularly known as the Blue Mosque for the blue tiles adorning the walls of its interior.

It was built between 1609 and 1616, during the rule of Ahmed I. Like many other mosques, it also comprises a tomb of the founder, a madrasah and a hospice. While still used as a mosque, the Sultan Ahmed Mosque has also become a popular tourist attraction.

After the Peace of Zsitvatorok (1606) and the unfavourable result of the wars with Persia, Sultan Ahmed I decided to build a large mosque in Istanbul as recompense. This would be the first imperial mosque to be built in more than forty years. Whereas his predecessors had paid for their mosques with their war booty, Sultan Ahmed I had to withdraw the funds from the treasury, because he had not won any notable victories. This provoked the anger of the ulema, the Muslim legal scholars.

The mosque was to be built on the site of the palace of the Byzantine emperors, facing the Hagia Sophia (at that time the most venerated mosque in Istanbul) and the hippodrome, a site of great symbolic significance.

Large parts of the southern side of the mosque rest on the foundation and vaults of the Great Palace. Several palaces had already built there, most notably the palace of Sokollu Mehmet Pa?a, so these first had to be bought at a considerable cost and pulled down. Large parts of the Sphendone (curved tribune with U-shaped structure of the hippodrome) were also removed to make room for the new mosque. Construction of the mosque started in August 1609 when the sultan himself came to break the first sod. It was his intention that this would become the first mosque of his empire. He appointed his royal architect Sedefhar Mehmet A?a, a pupil and senior assistant of the famous architect Mimar Sinan to be in charge of the construction. The organization of the work was described in meticulous detail in eight volumes, now found in the library of the Topkap? Palace. The opening ceremonies were held in 1617 (although the inscription on the gate of the mosque says 1616). The sultan could now pray in the royal box (hünkâr mahfil). The building was not yet finished in this last year of his reign, as the last accounts were signed by his successor Mustafa I. Known as the Blue Mosque, Sultan Ahmed Mosque is one of the most impressive monuments in the world. The mosque was depicted on the reverse of the Turkish 500 lira banknotes of 1953-1976.

Almudena Cathedral

Santa María la Real de La Almudena is a Catholic cathedral in Madrid.

When the capital of Spain was transferred from Toledo to Madrid in 1561, the seat of the Church in Spain remained in Toledo; so the new capital - unusually for a Catholic country - had no cathedral. Plans were discussed as early as the 16th century to build a cathedral in Madrid dedicated to the Virgin of Almudena, but construction did not begin until 1879.

The cathedral seems to have been built on the site of a medieval mosque that was destroyed in 1085 when Alfonso VI conquered Madrid.

Francisco de Cubas, the Marquis of Cubas, designed and directed the construction in a Gothic revival style. Construction ceased completely during the Spanish Civil War, and the project was abandoned until 1950, when Fernando Chueca Goitia adapted the plans of de Cubas to a baroque exterior to match the grey and white façade of the Palacio Real, which stands directly opposite. The cathedral was not completed until 1993, when it was consecrated by Pope John Paul II. On May 22, 2004, the marriage of Felipe, Prince of Asturias to Letizia Ortiz Rocasolano (known thereafter as Letizia, Princess of Asturias) took place at the cathedral.

The Neo-Gothic interior is uniquely modern, with chapels and statues of contemporary artists, in heretogeneous styles, from historical revivals to "pop-art" decor.

The Neo-Romanesque crypt houses a 16th century image of the Virgen de la Almudena. Nearby along the Calle Mayor excavations have unearthed remains of Moorish and medieval city walls.

On the 28th of April 2004, Cardinal Antonio María Rouco Varela, Archbishop of Madrid blessed the new paintings in the apse, painted by Kiko Arguello, founder of the Neocatechumenal Way. The cathedral is the seat of the Patriarch of the Indies and the Ocean Sea, an honorific patriarchate created in the sixteenth century, and subsequently an honorific title for the Spanish court's chaplain.

Baptistry of St. John in Florence

The Florence Baptistery or Battistero di San Giovanni (Baptistery of St. John) is a religious building in Florence (Tuscany), Italy, which has the status of a minor basilica.

The octagonal Baptistery stands in both the Piazza del Duomo and the Piazza di San Giovanni, across from the Duomo cathedral and the Giotto bell tower (Campanile di Giotto). It is one of the oldest buildings in the city, built between 1059 and 1128. The architecture is in Florentine Romanesque style.

The Baptistery is renowned for its three sets of artistically important bronze doors with relief sculptures. The south doors were done by Andrea Pisano and the north and east doors by Lorenzo Ghiberti. The east pair of doors was dubbed by Michelangelo "the Gates of Paradise".

The Italian poet Dante Alighieri and many other notable Renaissance figures, including members of the Medici family, were baptized in this baptistery. In fact, until the end of the nineteenth century, all Catholic Florentines were baptized here.

Basilica of St. John Lateran

The Papal Archbasilica of St. John Lateran (Italian: Arcibasilica Papale di San Giovanni in Laterano) is the cathedral of the Church of Rome, Italy, and the official ecclesiastical seat of the Bishop of Rome, who is the Pope. Officially named Archibasilica Sanctissimi Salvatoris et Sanctorum Iohannes Baptista et Evangelista in Laterano (English: Archbasilica of the Most Holy Saviour and Sts. John the Baptist and the Evangelist at the Lateran", Italian: Arcibasilica del Santissimo Salvatore e Santi Giovanni Battista ed Evangelista in Laterano), it is the oldest and ranks first among the four Papal Basilicas or major basilicas of Rome (having the cathedra of the Bishop of Rome). It claims the title of ecumenical mother church (mother church of the whole inhabited world) among Roman Catholics. The current archpriest of St. John Lateran is Agostino Vallini, Cardinal Vicar General for the Diocese of Rome. The President of the French Republic, currently Nicolas Sarkozy, is ex officio the "first and only honorary canon" of the basilica, a title inherited from the Kings of France, who have held it since Henry IV.

An inscription on the façade, Christo Salvatori, indicates the church's dedication to "Christ the Saviour", for the cathedrals of all patriarchs are dedicated to Christ Himself. As the cathedral of the Bishop of Rome, containing the papal throne (Cathedra Romana), it ranks above all other churches in the Catholic Church, including St. Peter's Basilica in the Vatican. For that reason, unlike all other Roman Basilicas, it holds the title of Archbasilica. The cathedral itself is located outside of the Vatican City boundaries, territorially located within the city of Rome in the Italian Republic. However it has been granted a special extraterritorial status as a property of the Holy See. This is also the case with several other buildings after the solving of the Roman Question with the Lateran Treaty. The Lateran Basilica is adjacent to the Lateran Palace.

Bethlehem Chapel

The Bethlehem Chapel (Betlémská kaple) is a medieval religious building in Prague, Czech Republic notable for its connection with the Czech reformer Jan Hus. It was founded in 1391 by Wenceslas Kriz (known as 'the Merchant', and John of Milheim, and taught solely in the Czech vernacular, thus breaking with German domination of the Medieval Bohemian church. The building was never officially called as a church, only a chapel, though it could contain 3,000 people; indeed, the chapel encroached upon the parish of Sts. Philip and James, and John of Milheim paid the pastor of that church 90 grossi as compensation. Hus became rector and preacher in March, 1402. After Hus's excommunication in 1412, the Pope ordered the Bethlehem chapel to be pulled down, although this action was rejected by the Czech majority on the Old Town council. After Hus's death, he was succeeded by Jacob of Mies.

In the 17th century, the building was acquired by the Jesuits. During reign of the Emperor Joseph II (1780s) converted into an apartment building. Under the Czechoslovakian communist regime the building was restored by the government to its state at the time of Hus. Most of the chapel's exterior walls and a small portion of the pulpit date back to the medieval chapel. The wall paintings are largely from Hus's time there, and the text below is taken from his work De sex erroribus, and contrast the poverty of Christ with the riches of the Catholic Church of Hus's time[4

Cathedral of Divine Saviour

Cathedral of the Divine Saviour (Czech: Katedrála Božského Spasitele), located in the center of Ostrava, is the second largest Roman Catholic cathedral in Moravia and Silesia (after the basilica in Velehrad near Uherské Hradišt?). This three-nave neorenaissance basilica with a semi-circular apse and two 67m high towers is dating since 1889 (building started in 1883). The church was designed by Gustav Meretta, the official architect of the Archbishop of Olomouc, and the interior by Max von Ferstel.

The main nave is 14 m wide and 22 m high, the two side aisles are 7 m wide and 10 m high each. The seating capacity of the cathedral is 4,000 people. On May 30, 1996 Pope John Paul II established the Diocese of Ostrava-Opava, and soon after the basilica has been dignified into a cathedral. In 1998, a new neo-baroque organ has been installed.

Cathedral of Fulda

Fulda Cathedral (German: Fuldaer Dom, also Sankt Salvator) is the former abbey church of Fulda Abbey and the burial place of Saint Boniface. Since 1752 it has also been the cathedral of the Diocese of Fulda, of which the Prince-Abbots of Fulda were created bishops. The abbey was dissolved in 1802 but the diocese and its cathedral have continued. The dedication is to Christ the Saviour (Latin: Salvator). The cathedral constitutes the high point of the Baroque district of Fulda, and is a symbol of the town.

Church of Our Lady before Týn

The Church of Our Lady before Týn (in Czech Kostel Matky Boží p?ed Týnem, also Týnský chrám (Týn Church) or just Týn) is a dominant feature of the Old Town of Prague, Czech Republic, and has been the main church of this part of the city since the 14th century. The church's towers are 80 m high and topped by four small spires. In the 11th century, this area was occupied by a Romanesque church, which was built there for foreign merchants coming to the near Týn Courtyard. Later it was replaced by an early Gothic Church of Our Lady in front of Týn in 1256. Construction of the present church began in the 14th century in the late Gothic style under the influence of Matthias of Arras and later Peter Parler. By the beginning of the 15th century, construction was almost complete; only the towers, the gable and roof were missing. The church was controlled by Hussites for some time, including John of Rokycan, future archbishop of Prague, who became the church's vicar in 1427.

The roof was completed in the 1450s, while the gable and northern tower were completed shortly thereafter during the reign of George of Podebrady. His sculpture was placed on the gable, below a huge golden chalice, the symbol of the Hussites. The southern tower was not completed until 1511, under Mat?j Rejsek. In 1626, after the Battle of White Mountain, the sculptures of George of Podebrady and the chalice were removed and replaced by a sculpture of the Virgin Mary, with a giant halo made from by melting down the chalice. In 1679 the church was struck by lightning, and the subsequent fire heavily damaged the old vault, which was later replaced by a lower baroque vault.

Renovation works carried out in 1876-1895 were later reversed during extensive exterior renovation works in the years 1973-1995. Interior renovation is still in progress.

Duomo di Pisa

Il Duomo di Santa Maria Assunta, al centro della omonima piazza, è la cattedrale medievale di Pisa nonché chiesa Primaziale. Capolavoro assoluto del romanico, in particolare del romanico pisano, rappresenta la testimonianza tangibile del prestigio e della ricchezza raggiunti dalla Repubblica marinara di Pisa nel momento del suo apogeo.

Florence Cathedral

The Basilica di Santa Maria del Fiore is the cathedral church (Duomo) of Florence, Italy, begun in 1296 in the Gothic style to the design of Arnolfo di Cambio and completed structurally in 1436 with the dome engineered by Filippo Brunelleschi. The exterior of the basilica is faced with polychrome marble panels in various shades of green and pink bordered by white and has an elaborate 19th century Gothic Revival facade by Emilio De Fabris.

The cathedral complex, located in Piazza del Duomo, includes the Baptistery and Giotto's Campanile. The three buildings are part of the UNESCO World Heritage Site covering the historic centre of Florence and are a major attraction to tourists visiting the region of Tuscany. The basilica is one of Italy's largest churches, and until the modern era, the dome was the largest in the world. It remains the largest brick dome ever constructed.

The cathedral is the mother church of the Roman Catholic Archdiocese of Florence, whose archbishop is currently Giuseppe Betori.

Southwark Cathedral

Southwark Cathedral or The Cathedral and Collegiate Church of St Saviour and St Mary Overie, Southwark, London, lies on the south bank of the River Thames close to London Bridge. It is the mother church of the Anglican Diocese of Southwark. It has been a place of Christian worship for over 1,000 years, but a cathedral only since 1905. The present building is mainly Gothic, from 1220 to 1420. The main railway line from London Bridge station to Cannon Street station passes close to the cathedral, blocking the view from the south side. Borough Market and the Hall of the Worshipful Company of Glaziers and Painters of Glass by the river are in the immediate vicinity.

St Paul's Cathedral

St Paul's Cathedral is an Anglican cathedral dedicated to Paul the Apostle. It sits at the top of Ludgate Hill, the highest point in the City of London, and is the seat of the Bishop of London. The present building dates from the 17th century and was designed by Sir Christopher Wren. It is generally reckoned to be London's fifth St Paul's Cathedral, all having been built on the same site since AD 604. The cathedral is one of London's most famous and most recognisable sights. At 365 feet (111m) high, it was the tallest building in London from 1710 to 1962, and its dome is also among the highest in the world.

Important services held at St Paul's include the funerals of Lord Nelson, the Duke of Wellington and Sir Winston Churchill; Jubilee celebrations for Queen Victoria; peace services marking the end of the First and Second World Wars; the launch of the Festival of Britain and the thanksgiving services for both the Golden Jubilee and 80th Birthday of Her Majesty the Queen. The Royal Family holds most of its important marriages, christenings and funerals at Westminster Abbey, but St Paul's was used for the marriage of Charles, Prince of Wales, and Lady Diana Spencer. St Paul's Cathedral is still a busy working church, with hourly prayer and daily services.

Transport in Europe

This page links to several topics related to transport in Europe. Transport in Europe provides for the movement needs of over 700 million people and associated freight. The political geography of Europe divides the continent into over 50 sovereign states and territories. This fragmentation, along with increased movement of people since the industrial revolution, has led to a high level of cooperation between European countries in developing and maintaining transport networks. Supranational and intergovernmental organisations such as the European Union (EU), Council of Europe and OSCE have led to the development of international standards and agreements that allow people and freight to cross the borders of Europe, largely with unique levels of freedom and ease.

Road, rail, air and water transportation are all prevalent and important across Europe. Europe was the location of the world's first railways and motorways and is now the location of some of the world's busiest ports and airports. The Schengen Area enables border control-free travel between 25 European countries. Freight transportation has a high level of intermodal compatibility and the European Economic Area allows the free movement of goods across 30 states.

Rail Transport

Powered rail transport began in England in the early 19th century with the invention of the steam engine. The modern European rail network spans the entire continent and provides passenger and freight movement. There are significant high-speed rail passenger networks such as the TGV in France and the LAV in Spain. The Channel Tunnel connects the United Kingdom with France, Belgium and thus the whole of the European rail system, and is considered one of the seven wonders of the modern world.

Various methods of rail electrification are used, as well as much unelectrified track. In all European countries, standard gauge is the most important rail gauge except for Russia, Finland and the ex-Soviet states. The European Rail Traffic Management System is an EU initiative to create a Europe-wide standard for train signalling.

Rail infrastructure, freight transport and passenger services are provided by a combination of local and national governments and private companies. Passenger ticketing varies from country to country and service to service. The Eurail Pass is a rail pass for 18 European countries; it is only available for persons who do not live in Europe, Morocco, Algeria and Tunisia. Inter Rail passes allow multi-journey travel around Europe for people living in Europe and surrounding countries.

Road Traffic

In the UK, Ireland, Malta and Cyprus, traffic drives on the left. In the rest of Europe, traffic mainly drives on the right with a few rare exceptions for certain stretches of motorway or a small country road. Toll roads are common in some European countries with the Vignette a particular notable road tax. The International E-road network is an international road numbering system covering major highways in Europe, but most road management and classification takes place at a local or national level.

Despite marked improvements since 1990, emissions from road transport continue to be the main source of health-damaging air pollutants, according to a 2008 report by the European Environment Agency (EEA). The report shows that road transport remains the single most important source of sulphur oxides (SOx), carbon monoxide (CO) and non-methane volatile organic compounds (NMVOCs) in the EU-27. It is also the second-most important source, behind the construction and residential sector, of fine particulate emissions (02 and PM2.5), which can cause respiratory diseases in humans.

Air Transport

Despite an extensive road and rail network, most long distance travel within Europe is by air. A large tourism industry also attracts many visitors to Europe, most of whom arrive into one of Europe's many large international airports. Heathrow Airport, London is the busiest airport in the world by number of international passengers (third busiest overall). The advent of low cost carriers in recent years has led to a large increase in air travel within Europe. Air transportation is now often the cheapest way of travelling between cities. This increase in air travel has led to problems of airspace overcrowding and environmental concerns. The Single European Sky is one initiative aimed at solving these problems.

Cheap air travel is spurred on by the trend for regional airports levying low fees to market themselves as serving large cities quite far away. Ryanair is especially noted for this, since it primarily flies out of regional airports up to 150 kilometres away from the city it has said to serve. A primary example of this is the Weeze-Skavsta flight, where Weeze mainly serves the Nijmegen/Kleve area, while Skavsta serves Nykoping/ Oxelosund. Ryanair however, markets this flight as Düsseldorf-Stockholm, which are both 80-90 kilometres away from these airports, resulting in up to four hours of ground transportation just to get to and from the airport.

Sea and River Transport

The Port of Rotterdam, Netherlands is the largest port in Europe and one of the busiest ports in the world, handling over 400 million metric tons of cargo in 2008. When the associated Europoort industrial area is included, Rotterdam is by certain measurements the world's busiest port.

The English Channel is one of the world's busiest seaways carrying over 400 ships per day between Europe's North Sea and Baltic Sea ports and the rest of the world.

As well as its role in freight movement, sea transport is an important part of Europe's energy supply. Europe is one of the world's major oil tanker discharge destinations. Energy is also supplied to Europe by sea in the form of LNG. The South Hook LNG terminal at Milford Haven, Wales is Europe's largest LNG terminal.

15 Religious Tourism Centers in America

The United States of America (also referred to as the United States, the U.S., the USA, or America) is a federal constitutional republic comprising fifty states and a federal district. The country is situated mostly in central North America, where its forty-eight contiguous states and Washington, D.C., the capital district, lie between the Pacific and Atlantic Oceans, bordered by Canada to the north and Mexico to the south. The state of Alaska is in the northwest of the continent, with Canada to the east and Russia to the west across the Bering Strait. The state of Hawaii is an archipelago in the mid-Pacific. The country also possesses several territories in the Caribbean and Pacific.

At 3.79 million square miles (9.83 million km2) and with over 308 million people, the United States is the third or fourth largest country by total area, and the third largest both by land area and population. It is one of the world's most ethnically diverse and multicultural nations, the product of large-scale immigration from many countries. The U.S. economy is the world's largest national economy, with an estimated 2009 GDP of $14.3 trillion (24% of nominal global GDP and 20% of global GDP at purchasing power parity).

Indigenous peoples of Asian origin have inhabited what is now the mainland United States for many thousands of years. This Native American population was greatly reduced by disease and warfare after European contact. The United States was founded by thirteen British colonies located along the Atlantic seaboard. On July 4, 1776, they issued the Declaration of Independence, which proclaimed their right to self-determination and their establishment of a cooperative union. The rebellious states defeated the British Empire in the American Revolution, the first successful colonial war of independence. The current United States Constitution was adopted on September 17, 1787; its ratification the following year made the states part of a single republic with a strong federal government. The Bill of Rights, comprising ten constitutional amendments guaranteeing many fundamental civil rights and freedoms, was ratified in 1791.

In the 19th century, the United States acquired land from France, Spain, the United Kingdom, Mexico, and Russia, and annexed the Republic of Texas and the Republic of Hawaii. Disputes between the agrarian South and industrial North over states' rights and the expansion of the institution of slavery provoked the American Civil War of the 1860s. The North's victory prevented a permanent split of the country and led to the end of legal slavery in the United States. By the 1870s, the national economy was the world's largest. The Spanish-American War and World War I confirmed the country's status as a military power. It emerged from World War II as the first country with nuclear weapons and a permanent member of the United Nations Security Council. The end of the Cold War and the dissolution of the Soviet Union left the United States as the sole superpower. The country accounts for 43% of global military spending and is a leading economic, political, and cultural force in the world.

The land area of the contiguous United States is approximately 1.9 billion acres (770 million hectares). Alaska, separated from the contiguous United States by Canada, is the largest state at 365 million acres (150 million hectares). Hawaii, occupying an archipelago in the central Pacific, southwest of North America, has just over 4 million acres (1.6 million hectares). The United States is the world's third or fourth largest nation by total area (land and water), ranking behind Russia and Canada and just above or below China. The ranking varies depending on how two territories disputed by China and India are counted and how the total size of the United States is calculated: the CIA World Factbook gives 3,794,101 square miles (9,826,675 km2), the United Nations Statistics Division gives 3,717,813 sq mi (9,629,091 km2), and the Encyclopædia Britannica gives 3,676,486 sq mi (9,522,055 km2). Including only land area, the United States is third in size behind Russia and China, just ahead of Canada.

The coastal plain of the Atlantic seaboard gives way further inland to deciduous forests and the rolling hills of the Piedmont. The Appalachian Mountains divide the eastern seaboard from the Great Lakes and the grasslands of the Midwest. The Mississippi-Missouri River, the world's fourth longest river system, runs mainly north-south through the heart of the country. The flat, fertile prairie of the Great Plains stretches to the west, interrupted by a highland region in the southeast. The Rocky Mountains, at the western edge of the Great Plains, extend north to south across the country, reaching altitudes higher than 14,000 feet (4,300 m) in Colorado. Farther west are the rocky Great Basin and deserts such as the Mojave. The Sierra Nevada and Cascade mountain ranges run close to the Pacific coast. At 20,320 feet (6,194 m), Alaska's Mount McKinley is the tallest peak in the country and in North America. Active volcanoes are common throughout Alaska's Alexander and Aleutian Islands, and Hawaii consists of volcanic islands. The supervolcano underlying Yellowstone National Park in the Rockies is the continent's largest volcanic feature.

The United States, with its large size and geographic variety, includes most climate types. To the east of the 100th meridian, the climate ranges from humid continental in the north to humid subtropical in the south. The southern tip of Florida is tropical, as is Hawaii. The Great Plains west of the 100th meridian are semi-arid. Much of the Western mountains are alpine. The climate is arid in the Great Basin, desert in the Southwest, Mediterranean in coastal California, and oceanic in coastal Oregon and Washington and southern Alaska. Most of Alaska is subarctic or polar. Extreme weather is not uncommon-the states bordering the Gulf of Mexico are prone to hurricanes, and most of the world's tornadoes occur within the country, mainly in the Midwest's Tornado Alley.

The U.S. ecology is considered "megadiverse": about 17,000 species of vascular plants occur in the contiguous United States and Alaska, and over 1,800 species of flowering plants are found in Hawaii, few of which occur on the mainland. The United States is home to more than 400 mammal, 750 bird, and 500 reptile and amphibian species. About 91,000 insect species have been described. The Endangered Species Act of 1973 protects threatened and endangered species and their habitats, which are monitored by the United States Fish and Wildlife Service. There are fifty-eight national parks and hundreds of other federally managed parks, forests, and wilderness areas. Altogether, the government owns 28.8% of the country's land area. Most of this is protected, though some is leased for oil and gas drilling, mining, logging, or cattle ranching; 2.4% is used for military purposes.

Famous Tourism Centers in America

National Cathedral

The Washington National Cathedral, officially named the Cathedral Church of Saint Peter and Saint Paul, is a cathedral of the Episcopal Church located in Washington, D.C., the capital of the United States. Of neogothic design, it is the sixth largest cathedral in the world, the second largest in the United States, and the fourth tallest structure in Washington, D.C. The cathedral is the seat of both the Presiding Bishop of the Episcopal Church, currently Katharine Jefferts Schori, and the Bishop of the Diocese of Washington, currently John Bryson Chane. In 2009, nearly 400,000 visitors toured the structure. The congregation numbers 800.

The Protestant Episcopal Cathedral Foundation, under the leadership of the nine Bishops of Washington, erected the cathedral under a charter passed by the United States Congress on January 6, 1893. Construction began on September 29, 1907, when the foundation stone was laid in the presence of President Theodore Roosevelt and a crowd of more than 20,000, and ended 83 years later when the last finial was placed in the presence of President George H. W. Bush in 1990. The foundation operates and funds the cathedral, which is not funded by the U.S. government.

The cathedral is located at Massachusetts and Wisconsin Avenues in the northwest quadrant of Washington. It is an associate member of the Washington Theological Consortium. It is listed on the National Register of Historic Places. In 2007, it was ranked third on the List of America's Favorite Architecture by the American Institute of Architects.

Salt Lake Temple

The Salt Lake Temple is the largest (of more than 130 around the world) and best-known temple of The Church of Jesus Christ of Latter-day Saints. It is the sixth temple built by the church overall, and the fourth operating temple built since the Mormon exodus from Nauvoo, Illinois.

The Salt Lake Temple is the centerpiece of the 10 acre (40,000 m^2) Temple Square in Salt Lake City, Utah. Although there are no public tours inside the temple (because it is considered sacred by the church and its members, a temple recommend is required), the temple grounds are open to the public and are a popular tourist attraction. Due to its location at LDS Church headquarters and its historical significance, it is patronized much by Latter-day Saints from many parts of the world.

The Salt Lake Temple is also the location of the weekly meetings of the First Presidency and the Quorum of the Twelve Apostles. As such, there are special meeting rooms in the Salt Lake Temple for these purposes, including the Holy of Holies, which are not present in other temples.

The official name of the Salt Lake Temple is also unique. In the early 2000s, as the building of LDS temples accelerated dramatically, the Church announced a formal naming convention for all existing and future temples. For temples located in the United States and Canada, the name of the temple is generally the city or town in which the temple is located, followed by the name of the applicable state or province (with no comma). For temples outside of the U.S. and Canada, the name of the temple is generally the city name (as above) followed by the name of the country. However, for reasons on which the Church did not elaborate (possibly due to the historical significance and worldwide prominence of the temple), the Salt Lake Temple was granted an exception to the new rule and thus avoided being renamed the Salt Lake City Utah Temple.

Some think the Temple is intended to evoke the Temple of Solomon at Jerusalem. It is oriented towards Jerusalem and the large basin used as a baptismal font is mounted on the backs of twelve oxen as was the brazen sea in Solomon's Temple. However this is only conjecture. At east end of the building, the height of the center pinnacle is 210 feet, or 120 cubits, making this Temple 20 cubits taller than the Temple of Solomon.

The location of the Temple is literally in "The Tops of the Mountains", with several mountain peaks closeby, in almost every direction, except to the northwest, where lies the Great Salt Lake. Very nearby, a shallow stream, City Creek, splits and flows both to the west and to the south, flowing into the deeper Jordan River, which flows northward into the large Great Salt Lake. There is a wall around the 10 acre Temple site. The surrounding wall became the first permanent structure on what has become known as Temple Square. The wall is a uniform fifteen feet high but varies in appearance because of the southwest slope of the site.

Baha'i House of Worship

A Bahá'í House of Worship, sometimes referred to by its Arabic name of Mashriqu'l-Adhkár, is the designation of a place of worship, or temple, of the Bahá'í Faith. The teachings of the religion envisage Houses of Worship being surrounded by a number of dependencies dedicated to social, humanitarian, educational, and scientific pursuits, although none has yet been built to such an extent.

Only eight Houses of Worship have been built around the world (this includes one in Ashgabat, Turkmenistan that has since been destroyed), with a ninth soon to be constructed in Chile. Bahá'í communities own many properties where Houses of Worship remain to be constructed as the Bahá'í community grows and develops further. The Houses of Worship are open to the public, and are exclusively reserved for worship, where sermons are prohibited and only scriptural texts may be read. Most Bahá'í meetings occur in local Bahá'í centres, individuals' homes, or rented facilities.

Cathedral of St. John the Divine

The Cathedral of St. John the Divine, officially the Cathedral Church of Saint John the Divine in the City and Diocese of New York, is the Cathedral of the Episcopal Diocese of New York. Located at 1047 Amsterdam Avenue, New York, NY 10025 (between West 110th Street, which is also known as "Cathedral Parkway", and 113th Street) in Manhattan's Morningside Heights, the cathedral disputes with Liverpool Anglican Cathedral the title of largest Cathedral and Anglican church and fourth largest Christian church in the world. The inside covers 121,000 sq ft (11,200 m2), spanning a length of 183.2 meters (601 ft) and height 70.7 meters (232 ft). The inside height of the nave is 37.8 meters (124 feet).

The cathedral is nicknamed St. John the Unfinished.

The cathedral, designed in 1888 and begun in 1892, has, in its history, undergone radical stylistic changes and the interruption of the two World Wars. Originally designed as Byzantine-Romanesque, the plan was changed after 1909 to a Gothic design. After a large fire on December 18, 2001, it was closed for repairs and reopened in November 2008. It remains unfinished, with construction and restoration a continuing process.

Chapel of the Holy Cross

The Chapel of the Holy Cross is a Roman Catholic chapel built into the mesas of Sedona, Arizona, which was inspired and commissioned by sculptor Marguerite Brunswig Staude, student of Frank Lloyd Wright. Richard Hein was chosen as project architect, and the design was executed by architect August K. Strotz, both from the firm of Anshen & Allen. The chapel is built on Coconino National Forest land; the late Senator Barry Goldwater assisted Staude in obtaining a special-use permit. The construction supervisor was Fred Courkos, who built the chapel in 18 months at a cost of US$300,000. The chapel was completed in 1956.

The American Institute of Architects gave the Chapel its Award of Honor in 1957. In the sculptor's words, "Though Catholic in faith, as a work of art the Chapel has a universal appeal. Its doors will ever be open to one and all, regardless of creed, that God may come to life in the souls of all men and be a living reality."

In 2007 Arizonans voted the Chapel to be one of the Seven Man-Made Wonders of Arizona, and it is also the site of one of the so-called Sedona vortices.

The Chapel is one of the main tourist attractions in the Sedona area. It is open from 9am to 5pm daily and closed Thanksgiving, Christmas, Good Friday and Easter.

Church of Scientology

The Church of Scientology is an organization devoted to the practice and the promotion of the Scientology belief system. The Church of Scientology International is the Church of Scientology's parent organization, and is responsible for the overall ecclesiastical management, dissemination and propagation of Scientology. Every Church of Scientology is separately incorporated and has its own local board of directors and executives responsible for its own activities and well-being, both corporate and ecclesiastical. The first Scientology church was incorporated in December 1953 in Camden, New Jersey, by American science fiction author L. Ron Hubbard. The church has been the subject of much controversy. The church's world headquarters are located in the Gold Base, unincorporated Riverside County, California.

Crystal Cathedral

The Crystal Cathedral is a Protestant Christian Church in the city of Garden Grove, in Orange County, California, United States. The prominent architect Philip Johnson designed the main sanctuary building, which was constructed using over 10,000 rectangular panes of glass and its sanctuary seats 2,736 people. The rectangular panes of glass are not bolted to the structure; instead they are glued to it using a silicone-based glue. This and other measures are intended to allow the building to withstand an earthquake of magnitude 8.0.

The name "Crystal Cathedral" is merely an alliterative colloquialism and does not mean that the church is a cathedral in the sense of being a church where there is a bishop's official seat; the Reformed Church in

America is governed by elders. Nor is the church made of crystal. The church is a Southern California architectural landmark.

On October 18, 2010, the board of the Crystal Cathedral filed for bankruptcy in Santa Ana, California.

First Unitarian Church

The First Unitarian Church of Philadelphia is a Unitarian Universalist congregation located at 2125 Chestnut Street in Philadelphia, Pennsylvania. As a regional Community Center it sponsors cultural, educational, civic, wellness and spiritual activities.

On June 12, 1796, twenty of Philadelphia's intellectual leaders formed the First Unitarian Society of Philadelphia, becoming the first continuously functioning church in the country to name itself "Unitarian". The founders were directed and encouraged by the Unitarian minister Joseph Priestley and its first settled minister was the Rev. Dr. William Henry Furness.

Grace Cathedral

Grace Cathedral is an Episcopal cathedral located on Nob Hill in San Francisco. It is the cathedral church of the Episcopal Diocese of California, once state-wide in area, now comprising parts of the San Francisco Bay Area. The cathedral community is known for its open-mindedness.

The cathedral has become an international pilgrimage center for church-goers and visitors alike, famed for its mosaics by De Rosen, a replica of Ghiberti's Gates of Paradise, two labyrinths, varied stained glass windows, Keith Haring AIDS Chapel altarpiece, and medieval and contemporary furnishings, as well as its 44 bell carillon, three organs, and choirs.

It contains one of only seven remaining Episcopal men and boys cathedral choirs, the Grace Cathedral Choir of Men and Boys, along with two other choirs with its corresponding boys K-8 school in the United States, along with Washington National Cathedral. Its director of music and choirmaster is Ben Bachmann. The Very Reverend Alan Jones retired as dean on January 31, 2009. He was also the moderator of The Forum at Grace Cathedral. On June 25, 2010, the Rev. Canon Dr. Jane Alison Shaw was named the eighth dean of Grace Cathedral, San Francisco.

Hsi Lai Temple

Hsi Lai Temple ((approximate pronunciation She Lye) is a traditional Chinese Buddhist mountain monastery in the United States. It is located on the foothill region of Hacienda Heights, California, USA, a suburb of Los Angeles County. The name "Hsi Lai" means Coming West in the sense of the "Great Buddhadharma Coming West."

The temple is affiliated with one of Taiwan's largest religious organizations, the Fo Guang Shan Buddhist order. It is one of the first overseas branch temples, and is often called the "Western torch of Dharma" by order members. Hsi Lai was the site of the founding of Buddha's Light International Association, established in 1991. The temple, like its mother temple in Taiwan, practices Humanistic Buddhism, which incorporates all of the eight traditional schools of Chinese Buddhism - especially the Linji Chan and Pure Land schools - to provide guidance deemed most useful to modern life.

Islamic Center of Washington

The Islamic Center of Washington is a mosque and Islamic cultural center in Washington, D.C., United States. It is located on Embassy Row on Massachusetts Avenue just east of the bridge over Rock Creek. When it opened in 1957 it was the largest Muslim place of worship in the Western Hemisphere. Some 6000 people attend prayers there each Friday.

The center was originally conceived in 1944 when the Turkish ambassador Münir Ertegün died and there was no mosque in which to hold his funeral. The Washington diplomatic community played a leading role in the effort to have a mosque constructed. Support came from most of the Islamic nations of the world which donated funds, decorations, and craftsmen to the project. Support for the project also came from the American-Muslim community. The site was purchased in 1946 and the cornerstone was laid on January 11, 1949. The building was designed by Italian architect Mario Rossi and was dedicated on June 28, 1957 with President Dwight D. Eisenhower in attendance. The main prayer hall of the center is covered by Persian carpets dedicated by the late Shah of Iran. The center continues to be controlled by a board of governors made up of various ambassadors. Around the building are arrayed the flags of the Islamic nations of the world.

The mosque has been visited by many high profile dignitaries, including several presidents. The highest profile visit was by President George W. Bush on September 17, 2001, only days after the attacks of September 11. On national television, Bush quoted from the Qur'an and worked to assure Americans that the vast majority of Muslims are peaceful.

In addition to the mosque, the center contains a library and classrooms where courses on Islam and the Arabic language are taught.

Lovely Lane Methodist Church

Lovely Lane United Methodist Church, formerly known as First Methodist Episcopal Church, is a historic United Methodist church located at Baltimore, Maryland, United States. It was designed by renowned architect Stanford White (1853-1906) in 1884, built in the Romanesque Revival style. It is patterned after the early churches and basilicas in Ravenna, Italy. The exterior is constructed of a gray ashlar granite with limited ornamentation. It features a square bell tower patterned after the campanile of the 12th-century church of Santa Maria, Abbey of Pomposa, near Ravenna. The pulpit is a reproduction of the one at St. Apollinaris, in Ravenna. It is also known as the Mother Church of American Methodism.

Lovely Lane Methodist Church was listed on the National Register of Historic Places in 1973.

St. John's Church

St. John's is an Episcopal church located in Richmond, Virginia. St. John's Episcopal Church is the oldest church in Richmond, built by Col. Richard Randolph in 1741 and giving its name to the Church Hill district. St. John's was formed from several earlier churches. It was the site of two important conventions in the period leading to the American Revolutionary War, and is most famous as the location where Patrick Henry gave his closing speech at the Second Virginia Convention with the famous quotation "Give me liberty or give me death."

Transportation

Everyday personal transportation in the United States is dominated by the automobile driving on one of 13 million roads. As of 2003, there were 759 automobiles per 1,000 Americans, compared to 472 per 1,000 inhabitants of the European Union the following year. About 40% of personal vehicles are vans, SUVs, or light trucks. The average American adult (accounting for all drivers and nondrivers) spends 55 minutes driving every day, traveling 29 miles (47 km).

The civil airline industry is entirely privately owned, while most major airports are publicly owned. The four largest airlines in the world by passengers carried are American; Southwest Airlines is number one. Of the world's thirty busiest passenger airports, sixteen are in the United

States, including the busiest, Hartsfield-Jackson Atlanta International Airport. While transport of goods by rail is extensive, relatively few people use rail to travel, within or between cities. Mass transit accounts for 9% of total U.S. work trips, compared to 38.8% in Europe. Bicycle usage is minimal, well below European levels.

16 Religious Tourism Centers in Australia

Australia, officially the Commonwealth of Australia, is a country in the Southern Hemisphere comprising the mainland of the Australian continent, the island of Tasmania and numerous smaller islands in the Indian and Pacific Oceans.N4 Neighbouring countries include Indonesia, East Timor and Papua New Guinea to the north, the Solomon Islands, Vanuatu and New Caledonia to the northeast and New Zealand to the southeast.

For at least 40,000 years before European settlement in the late 18th century, Australia was inhabited by indigenous Australians, who belonged to one or more of roughly 250 language groups. After discovery by Dutch explorers in 1606, Australia's eastern half was claimed by Britain in 1770 and initially settled through penal transportation to the colony of New South Wales, formally founded on 7 February 1788 (although formal possession of the land had occurred on 26 January 1788). The population grew steadily in subsequent decades; the continent was explored and an additional five self-governing Crown Colonies were established.

On 1 January 1901, the six colonies became a federation and the Commonwealth of Australia was formed. Since Federation, Australia has maintained a stable liberal democratic political system and is a Commonwealth realm. The population is 22 million, with approximately 60 per cent concentrated in and around the mainland state capitals of Sydney, Melbourne, Brisbane, Perth and Adelaide. The nation's capital city is Canberra, in the Australian Capital Territory. Approximately 56 per cent of Australia's population live in either Victoria or New South Wales, and approximately 77 per cent live on the mainland's east coast.

A prosperous developed country, Australia is the world's thirteenth largest economy. Australia ranks highly in many international comparisons of national performance such as human development, quality of life, health care, life expectancy, public education, economic freedom and the protection of civil liberties and political rights. Australia is a member of the United Nations, G20, Commonwealth of Nations, ANZUS, OECD, APEC, Pacific Islands Forum and the World Trade Organization.

Australia's landmass of 7,617,930 square kilometres (2,941,300 sq mi) is on the Indo-Australian Plate. Surrounded by the IndianN4 and Pacific oceans, it is separated from Asia by the Arafura and Timor seas. The world's smallest continent and sixth largest country by total area, Australia-owing to its size and isolation-is often dubbed the 'island continent' and variably considered the world's largest island. Australia has 34,218 kilometres (21,262 mi) of coastline (excluding all offshore islands) and claims an extensive Exclusive Economic Zone of 8,148,250 square kilometres (3,146,060 sq mi). This exclusive economic zone does not include the Australian Antarctic Territory. Excluding Macquarie Island, Australia lies between latitudes 9° and 44°S, and longitudes 112° and 154°E.

The Great Barrier Reef, the world's largest coral reef, lies a short distance off the north-east coast and extends for over 2,000 kilometres (1,240 mi). Mount Augustus, claimed to be the world's largest monolith, is located in Western Australia. At 2,228 metres (7,310 ft), Mount Kosciuszko on the Great Dividing Range is the highest mountain on the Australian mainland, although Mawson Peak on the remote Australian territory of Heard Island is taller at 2,745 metres (9,006 ft).

Australia is the flattest continent, with the oldest and least fertile soils; desert or semi-arid land commonly known as the outback makes up by far the largest portion of land. The driest inhabited continent, only its south-east and south-west corners have a temperate climate. The population density, 2.8 inhabitants per square kilometre, is among the lowest in the world, although a large proportion of the population lives along the temperate south-eastern coastline.

Eastern Australia is marked by the Great Dividing Range that runs parallel to the coast of Queensland, New South Wales and much of Victoria - although the name is not strictly accurate, as in parts the range consists of low hills and the highlands are typically no more than 1,600 metres (5,249 ft) in height. The coastal uplands and a belt of Brigalow grasslands lie between the coast and the mountains while inland of the dividing range are large areas of grassland. These include the western plains of

New South Wales and the Einasleigh Uplands, Barkly Tableland and the Mulga Lands of inland Queensland. The northern point of the east coast is the tropical rainforested Cape York Peninsula.

The landscapes of the northern part of the country, the Top End and the Gulf Country behind the Gulf of Carpentaria, with their tropical climate, consist of woodland, grassland and desert. At the northwest corner of the continent is the sandstone cliffs and gorges of The Kimberley and below that the Pilbara while south and inland of these lie more areas of grassland, the Ord Victoria Plain and the Western Australian Mulga shrublands. The heart of the country is the uplands of central Australia while prominent features of the centre and south include the inland Simpson, Tirari and Sturt Stony, Gibson, Great Sandy, Tanami and Great Victoria Deserts with the famous Nullarbor Plain on the southern coast.

The climate of Australia is significantly influenced by ocean currents, including the Indian Ocean Dipole and the El Niño-Southern Oscillation, which is correlated with periodic drought, and the seasonal tropical low pressure system that produces cyclones in northern Australia. These factors induce rainfall to vary markedly from year to year. Much of the northern part of the country has a tropical predominantly summer rainfall (monsoon) climate. Just under three quarters of Australia lies within a desert or semi-arid zone. The southwest corner of the country has a Mediterranean climate. Much of the southeast (including Tasmania) is temperate.

Religion

Australia has no state religion. In the 2006 census, 64% of Australians listed themselves as Christian, including 26% as Roman Catholic and 19% as Anglican. About 19% of the population cited "No religion" (which includes humanism, atheism, agnosticism, and rationalism), which was the fastest-growing group from 2001 to 2006, and a further 12% did not answer (the question is optional) or did not give a response adequate for interpretation. The largest non-Christian religion in Australia is Buddhism (2.1%), followed by Islam (1.7%), Hinduism (0.8%), and Judaism (0.5%). Overall, fewer than 6% of Australians identify with non-Christian religions. Weekly attendance at church services in 2004 was about 1.5 million: about 7.5% of the population. Religion does not play a central role in the lives of much of the population.

Christianity

The churches with the largest number of members are the Roman Catholic Church in Australia, the Anglican Church of Australia and the Uniting Church in Australia, The Pentecostal churches and charismatic movement are also present with megachurches being found in most states (for example, Hillsong Church and Paradise Community Church). The National Council of Churches in Australia is the main Christian ecumenical body.

In his welcoming address to the Catholic World Youth Day 2008 in Sydney, the Prime Minister of Australia, Kevin Rudd, said that Christianity had been a positive influence on Australia: "It was the church that began first schools for the poor, it was the church that began first hospitals for the poor, it was the church that began first refuges for the poor and these great traditions continue for the future." Christian charitable organisations, hospitals and schools have played a prominent role in welfare and education since Colonial times, when First Fleet chaplain Richard Johnson was credited as "the physician both of soul and body" during the famine of 1790, and was charged with general supervision of schools.

Today, the Catholic education system is the second biggest sector after government schools, with more than 650,000 students (and around 21 per cent of all secondary school enrolments). The Anglican Church educates around 105,000 students and the Uniting Church has around 48 schools. Smaller denominations, including the Lutheran Church also have a number of schools in Australia. The Australian Catholic University opened in 1991 following the amalgamation of four Catholic tertiary institutions in eastern Australia.

Catholic Social Services Australia's 63 member organisations help more than a million Australians every year. Anglican organisations work in health, missionary work, social welfare and communications; and the Uniting Church does extensive community work, in aged care, hospitals, nursing, family support services, youth services and with the homeless. Christian charities like the Saint Vincent de Paul Society, the Salvation Army and Youth Off the Streets receive considerable national support. Religious orders founded many of Australia's hospitals, such as St Vincent's Hospital, Sydney, which was opened as a free hospital in 1857 by the Sisters of Charity and is now Australia's largest not-for-profit health provider and has trained prominent Australian surgeons such as Victor Chang.

Notable Australian Christians have included: Mary MacKillop - educator, foundress of the Sisters of St Joseph of the Sacred Heart and the first Australian to be recognised as a saint by the Roman Catholic Church; David Unaipon - an Aboriginal writer, inventor and Christian preacher currently featured on the Australian $50 note; Archbishop Daniel Mannix of Melbourne - a controversial voice against Conscription during World War One and against British policy in Ireland; The Reverend John Flynn - founder of the Royal Flying Doctor Service, currently featured on the Australian $20 note; Sir Douglas Nicholls - Aboriginal rights activist, athlete, preacher and former Governor of South Australia.

Sectarianism in Australia tended to reflect the political inheritance of Britain and Ireland. Until 1945, the vast majority of Catholics in Australia were of Irish descent, causing the British majority to question their loyalty to the British Empire. The first Catholic priests arrived in Australia as convicts in 1800, but the Castle Hill Rebellion of 1804 alarmed the British authorities and no further priests were allowed in the colony until 1820, when London sent John Joseph Therry and Philip Connolly. In 1901, the Australian Constitution guaranteed Separation of Church and State. A notable period of sectarianism re-emerged during the First World War and the 1916 Easter Uprising in Ireland, but the significance of sectarian division declined dramatically after World War Two. There was a growth in non-religious adherence, but also a diversification of Christian churches (especially the growth of Greek, Macedonian, Serbian and Russian Orthodox churches), together with an increase in ecumenism among Christians, through organisations such as the National Council of Churches in Australia.

One of the most visible signs of the historical importance of Christianity to Australia is the prominence of churches in most Australian towns and cities. One of Australia's oldest is the Anglican St James Church, Sydney, built between 1819 and 1824 by Governor Macquarie's architect, Francis Greenway. St Mary's Cathedral, Sydney was built to a design by William Wardell from a foundation stone laid in 1868, the spires of the cathedral were not finally added until the year 2000. Wardell also worked on the design of St Patrick's Cathedral, Melbourne - among the finest examples of ecclesiastical architecture in Australia. The Anglican St Paul's Cathedral, Melbourne in the iconic hub of the city opposite Flinders Street Station. Adelaide is known as the "City of Churches" but churches extend far into the Australian

Outback, as at the historic Lutheran Mission Chapel at Hermannsburg, Northern Territory. Along with community attitudes to religion, church architecture changed significantly during the 20th century. Urban churches, such as the Wayside Chapel (1964) in Sydney, differed markedly from traditional ecclesiastical designs. In the later 20th century, distinctly Australian approaches were applied at places such as Jambaroo Benedictine Abbey, where natural materials were chosen to "harmonise with the local environment" and the chapel sanctuary is of glass overlooking rainforest. Similar design principles were applied at Thredbo Ecumenical Chapel built in the Snowy Mountains in 1996.

The Christian festivals of Christmas and Easter are national public holidays in Australia. Christmas, which recalls the birth of Jesus Christ, is celebrated on 25 December during the Australian summer and is an important cultural festival even for many non-religious Australians. The European traditions of Christmas trees, roast dinners, carols and gift giving are all continued in Australia - though they might be conducted between visits to the beach - and Santa Claus is said in song to be drawn on his sleigh by six white boomer kangaroos.

Some Christian denominations with Australian articles:

- Anglican Church of Australia (formerly Church of England)
- Australian Christian Churches (formerly Assemblies of God in Australia)
- Australian Union Conference of Seventh-day Adventists
- Baptist Union of Australia
- Christian City Churches
- Christian Outreach Centre
- Churches of Christ in Australia
- Fellowship of Congregational Churches
- CRC Churches International
- Lutheran Church of Australia
- Presbyterian Church of Australia
- Presbyterian Church of Eastern Australia
- Presbyterian Reformed Church (Australia)
- Roman Catholic Church in Australia
- Uniting Church in Australia

Hinduism

Hindus are a religious minority in Australia of about 150,000 adherents according to the 2006 census. In the 19th century, Hindus first came to Australia to work on cotton and sugar plantations. Many remained as small businessmen, working as camel drivers, merchants and hawkers, selling goods between small rural communities. Their population increased dramatically from the 1960s and 1970s and more than doubled between the 1996 and 2006 censusus to around 148,000 people. Most were migrants, from countries such as Fiji, India, Sri Lanka and South Africa. At present many Hindus are well-educated professionals in fields such as medicine, engineering, commerce and information technology. Among Australia's best-known Hindus is the singer Kamahl. There are around 34 Hindu temples in Australia. Sri Mandir Temple in multicultural Auburn, Sydney was the first Hindu temple in Australia. It was established in 1977 to meet the needs of the growing Hindu community.

Islam.

The first contacts that Islam had with Australia was when Muslim fishermen native to Makassar, which is today a part of Indonesia, visited North-Western Australia long before British settlement in 1788. This contact of South East Asian ethnic groups of Islamic faith can be identified from the graves they dug for their comrades who died on the journey, being that they face Mecca (in Arabia), in accordance with Islamic regulations concerning burial, as well as evidence from Aboriginal cave paintings and religious ceremonies which depict and incorporate the adoption of Makassan canoe designs and words.[51]

In later history, throughout the 19th century following British settlement, other Muslims came to Australia in order to perform specialised labour jobs - most famously the Muslim 'Afghan' cameleers, who used their camels to transport goods and people through the otherwise unnavigable desert and pioneered a network of camel tracks that later became roads across the Outback. Australia's first mosque was built for them at Marree, South Australia in 1861. Between the 1860s and 1920s around 2000 cameleers were brought from Afghanistan and the north west of British India (now Pakistan) and perhaps 100 families remained in Australia. Other outback mosques were established at places like Coolgardie, Cloncurry, and Broken Hill - and more permanent mosques in Adelaide, Perth and later Brisbane. A legacy of this pioneer era is the presence of wild camels in Outback and the oldest Islamic structure in the southern hemisphere, at Central Adelaide Mosque. Nonetheless, despite their significant role in Australia prior to the establishment of rail and road networks, the formulation of the White Australia policy at the time of Federation made immigration difficult for the 'Afghans' and their memory slowly faded during the 20th century, until a revival of interest began in the 1980s.

In the early 20th century, most Muslims could not legally immigrate to Australia because of the White Australia policy which restricted immigration to Europeans or those of European descent, very few of whom were Muslim. However, European Muslims from Albania and Bosnia did arrive in numbers especially in the 1920s and 1930s. In 1947, out of 7,579,358 Australian inhabitants, there were 2,704 or 0.04% Muslims.

Successive Australian governments dismantled the White Australia Policy in the Post-WW2 period. From the 1970s onwards, under the leadership of Gough Whitlam and Malcolm Fraser, Australia began to pursue multiculturalism. Australia in the later 20th century became a refuge for many Muslims fleeing conflicts including those in Lebanon, the former Yugoslavia, Iraq, Iran, Sudan and Afghanistan. General immigration, combined with religious conversion to Islam by Christians and other Australians, as well as Australia's participation in UN refugee efforts has increased the overall Muslim population. Around 36% of Muslims are Australian born. Overseas born Muslims come from a great variety of nations and ethnic groups - with large Lebanese and Turkish communities.

Following the 11 September 2001 terrorist attacks, associations drawn between the political ideology of Osama Bin Laden and the religion of Islam have stirred debate in some quarters in Australia regarding Islam's relationship with the wider community - with some advocating greater emphasis on assimilation, and others supporting renewed commitment to diversity. The deaths of Australians in bombings by militant Islamic fundamentalists in New York in 2001, Bali in 2002-5 and London in 2005; as well as the sending of Australian troops to East Timor in 1999, Afghanistan in 2001 and Iraq in 2003; the arrest of bomb plotters in Australia; and concerns about certain cultural practices such as the wearing of the Burkha have all contributed to a degree of tension in recent times A series of comments by a senior Sydney cleric, Sheikh Taj El-Din Hilaly also stirred controversy, particularly his remarks regarding "female modesty" following an incident of gang rape in Sydney Australians were among the targets of Islamic Fundamentalists in the Bali bombings[disambiguation needed] in Indonesia and attack on

Australian Embassy in Jakarta and the South East Asian militant group Jemaah Islamiyah has been of particular concern to Australians.

The Australian government's mandatory detention processing system for asylum seekers became increasingly controversial after the 11 September 2001 terrorist attacks. A significant proportion of recent Asylum seekers arriving by boat have been Muslims fleeing the conflicts in Iraq and Afghanistan and elswhere.

Some Islamic leaders and social commentators claim that Islam has suffered from unfair stereotyping Violence and intimidation was directed against Muslims and people of Middle Eastern appearance during southern Sydney's Cronulla riots in 2005.

In 2005, the Howard Government established the Muslim Community Reference Group to advise on Muslim community issues for one year, chaired by Ameer Ali. Inter-faith dialogues were also established by Christian and Muslim groups such as The Australian Federation of Islamic Councils and the National Council of Churches in Australia. Australia and Indonesia co-operated closely following the Bali-bombings, not only in law-enforcement but in improving education and cross-cultural understanding, leading to a marked improvement in relations. After a series of controversies, Sheikh Taj El-Din Hilaly retired as Grand mufti of Australia in 2007 and was replaced by Fehmi Naji El-Imam AM.

Today, over 360,000 people in Australia identify as Muslim. with diverse communities concentrated mainly in Sydney and Melbourne. Since the 1970s Islamic schools have been established as well as more than 100 mosques and prayer centres. Many notable Muslim places of worship are to be found in Australian cities, including the Central Adelaide Mosque, which was constructed during the 1880s; and Sydney's Classical Ottoman style Auburn Gallipoli Mosque, which was largely funded by the Turkish community and the name of which recalls the shared heritage of the foundation of modern Turkey and the story of the ANZACs. Notable Australian Muslims include boxer Anthony Mundine; community worker and rugby league star Hazem El Masri; cricketer Usman Khawaja and academic Waleed Aly.

Judaism

The history of the Judaism in Australia began with the transportation of eight Jewish convicts aboard the First Fleet in 1788 when the first European settlement was established on the continent. An estimated 110,000 Jews currently live in Australia, the majority being Ashkenazi

Jews of Eastern European descent, with many being refugees and Holocaust survivors who arrived during and after World War II.

The Jewish population has increased slightly in recent times due to immigration from South Africa and the former Soviet Union. The largest Jewish community in Australia is in Melbourne, with about 60,000, followed by Sydney with about 45,000 members. Smaller communities are dispersed among the other state capitals.

Following the conclusion of the British Colonial period, Jews have enjoyed formal equality before the law in Australia and have not been subject to civil disabilities or other forms of state-sponsored anti-Semitism which exclude them from full participation in public life.

JewishCare is among Australia's largest and oldest Jewish aid organisations, started in 1935 to assist with Jewish migration from Nazi Germany. It is still engaged in assisting migrants and other services. Sydney's gothic design Great Synagogue, consecrated in 1878, is a notable place of Jewish worship in Australia. Notable Australian Jews have included the Sir John Monash, the notable World War I general who opened the Maccabean Hall in Sydney in 1923 to commemorate Jews who fought and died in the First World War and who is currently featured on the Australian $100 note; and Sir Isaac Isaacs who became the first Australian born governor general in 1930. The Sydney Jewish Museum opened in 1992 to commemorate the Holocaust "challenge visitors' perceptions of democracy, morality, social justice and human rights".

Buddhism

Although the first definite cases of Buddhist settlement in Australia were in 1848, there has been speculation from some anthropologists that there may have been contact some hundreds of years earlier. Buddhists began arriving in Australia in significant numbers during the goldrush of the 1850s, with an influx of Chinese miners. However, the population remained low until the 1960s. Buddhism is now one of the fastest growing religions in Australia. Immigration from Asia has contributed to this, but some people of non-Asian origin have also converted. The three main traditions of Buddhism - Theravada, East Asian and Tibetan) - are now represented in Australia.

According to the Australian census in 2006, Buddhism is the largest non-Christian religion in Australia, with 418,000 adherents, or 2.1% of the total population. It was also the fastest growing religion in terms of percentage, having increased its number of adherents by 109.6% since 1996.

The Nan Tien Temple, or "Southern Paradise Temple" in Wollongong, New South Wales began construction in the early 1990s, adopting the Chinese palace building style and is today the largest Buddhist temple in the Southern Hemisphere. The temple follows the Venerable Master Hsing Yun of the Fo Guang Shan Buddhist order.

Sikhism

Sikhs have been in Australia since the 1830s, initially coming to work as labourers in the cane fields and as cameleers, known as Ghans. At the turn of the century a number of them were working as hawkers, opening up stores. After World War I, Sikhs in Australia were given rights far greater than other Asians and made use of them by emigrating to Australia and working as labourers. As the decades passed they formed a sizable community in Woolgoolga, where the first Gurdwara, named the First Sikh Temple, was built. Following the end of the White Australia Policy there has been a great increase in the number of Sikhs from a number of countries including India, Malaysia, Fiji and the United Kingdom. The 2006 Australian Census shows about 26,500 followers, up from 17,000 in 2001 and 12,000 in 1996.

Bahá'í

The Bahá'í faith in Australia has a long history and a growing visible presence in the country since 1922. A Bahá'í House of Worship exists in Sydney, dedicated on 17 September 1961 and opened to the public after four years of construction. The 1996 Australian Census lists Bahá'í membership at just under 9000. The 2001 second edition of A Practical Reference to Religious Diversity for Operational Police and Emergency Services added the Bahá'í faith in its coverage of religions in Australia and noted that the community had grown to over 11,000. The Association of Religion Data Archives (relying on World Christian Encyclopedia) estimated some 17,700 Bahá'ís in 2005.

Transport in Australia

Roads

Australia has the second highest level of car ownership in the world. It has three to four times more road per capita than Europe and seven to nine times more than Asia. Australia also has the third highest per capita rate of fuel consumption in the world. Perth, Adelaide and Brisbane are rated among the most car-dependent cities in the world, with Sydney and Melbourne close behind. Furthermore, the distance travelled by car (or similar vehicle) in Australia is among the highest in the world, being exceeded by USA and Canada.

There are 3 different categories of Australian roads:

- Federal Highways
- State Highways
- Local Roads

The road network comprises a total of 913,000 km broken down into:

- Paved: 353,331 km (including 3,132 km of expressways)
- Unpaved: 559,669 km (1996 estimate)

The majority of road tunnels in Australia have been constructed since the 1990s to relieve traffic congestion in metropolitan areas, or to cross significant watercourses.

Public Transport in Australia

Rising petrol prices and increasing traffic congestion are thought to be factors contributing to renewed growth in use of urban public transport.

Intra-city Public Transport Networks

The table below lists major cities in Australia with currently operating multi-modal intra-city (as opposed to inter-city or regional) public transportation networks.

The only Australian capital cities without such networks are Canberra and Darwin.

Trams in Australia historically serviced many Australian towns and several cities formerly operated tram networks, however the majority of these were shut down before the 1970s. Melbourne is an exception here however, and today boasts the largest tram network of any city in the world. Major regional cities where trams formerly facilitated multi-modal public transport networks Launceston, Geelong, Ballarat, Bendigo and Rockhampton.

Most major cities have at minimum bus services and these cities have been excluded services as have any with tourist or heritage transport (such as the private monorail at Sea World or the tourist Victor Harbor Horse Drawn Tram).

The railway network is large, comprising a total of 33,819 km (2,540 km electrified) of track: 3,719 km broad gauge, 15,422 km standard gauge, 14,506 km narrow gauge and 172 km dual gauge. Rail transport started in the various colonies at different dates. Privately owned railways started the first lines, and struggled to succeed on a remote, huge, and sparsely populated continent, and government railways dominated. Although the various colonies had been advised by London to choose a common gauge, the colonies ended up with different gauges.

Inter-state Rail Services

The Great Southern Railway, owned by Serco Asia Pacific, operates three trains: the Indian Pacific (Sydney-Adelaide-Perth), The Ghan (Adelaide-Alice Springs-Darwin), and The Overland (Melbourne-Adelaide) . NSW owned CountryLink services link Brisbane, Canberra and Melbourne via Sydney. Since the extension of the Ghan from Alice Springs to Darwin was completed in 2004, all mainland Australian capital cities are linked by standard gauge rail, for the first time.

Intra-state and City Rail Services

There are various state and city rail services operated by a combination of government and private entities, the most prominent of these include V/Line (regional trains and buses in Victoria); Metro Trains Melbourne which operates the Melbourne rail network; RailCorp operating all passenger rail services in New South Wales including (CityRail and CountryLink);Queensland Rail (QR) operating Traveltrain and the Citytrain network, South-East Queensland's commuter railway network under the TransLink scheme, and Transwa operating train and bus services in Western Australia.

Metro

Major cities in Australia do not have full-fledged rapid transit systems. Melbourne, Sydney, Brisbane and Perth's systems are all partially underground. Melbourne has plans for a new train service branded as a metro, but as it will interact with the suburban system and won't be grade-separated from Footscray out, it will fall short of the criteria of a metro. Plans for a "Euro-style" metro in Sydney have been shelved in favor of additional underground lines on the suburban network.

Mining Railways

Four heavy-duty mining railways carry iron ore to ports in the northwest of Western Australia. These railways carry no other traffic, and are isolated by deserts from all other railways. The lines are standard gauge and are built to the heaviest US standards.

In 2006, a fifth iron ore railway is proposed by the Fortescue Metals Group, while a sixth common carrier railway is proposed to serve the port of Oakajee just north of Geraldton.

Cane Railways

In Queensland about 15 sugar mills have narrow gauge (2 ft (610 mm) gauge) cane tramways that deliver sugar cane to the mills.

Waterways

Australia's inland waterways are not a significant means commercial transport. In the 19th century, paddle steamers were used on the Murray-Darling Basin to transport produce such as wool and wheat but the water levels are highly unreliable, making the river impassable for large parts of the year. The steamers proved unable to compete with rail, and later, road transport. Traffic now on inland waterways is therefore largely restricted to private recreational craft.

17 Religious Tourism Centers in Africa

Africa is the world's second-largest and second most-populous continent, after Asia. At about 30.2 million km² (11.7 million sq mi) including adjacent islands, it covers 6% of the Earth's total surface area and 20.4% of the total land area. With 1.0 billion people (as of 2009, see table) in 61 territories, it accounts for about 14.72% of the world's human population.

The continent is surrounded by the Mediterranean Sea to the north, both the Suez Canal and the Red Sea along the Sinai Peninsula to the northeast, the Indian Ocean to the southeast, and the Atlantic Ocean to the west. The continent has 54 sovereign states, including Madagascar, various island groups, and the Sahrawi Arab Democratic Republic, a member state of the African Union whose statehood is disputed by Morocco.

Africa, particularly central eastern Africa, is widely regarded within the scientific community to be the origin of humans and the Hominidae clade (great apes), as evidenced by the discovery of the earliest hominids and their ancestors, as well as later ones that have been dated to around seven million years ago - including Sahelanthropus tchadensis, Australopithecus africanus, A. afarensis, Homo erectus, H. habilis and H. ergaster - with the earliest Homo sapiens (modern human) found in Ethiopia being dated to circa 200,000 years ago.

Africa straddles the equator and encompasses numerous climate areas; it is the only continent to stretch from the northern temperate to southern temperate zones. The African expected economic growth rate is at about 5.0% for 2010 and 5.5% in 2011.

Africa is the largest of the three great southward projections from the largest landmass of the Earth. Separated from Europe by the

Mediterranean Sea, it is joined to Asia at its northeast extremity by the Isthmus of Suez (transected by the Suez Canal), 163 km (101 miles) wide. (Geopolitically, Egypt's Sinai Peninsula east of the Suez Canal is often considered part of Africa, as well.)

From the most northerly point, Ras ben Sakka in Tunisia (37°21' N), to the most southerly point, Cape Agulhas in South Africa (34°51'15" S), is a distance of approximately 8,000 km (5,000 miles); from Cape Verde, 17°33'22" W, the westernmost point, to Ras Hafun in Somalia, 51°27'52" E, the most easterly projection, is a distance of approximately 7,400 km (4,600 miles). The coastline is 26,000 km (16,100 miles) long, and the absence of deep indentations of the shore is illustrated by the fact that Europe, which covers only 10,400,000 km² (4,010,000 square miles) - about a third of the surface of Africa - has a coastline of 32,000 km (19,800 miles).

Africa's largest country is Sudan, and its smallest country is the Seychelles, an archipelago off the east coast. The smallest nation on the continental mainland is The Gambia.

According to the ancient Romans, Africa lay to the west of Egypt, while "Asia" was used to refer to Anatolia and lands to the east. A definite line was drawn between the two continents by the geographer Ptolemy (85-165 AD), indicating Alexandria along the Prime Meridian and making the isthmus of Suez and the Red Sea the boundary between Asia and Africa. As Europeans came to understand the real extent of the continent, the idea of Africa expanded with their knowledge.

Geologically, Africa includes the Arabian Peninsula; the Zagros Mountains of Iran and the Anatolian Plateau of Turkey mark where the African Plate collided with Eurasia. The Afrotropic ecozone and the Saharo-Arabian desert to its north unite the region biogeographically, and the Afro-Asiatic language family unites the north linguistically.

The climate of Africa ranges from tropical to subarctic on its highest peaks. Its northern half is primarily desert or arid, while its central and southern areas contain both savanna plains and very dense jungle (rainforest) regions. In between, there is a convergence where vegetation patterns such as sahel, and steppe dominate.

Religion in Africa

Religion in Africa is multifaceted. Most Africans adhere to either Christianity or Islam. Many adherents of either religion also practice African traditional religions, with traditions of folk religion or syncretism practised alongside an adherent's Christianity or Islam. Judaism also has roots in Africa, due to the time the Israelites spent in Egypt before the Exodus. Around 15% of Africans follow one of the traditional African religions and a small minority of Africans are non-religious.

The original religions of Africa have been declining over the past century due to the influences of colonialism, acculturation and increasing proselytizing by Christianity and Islam. However, in the Americas and Caribbean, syncretistic religions involving African religions are growing. Religious adherents in Africa are often of a syncretic nature.

Not all communities in East AFrica are the same when it comes to religioin. There is one thing that remains the same throughout the religions though, that is the cecept of unity. In East Africa they show their unity not just in words or in church, but through their actions. Unity is not the only simmilarities between all the religions though. African communities are also big on the concept of harmony within the community, love within the community and the conccept of common good. Africans stress on the concpet of family and its importance, their family is part of their community and it gives them a sense of belonging.

Africa encompass a wide variety of traditional beliefs. Traditional religious customs are sometimes shared by many African societies, but they are usually unique to specific ethnic groups. Traditional African religions used to be adhered to by the majority of Africa's population, however since the rapid expansion of Christianity and Islam they have become a minority across much of their own continent. Many African Christians and Muslims maintain some aspects of their original traditional religions.

Some indigenous African religions worship a single God (Chukwu, Nyame, Olodumare, Ngai etc.), and some recognize a dual or complementary twin God such as Mawu-Lisa. Obeisance can be paid to the primary God through lesser deities (Ogoun, Da, Agwu, Esu, Mbari, etc.). Some societies also deify entities like the earth, the sun, the sea, lightning, or Nature. Each deity can have its own priest or priestess.Jacob Olupona and Charles E. Long, Editors, African Spirituality. New York: Cross Road Publishing Co., 2000. Sabine Jell-Bahlsen, The Water Goddess in Igbo Cosmology; Ogbuide of Oguta Lake. Trenton, NJ: Africa World Press, 2008. The Ndebele and Shona ethnic groups of Zimbabwe have a trinity - a fundamental family group - made up of God the Father, God the Mother, and God the Son. Among the Fon of West Africa and Benin, God, who is called "Vondu", is androgynous, with both male and female traits.

The Ewe people of southern Ghana have a conception of the high God as a female-male partnership. Mawu who is female is often spoken of as gentle and forgiving. Lisa who is male renders judgment and punishes. Among the Ewe it is believed that when Lisa punishes, Mawu may grant forgiveness. Here we see the complementarity of male and female that characterizes many of the traditional African religions.

The only example in Africa of a female high Goddess is among the Southern Nuba of Sudan, whose culture has matriarchal traits. The Nuba conceive of the creator Goddess as the "Great Mother" who gave birth to earth and to mankind. (Mbiti, J.S., Introduction to African Religion, Oxford, 1975, p. 53.)

Polytheism in Africa has developed several times independently and in very different ways. For example in the case of ancient Egypt where a pantheon was worshipped or in the case of the Orisha religion in West Africa.

Abrahamic Religions

The majority of Africans are adherents of Christianity or Islam. Both religions are widespread throughout Africa. They have both spread at the expense of indigenous African religions, but are often adapted to African cultural contexts and belief systems. It was estimated in 2002 that Christians form 40% of Africa's population, with Muslims forming 45%.

Christianity

Although Christianity existed far before the rule of King Ezana the Great of the Kingdom of Axum, the religion took a strong foot hold when it was declared a state religion in 330 AD. The earliest and best known reference to the introduction of Christianity to Africa is mentioned in the Christian Bible's Acts of the Apostles, and pertains to the evangelist Phillip's conversion of an Ethiopian traveler in the 1st Century AD. Although the Bible refers to them as Ethiopians, scholars have argued that Ethiopia was a common term encompassing the area South-Southeast of Egypt.

Other traditions have the convert as a Jew who was a steward in the Queen's court. All accounts do agree on the fact that the traveler was a member of the royal court who successfully succeeded in converting the Queen, which in turn caused a church to be built.

Rufinus of Tyre, a noted church historian, also has recorded a personal account as do other church historians such as Socrates and Sozemius.

After being shipwrecked and captured at an early age, Frumentius was carried to Axum where he was treated well with his companion Edesius. At the time, there was a small population of Christians living there who sought refuge from Roman persecution. Once of age, Frumentius and Edesius were allowed to return to their homelands, however they chose to stay at the request of the queen. In doing so, they began to secretly promote Christianity through the lands.

During a trip to meet with church elders, Frumentius met with Athanasius, Archbishop of Alexandria who was second in line to the pope. After recommending that a bishop be sent to proselytize, a council decided that Frumentius be appointed as a bishop to Ethiopia.

By 430 AD, Frumentius returned to Ethiopia, he was welcomed with open arms by the rulers who were at the time not Christian. Ten years later, through the support of the kings, the majority of the kingdom was converted and Christianity was declared the official state religion.

Rastafari

There are also Rasta communities in Africa. In the Ivory Coast presidential candidates tried to reach out to voters in the Rasta village of Port Bouet.

Islam

According to the World Book Encyclopedia, Islam is the largest religion in Africa, with 47% of the population being Muslim. Its historic roots in Africa stem from the time Muhammad whose relatives and the epic followers migrated on a hijra to Abyssinia in fear of persecution from the pagan Arabs.

The main spread of Islam came with the invasion of Egypt under Caliph Umar, through the Sinai Peninsula - followed by the rapid conquest of North Africa by the Arab armies - as well as through Islamic Arab and Persian traders and sailors.

Islam is the dominant religion in North Africa and the Horn of Africa, and it has also become the predominant and historical religion of the West African interior and the far west coast of the continent as well as the coast of East Africa. There have been several Muslim empires in Western Africa which exerted considerable influence, notably the Mali Empire, which flourished for several centuries and the Songhai Empire, under the leadership of Sonni Ali and Askia Mohammed.

The Ahmadiyya Muslim Community is relatively modern community which is progressing relatively rapidly, particularly in West Africa.

Judaism

Adherents of Judaism too can be found scattered across Africa. Perhaps not as well known as the history of Christianity and Islam in Africa to the outside observer, Judaism has an ancient and rich history on the African continent. Today, there are Jewish communities in many countries; including the Beta Israel of Ethiopia, the Abayudaya of Uganda, the House of Israel in Ghana, the Igbo Jews of Nigeria and the Lemba of Southern Africa.

Baha'i

Baha'i Faith is the 3rd most widespread organized Abrahamic religion in Africa after Islam and Christianity. African Bahá'í Community statistics are also hard to come by. However, Africans have a long history with the Bahá'í Faith; several of the earliest followers of both the Báb and Bahá'u'lláh were reportedly African. From 1924 to 1960 the religion was declared one of the legally sanctioned faiths in Egypt, but has since then been subject to restrictions and outright persecution by authorities and others

Hinduism

The history of Hinduism in Africa is, by most accounts, very short in comparison to that of Islam, Christianity, or Judaism. However, the presence of its practitioners in Africa dates back to pre-colonial times and even medieval times. There are sizable of Hindu populations in South Africa and the East African coastal nations.

Transport in South Africa

Roads

Approximately ten thousand people die on roads in South Africa yearly.

The national speed limit is between 40 or 80 km/h in residential areas and 120 km/h on national roads/freeways/motorways.

In 2002 the country had 362,099 km of highways, 73,506 km (17%) of which was paved (including 239 km of expressways)..

Railways

In 2000, South Africa had 20,384 km of rail transport, all of it narrow gauge. 20,070 km was 1,067 mm (3 ft 6 in) gauge (9,090 km of that electrified), with the remaining 314 km 610 mm (2 ft) gauge. The operation of the country's rail systems is accomplished by Transnet subsidiaries Spoornet, Shosholoza Meyl, Metrorail, Transwerk, Protekon et al.

A feasibility study is to be conducted into the construction of a 720 km of 1,435 mm (4 ft 8 1?2 in) (standard gauge) line from Johannesburg to Durban for double-stack container trains.

On 2010-06-07 the Gautrain opened between Oliver R Tambo International Airport (ORTIA) and Sandton. This is the first stage of a standard gauge passenger line connecting Johannesburg, Pretoria and ORTIA.

Links exist to Botswana, Lesotho, Namibia, Swaziland, and Zimbabwe. Railways linking Mozambique are under repair.

Water Ways

South Africa's major ports and harbours are Cape Town, Durban, East London, Mossel Bay, Port Elizabeth, Richards Bay, and Saldanha Bay. In 2006 the new port is to open: Ngqura, at Coega, which is 20 km northeast of Port Elizabeth. The administration and operation of the country's port facilities is done by two subsidiaries of Transnet, the Transnet National Ports Authority and South African Port Operations (SAPO).

In 2002, the merchant marine consisted of eight ships of 1,000 GRT or over, totaling 271,650 GRT/268,604 metric tons deadweight (DWT). Six were container ships, and two were petroleum tankers (including foreign-owned ships registered as a flag of convenience: Denmark: 3, Netherlands: 1).

Tramways

A number of urban tramway systems used to operate in South Africa, but the last system (Johannesburg) closed in 1961.

18 Religious Tourism Information Source

Religion is historically associated with tourism. Some of our most popular tourist destinations are founded on ancient places of worship: the Temple of Hathor - the Pharaonic Mother Goddess at Dendera in Upper Egypt; Dodona, location of the oracle devoted to Zeus, in prehistoric Greece, Bodhgaya and other sacred places in India associated with the life and teachings of the Buddha. Jerusalem, Amritsar, Mount Fuji: pilgrims travelling to these holy places were effectively the world`s first tourists. In fact pilgrim hospices in Europe were the forerunners of modern hotels. And pilgrims are on the move as never before. The collapse of Communism in the former Soviet republics sees people now able to worship legally in churches and at historic shrines. Countries such as Italy, Spain and the Slavic states are experiencing an explosive interest in the old pilgrim routes subsequent to the..2000th anniversary of the birth of Christ. More than 10 million Christians are expected to visit Lourdes in 2008 for the 150th anniversary of the apparition of the Virgin Mary. Muslims performing the annual hajj pilgrimage to Mecca number three million while the Kumbh Mela held every 12 years in Allahabad northern India attracted 75 million Hindus on the last occasion in 2001. Joining the colourful melting-pot at Allahabad are tourists staying in luxuriously equipped tents to view but not to participate in the devotional when river water is elevated to.the status of "Divine"

Cultural tourism frequently overlaps places of worship considered to have special artistic merit. Tour groups visiting Chartres Cathedral in France or the Hassan II Mosque in Casablanca are notable examples. And somehow, despite the dangers posed by religious extremism, moderate believers are finding new confidence to practise their chosen faith resulting in an emergent interest in undertaking sacred journeys. Accompanying them are more and more of the `uncommitted`; persons who for various reasons - the death of a loved one, the loss of a job or other emotional setback are seeking somewhere, usually ancient and well trod, offering solace, enlightenment or at least a temporary escape from the stresses of modern life. Delegates to ICORET the first ever international conference on religious tourism hosted by the Cyprus Tourism Organisation in 2006 emphasised that spiritual travel is set to become a tour de force across all age-groups in the 21st century. Cyprus with its rich Christian history and numerous Byzantine churches was an ideal starting point for religious discourse. A World Religious Tourism Association has since been formed to facilitate the exchange of dialogue between faith groups and travel agents while a charter airline launched by the Vatican is forecast to carry some 18 million religious tourists visiting sacred Christian sites.

SACRED SITES

Since time immemorial, devout believers have built places of worship to celebrate their faith along with shrines & monuments erected to prophets, gurus and saints. Natural phenomena have also been harnessed for worship & ritual & together with man-made edifices many are inscribed on the UNESCO World Heritage List of items having special cultural & religious significance. While due to their great age some are in ruins, such sacred sites continue to weave their magic on modern-day pilgrims & tourists.

We feel that the Lord cannot be Pleased with how hate-filled so many of His followers are toward others who do not agree with their views or beliefs, especially other Believers in Him! Over half of all the six billion people on our planet believe in Him, the One True God of Abraham (which includes Christians, Jews, Muslims and others), yet the vast majority of them feel extreme hatred toward others of His followers. Because each of the many different religions and Denominations have made their own individual assumptions regarding exactly what he meant to teach us, and therefore each chooses to Teach selective, and sometimes distorted information about all other belief systems. Can the Lord be Pleased with this sort of behavior? We think not.

We think that He would wish All people to have access to and understanding of Accurate and Honest information on all religious subjects. Christians believe that He has installed an Indwelling Holy Spirit in each person such that the person then has Divine assistance regarding Discerning what is correct regarding the best way of Worshipping the one true Lord. Religious systems tend to try to force followers to accept only what they Teach them, and to be deaf or even adversarial to things anyone else might say. There is nothing wrong with Trusting and following your religious leader, and indeed, it is important to do so. But there also needs to be some system of checks and balances where the Lord's True Message might not be distorted.

We have recently realized that if Jesus Himself would arrive at any of many thousands of Christian Churches, in His robe and with His long hair and general appearance, He would certainly be denied admission to the Church! What does that say about our modern understanding of what He tried to Teach us?

The different religions, and Denominations each absolutely insist that THEIR interpretation is superior to all others. Isn't that Arrogance, something that the Lord Wished us to avoid? Didn't He Try to Teach us Humility and Tolerance of others? It seems to us that if a religion chooses to refer to the One True God by a somewhat confusing collection of Three Different Names (Father, Son and Holy Spirit) or to see Him as very Harsh (Jewish) or Loving (Christianity), does it necessarily mean that HE is any Different? Probably not. It probably simply indicates that we humans are not nearly as smart as we often want to claim, and that there are many, many things that we only vaguely comprehend. There actually seems a credible possibility that we are all actually "speaking the same language of Love and Adoration for the One True God of Abraham" but simply do not (yet) realize it!

Each religion encourages Passion regarding believing what they believe. Fine. But that commonly then includes hatred for strangers who believe differently than themselves. That Cannot be what the Lord had in Mind! Especially when those strangers happen to also be trying to Worship the very same Lord! It is sad that thousands of different groups of Christians read English translations of the exact same Original Ancient Hebrew and Greek texts, and interpret what they read differently than the Church down the street, and then find causes to develop insults and hatred for neighbors who attend that Church. How is it possible that we are so shallow to fall into such things? And that other Church Teaches the same Arrogance regarding this Church? Are either of those Churches right in such postures of superiority that can seem rather disgusting to observers? Didn't Jesus Teach Humility and not Arrogance?

A central reason for the existence of the Believe resource is to try to provide the best such information that we could accumulate. Many of our subject presentations include (separate) articles written by Protestant Christian scholars, Catholic scholars, Jewish scholars, Orthodox scholars, Muslim scholars, etc, to try to provide the broadest possible view of a subject, by including perspectives from many different (scholarly) directions. We have also included excerpts from important Buddhist, Hindu, Muslim and other religious texts, which often seem to show the same charity, kindness, patience and other characteristics which are familiar in nearly all religions.

Churches each Interpret many different things to generate their own ideas about how a Church is supposed to be. An interesting example to ponder might be a few paragraphs from a respected Christian scholar's discussion regarding Jesus' 'self awareness' during His earthly activities. That scholar notes that at NO time did Jesus ever refer to Himself as Son of God or as anything very different from terms used for Jewish Rabbis of the time, such as "my Lord.". The Post-Easter Church, After He had Died, developed nearly all of the titles by which we now refer to Jesus. But modern Christians and modern Churches all believe that they were applied to Jesus while He was Alive on Earth. That was not the case. Jesus clearly realized that He had an unique and intimate relationship with the Lord, but He never implied that He felt it was as Son or as any other Divine Being! It IS possible that He made such comments As an assumption, based on the fact that each time that He requested a Miracle, it occurred! The reality that He Was the One True God of the Universe meant that such Miracles would occur because He wished them! But HE did not realize all of that, and He believed that He had to Request Miracles "from the Father"! Churches have Taught for centuries that those things were accurate and true statements, but they appear to have been primarily Opinions of leaders of the Post-Easter Church as it was developing. We feel that the Lord Wishes us all to know the actual Truth, and not necessarily just the opinions of that Truth held by Ministers of any specific Church. Doesn't that seem what He would Want?

Believe is currently a collection of over 7,000 articles by respected scholars on around 2,300 religious subjects. Protestant Christian Churches, the Roman Catholic Church, and the Orthodox Church, all follow Faiths which involve hundreds of individual subjects, which are each thoroughly presented in believe. Many of these subjects are very important to Faith, like Eschatology, but which are seldom presented in Church Services or during

Bible Study. Others are commonly known religious subjects, like Salvation, or Baptism, that we just present more thoroughly than is usually available.

We think you might find it refreshing that we have no intention of pushing you toward any specific attitudes or positions. We also have no intention of trying to get you to like or dislike any specific group or Denomination or Faith. Our intent is only to present you with enough accurate, unbiased information such that you can make your own thoughtful conclusion about any particular subject. If you have questions, concerns, doubts, skepticism, you're probably in the right place to get actual information on which to form your own conclusions. We have tried hard not to include opinions or unsupported logic. Our attitude is that you must find your own conclusions (as long as you have accurate information to work with) and it is not our place to try to drag you anywhere!

A concept that we have tried to keep in mind in assembling believe is:

Whatever you do, work at it with all your heart, as though you were working for the Lord and not for men. (Col. 3: 23) (NIV). In that regard, we have added nearly 4,000 complete texts of Early Christian Manuscripts (translated into English). We think that cynics might be surprised in browsing through some of them, as, for example, the single presentation on Tatian's Diatessaron includes over 3,800 footnotes! An access to the entire assemblage is at 4,000 Early Christian Manuscripts. The level of intellectual care and attention to accuracy is really impressive!

Tourism Offices Worldwide Directory

The Tourism Offices Worldwide Directory is your guide to official tourist information sources: government tourism offices, convention and visitors bureaus, chambers of commerce, and similar organizations that provide free, accurate, and unbiased travel information to the public. Businesses such as travel agents, tour operators, and hotels are not included.

Association of National Tourist Office Representatives

If you are located in one of the following countries, you may wish to also try the services offered by the Associations of National Tourist Office Representatives (ANTOR), which are industry membership associations of the tourist information offices located in: Australia - Belgium - Canada - France - Norway - Taiwan - United Kingdom

2. Religious Tourism Booms
3. Modern Issues in Religious Tourism

19 Religious Tourism Boom

The plain classrooms of the Hue Tourism School come alive with color when the female students take their seats. They are dressed in shimmering red or blue ao dai, the flowing tunic and wide-bottomed trousers that make up Viet Nams national costume. The school began only 5 years ago with capacity for 300 students. Yet so great has been the demand that 800 full-time and 500 part-time students now cram into eight classrooms that are used in three shifts.

Many of the young men and women are from the Central Regionone of Viet Nams poorest areasand are taking advantage of the current tourism boom to improve their lives. The studentsmore than 80% young women are enrolled in either 1-year professional or 2-year college courses. Some 30% of our students are from poor households, including ethnic minorities. They come because of the strong development of tourism in central Viet Nam, says Le Duc Trung, the schools affable vice director. They know tourism is an important means to escape poverty.

The tourism boom is spurred in part by the improved East-West Economic Corridor, also known as Highway 9, which provides easier access to Viet Nams Central Region from the Lao Peoples Democratic Republic (Lao PDR) and Thailand, as well as other parts of the country The rehabilitation of the highway in the Lao PDR and Viet Namwhich the Asian Development Bank (ADB) helped cofinance under the GMS Economic Cooperation Programis nearing completion.

Easing Access for Tourists

The GMS countries Cambodia, Peoples Republic of China, Lao PDR, Myanmar, Thailand, and Viet Nam are promoting the subregion as a single tourist destination. They have relaxed visa regimes, upgraded and improved airports, developed roads, initiated tourism training programs, and intensified joint marketing efforts.

Tourist arrivals in the six countries last year totaled nearly 16 million, and these are expected to soar to 20 million in 2006. By 2010, tourist arrivals are expected to increase to nearly 30 million.

At the ochre-colored An Dinh Palace, by the Perfume River that runs through Hue, Ngo Hoa, Vice Chairman of the Peoples Committee of Thua Thien Hue Province, says improved road and rail links are contributing to a boom that has seen a rise in the number of visitors to the province by about 17-20% annually in recent years. This is well above the national average.

Our tourism drive includes stepping up advertising as well as using the Internet more, says Mr. Hoa. The Central Region has a strong attraction for ecotourists as well as those interested in history and culture.

Ancient History Attracts

Major Central Region tourist attractions?which include the Ho Chi Minh Trail, the Imperial City of Hue, and the 17th century trading port of Hoi An? are expected to play a key role in that increase.

Hue?s hotels are also gearing up to handle increased business. At the historic Saigon Morin Hotel, general manager Tao Van Nghe sends his staff for training to cope with the demands of rising occupancy rates, with 60% of the guests coming from Europe.

Meanwhile, the Hue Tourism School is planning to expand its facilities to cater to the ever-increasing number of students. In 2006, the 2-year college course will be upgraded to a 3-year course. Despite strained resources, Mr. Trung says the school waives tuition fees for the poorest students.

Some students come from neighboring countries, says Mr. Trung. Currently, 10 students are from the Lao PDR. Most are male, but the contingent includes Manohay Sindonthan, who wants to work as a travel agent when she returns home to Champassak in Southern Lao PDR.

The Hue Tourism School receives financing from the European Union. Vincent Gibbon, an Irish senior technical advisor with the Luxembourg Development Agency, helps ensure training is up to international standards. ?We?ve supported the training program and have developed the examination and certification system under the Viet Nam Tourism Certification Board,? he says. English language skills are the top priority.

By easing access to and within the subregion, improving training in the tourism industry, and promoting the GMS as a single tourist destination, new opportunities for both poor people and tourists will be developed. The poor are improving their lives through training and greater availability and diversity of employment, and the tourists can now enjoy more of the subregion?s geographical beauty and historical and cultural richness while availing of good service from an increasingly professional industry.

Holiday Weekend Tourism Boom

Buenos Aires is preparing for a huge surge in people entering and leaving the city this weekend as the reinstated national bank holiday means two days off work. The holiday will see tourism soar almost to the same level as Semana Santa and Christmas. Some are travelling in order to celebrate Mardi Gras at one of the eighty carnivals happening across the country whilst others plan to relax over the long weekend. To cope with the exodus and influx, 1339 buses will depart from Retiro station and 869 will arrive. According to tourist operators, 80% of accommodation on the Atlantic Coast and in Córdoba is already reserved and there are no rooms left in Gualeguaychú, where the national carnival will take place. In Capital Federal, 77% of accommodation is already booked. Reservation numbers are helped by the fact that sunshine is forecast and temperatures are set to rise between now and Tuesday. The celebrations across the country will be "a great incentive to boost tourism in the interior provinces," said Patricia Vismara, the vice-secretary of National Tourism Promotion.

Indian Hotels: Tourism Boom

Indian Hotels Company (IHC), the owner of a chain of luxury restaurants, including the Taj Hotels, looks well geared up to take advantage of revival in tourist arrivals. The company has recently reopened its property in South Mumbai, which alone is likely to boost its annual revenue by more than 10%, feel analysts.

IHC recently made its Taj Mahal Palace & Tower property fully operational, nearly two years after the terrorist attack in South Mumbai. This means the hotel would now operate some 500 rooms, including the Palace wing.

Historically on a full operational basis, the hotel has exhibited the potential of contributing around Rs 200 crore to the topline on an annualised basis. Take, for instance, in FY08, when the hotels business was still to get impacted by slowdown and hotels players were making good business, the hotel yielded revenues of around Rs 180 crore or nearly 10% of total revenue.

Tourism Boom in the GCC

Skyscrapper hotels and massive shopping centres continue to rise. Wide roads are being laid. New ideas, such as building water and theme parks, to lure people are being introduced and implemented.

Several plans, ranging from holding shopping festivals in the UAE, to cultural and entertainment events in Oman, to sports activities in Qatar, have been drawn to attract tourists, mainly from other GCC countries.

The tourism sector in the GCC region is booming, and mega projects are mushrooming to elevate the region on the world's tourism map. To put things in perspective in financial terms, here are some of the examples that made headlines recently in the Gulf.

The UAE expects to receive 10 million tourists in 2008 compared to 8.8 million last year. More than 30 multi-faceted entertainment resorts and theme parks are being built until 2012 with a projected investment of Dh228 billion ($62 billion), according to CMPi UAE, organisers of Middle East Attractions, Amusements, Parks, Leisure and Entertainment International Trade Exhibition (MEAAPLE) which will run in February.

And beyond the UAE, every year, nearly 17 million travellers cross the bridge linking Saudi Arabia and Bahrain. Hakeer, the giant Saudi developer, plans to build seven International hotels in the main Saudi cities as well as Dubai with the cost of one billion Saudi riyals. Qatar has allocated $1.4 billion to build a number of shopping centres by 2009.

In Bahrain, plans are under way to open a giant shopping centre at a cost of 25 million Bahraini dinars. Oman plans to build a tourism city or tourism integrated project, including hotels, tourist village, market, natural park, golf hotel, and malls, at a cost of $15-20 billion on an area of 34 square km. The first phase is expected to be completed in 2010. Some press reports have estimated the overall investment in internal tourism projects in GCC to reach nearly $380 billion in the next 10 years.

But GCC officials say these figures as "conservative estimates" in view of the contributions of both public and private sectors.

Religious Boom in China

Alongside China's astonishing economic boom, an almost unnoticed religious boom has quietly been taking place. In the country's first major survey on religious beliefs, conducted in 2006, 31.4 percent of about 4,500 people questioned described themselves as religious. That amounts to more than 300 million religious believers, an astonishing number in an officially atheist country, and three times higher than the last official estimate, which had largely remained unchanged for years.

The collapse of the communist ideology created a void that has left many Chinese staring into a spiritual vacuum, looking for a value system to counterbalance the rampant materialism that seems to govern life in China.

"Chinese people don't know what to believe in anymore," says Liu Zhongyu, a professor at East China Normal University in Shanghai, who conducted the survey. "And since the political atmosphere has relaxed, they turn to religion for comfort."

One young evangelical Christian missionary travels from rural village to village in the Protestant heartland in eastern China to proselytize. She attributed her own conversion to the overwhelming pressures of China's education system.

"In high school, I felt very depressed," said the bright-eyed young woman, who gave her name as Nicole. "I felt people had no direction, and I felt life was dry and boring. I felt the pressure of school was very high. God helped me and liberated me."

Although proselytizing is still illegal in China today, she and a group of friends are openly preaching in villages, without official interference. China has come a long way from the dark days of the Cultural Revolution, which ended in 1976, when all religious practice was banned, and monks and clergy were sent to prison or to perform hard labor.

Tourism Boom in Turkey

Turkish tourism, long restricted within the "sea-sun-beach" triangle, has begun to reap the fruits of advertising its historical and cultural heritage. The number of tourists who visited such cities as Sanliurfa, Mardin, Konya, and Trabzon renowned for their rich historical heritage is growing. The tourism boom in Mardin is particularly striking. The number of tourists that visited Mardin grew ten fold in four years to reach 400,000. Tradesmen in Mardin are pleased with the number of tourists that visited Mardin in the first half of 2005 that reached nearly 250,000. "It is very gratifying that faith and cultural tourism have gained popularity. If the deficiencies in the hosting and other facilities are corrected, faith and cultural tourism can generate as much revenue as coastal tourism," say tourism sector officials. The growth in cultural tourism also directs tourism sector auxiliaries towards these cities.

Faith and cultural tourism have great potential in Turkey that already receives a great deal of income through coastal tourism, as local prices are considerably lower than European countries. Through promotional advertisements and cultural events, tourists are flocking to Anatolia that harbors a rich array of cultures and religions. According to figures released by the Turkish Tourism Ministry, the number of tourists coming to Turkey for culture and faith tourism grows exponentially. The other most important cities in faith tourism after Mardin are Sanliurfa, Konya, Adiyaman, and Trabzon.

The Sumela Monastery in Trabzon is a major pilgrimage destination for Christians. The cave where Prophet Abraham was born, Mevlid-i Halil Mosque, Prophet Eyyup's Cave and Harran are the main tourist attractions in Sanliurfa. The city hosted 500,000 tourists in 2004 and 300,000 tourists in the first half of 2005. Mevlana Museum in Konya attracts hundreds of thousands of tourists. During 2004, Konya received 1,505,000 tourists. Among them are Norwegians Claudio Sandor and Halvor Bodin who came to Konya after reading books about Mevlana Celaleddin-i Rumi. They related that they were fascinated by Mevlana's mystical atmosphere and that they were mostly awed by the spectacle of the Sama, a whirling dervish ceremony. "Rumi is a well known figure in our country. Many people admire him," they say. Ahmet Yenikenli who came from Kastamonu to visit the Mevlana Museum for the second time relates that they come to Konya for a holiday whenever they find the time.

Besides European tourists, tourists from all around Turkey flock to Mardin on one-day tours as well. The number of tourists visiting 6,000-yearold Mardin exceeded one million over the last five years. Tourists enchanted by the historical and cultural nature of the city say: "The inns, baths, caravanserais, madrasahs and mansions are all magnificent. Walking in the 6,000 years old Deyrulzafaran monastery incites inexplicable feelings."

Kristen Moleyn from The Netherlands strongly affected by the mystical atmosphere of the city, says: "This is my second visit. It is amazing and beautiful to be in one of those rare cities where different religions and languages live together in peace. The kindness and the hospitality of the people attracts us here." Helain Kristean from Germany, visiting Mardin for the second time in two years, noting that she has traveled much but she have never seen a city as beautiful as Mardin, says: "That different religions and languages peacefully shared this place sets an important example for us. I want to come here every year." Maria Micheail, a writer from the US relating that she heard of Mardin last year after watching a television program on inter-religious clemency says: "I am particularly moved by the ancient madrasahs and the mosques. These are superb buildings. We are also gratified by the kindness and the hospitality of the local people."

Hotels in the city are now full due to huge influx of tourists. Hoteliers pleased with the situation consider new investment plans, as shop owners in the bazaars are also happy with the situation. A total of 11 hotels currently serve the city. Businessmen open "boutique hotels", from restored historic mansions and caravansaries to meet the tourist demand. Historic Erdoba Mansion with 30 rooms and 60 beds was opened in 2003. The Artuklu Caravansary with 43 rooms and 100-bed capacity and the Maria Mansion with nine rooms and 23-bed capacity were opened in 2005. Construction of a 400-bed capacity hotel with 200 rooms on the road to Diyarbakir is soon to be finished. It is said the "Symposium on Inter-Religious Tolerance" in 2004 made a considerable contribution to the tourism boom in the city. Mardin preparing to be included in the UNESCO's "World Heritage List" aims to host one million tourists in 2005.

Mardin's governor Mustafa Temel Kocaklar indicating activities held in 2004 promoted Mardin on the global scale says, "We currently organize promotion campaigns for more people to visit Mardin. We invite businessmen from Mardin to invest in their homeland." Mardin's proxy tourism director Alaaddin Aydin, on the other hand, notes mostly foreign and domestic day-trippers visit Mardin due to the insufficient accommodation capacity. Konya's Culture and Tourism Association President Fevzi Halici informs that tourists coming to Konya mostly visit the Mevlana Museum. They do not leave the city without a visit to

Rumi's tomb. Hoteliers and Guest House Chamber President Mustafa Sarioglu urges more activities need to be conducted to encourage tourists to stay in the city longer. According to Sarioglu, both national and international tourists visit the city for sightseeing, but they do not stay longer. Another tourism boom erupted in Sanliurfa, one of Turkey's cultural tourism centers and it is almost impossible to find an empty bed any of the hotels in the city with a 700-bed capacity. National and international tourists mostly show an interest in Balikligol, Dergah, the cave of Prophet Eyyub, his tomb in Eyyub Nebi village in Viransehir town, as well as Harran Township, which is famous for its cupola houses and the first university in history.

Adiyaman's hotels are also full to capacity and even reservations for next year have already been made. Mount Nemrut with the 2000 year-old giant sculptures that are seen as the "8th Wonder of the World" is Adiyaman's tourism magnet. Walking, paragliding and water sports held on Ataturk Dam Lake are the just some of the sports conducted in the region. Speleology, the exploration of caves, is also promoted in the region. Nemrut Volcanic Lake in the Tatvan town of Bitlis is the most popular place visited by foreign and domestic tourists.

20 Modern Issues in Religious Tourism

Interfaith cooperation

Because religion continues to be recognized in Western thought as a universal impulse, many religious practitioners have aimed to band together in interfaith dialogue and cooperation. The first major dialogue was the Parliament of the World's Religions at the 1893 Chicago World's Fair, which remains notable even today both in affirming "universal values" and recognition of the diversity of practices among different cultures. The 20th century has been especially fruitful in use of interfaith dialogue as a means of solving ethnic, political, or even religious conflict, with Christian-Jewish reconciliation representing a complete reverse in the attitudes of many Christian communities towards Jews.

Recent interfaith initiatives include "A Common Word", launched in 2007 and focused on bringing Muslim and Christian leaders together, the "C1 World Dialogue", the "Common Ground" initiative between Islam and Buddhism, and a United Nations sponsored "World Interfaith Harmony Week".

Secularism and Irreligion

As religion became a more personal matter in western culture, discussions of society found a new focus on political and scientific meaning, and religious attitudes (dominantly Christian) were increasingly seen as irrelevant for the needs of the European world. On the political side, Ludwig Feuerbach recast Christian beliefs in light of humanism, paving the way for Karl Marx's famous characterization of religion as "the opium of the people". Meanwhile, in the scientific community, T.H. Huxley in 1869 coined the term "agnostic," a term-subsequently adopted by such figures as Robert Ingersoll-that, while directly conflicting with and novel to Christian tradition, is accepted and even embraced in some other religions. Later, Bertrand Russell told the world Why I Am Not a Christian, which influenced several later authors to discuss their breakaway from their own religious uprbringings from Islam to Hinduism.

The terms "atheist" (lack of belief in any gods) and "agnostic" (belief in the unknowability of the existence of gods), though specifically contrary to theistic (e.g. Christian, Jewish, and Muslim) religious teachings, do not by definition mean the opposite of "religious". There are religions (including Buddhism and Taoism), in fact, that classify some of their followers as agnostic, atheistic, or nontheistic.

The true opposite of "religious" is the word "irreligious". Irreligion describes an absence of any religion; antireligion describes an active opposition or aversion toward religions in general.

Critics of religious systems as well as of personal faith have posed a variety of arguments against religion.[clarification needed] Some modern-day critics hold that religion lacks utility in human society; they may regard religion as irrational. Some[who?] assert that dogmatic religions are morally deficient, elevating as they do to moral status ancient, arbitrary, and ill-informed rules.

Religion and Philosophy

Religion and philosophy meet in several areas - notably in the study of metaphysics and cosmology. In particular, a distinct set of religious beliefs will often entail a specific metaphysics and cosmology. That is, a religion will generally offer answers to metaphysical and cosmological questions about the nature of being, of the universe, humanity, and the divine.

Religion and Superstition

Superstition has been described as "the incorrect establishment of cause and effect" or a false conception of causation. Religion is more complex and includes social institutions and morality. But religions may include superstitions or make use of magical thinking. Members of one religion often think other religions as superstition|superstitious. Some atheists, agnostics, deists, and skeptics regard religious belief as superstition. Religious practices are likely to be labeled "superstitious" when they include belief in miracles or extraordinary events, supernatural interventions, apparitions, charms, omens, incantations, an afterlife or the efficacy of prayer..

Greek and Roman pagans, who saw their relations with the gods in political and social terms, scorned the man who constantly trembled with fear at the thought of the gods (deisidaimonia), as a slave might fear a cruel and capricious master. The Romans called such fear of the gods superstitio. Early Christianity was outlawed as a superstitio Iudaica, a "Jewish superstition", by Domitian in the 80s AD. In AD 425, when Rome had become Christian, Theodosius II outlawed pagan traditions as superstitious.

The Roman Catholic Church considers superstition to be sinful in the sense that it denotes a lack of trust in the divine providence of God and, as such, is a violation of the first of the Ten Commandments. The Catechism of the Catholic Church states that superstition "in some sense represents a perverse excess of religion". "Superstition," it says, "is a deviation of religious feeling and of the practices this feeling imposes. It can even affect the worship we offer the true God, e.g., when one attributes an importance in some way magical to certain practices otherwise lawful or necessary. To attribute the efficacy of prayers or of sacramental signs to their mere external performance, apart from the interior dispositions that they demand is to fall into superstition.

Myth

The word myth has several meanings.

1. A traditional story of ostensibly historical events that serves to unfold part of the world view of a people or explain a practice, belief, or natural phenomenon;
2. A person or thing having only an imaginary or unverifiable existence; or
3. A metaphor for the spiritual potentiality in the human being.

Ancient polytheistic religions, such as those of Greece, Rome, and Scandinavia, are usually categorized under the heading of mythology. Religions of pre-industrial peoples, or cultures in development, are similarly called "myths" in the anthropology of religion. The term "myth" can be used pejoratively by both religious and non-religious people. By defining another person's religious stories and beliefs as mythology, one implies that they are less real or true than one's own religious stories and beliefs. Joseph Campbell remarked, "Mythology is often thought of as other people's religions, and religion can be defined as mis-interpreted mythology."

In sociology, however, the term myth has a non-pejorative meaning. There, myth is defined as a story that is important for the group whether or not it is objectively or provably true. Examples include the death and resurrection of Jesus, which, to Christians, explains the means by which they are freed from sin and is also ostensibly a historical event. But from a mythological outlook, whether or not the event actually occurred is unimportant. Instead, the symbolism of the death of an old "life" and the start of a new "life" is what is most significant. Religious believers may or may not accept such symbolic interpretations.

Religion and Violence

Charles Selengut characterizes the phrase "religion and violence" as "jarring", asserting that "religion is thought to be opposed to violence and a force for peace and reconciliation. He acknowledges, however, that "the history and scriptures of the world's religions tell stories of violence and war as they speak of peace and love."

Hector Avalos argues that, because religions claim divine favor for themselves, over and against other groups, this sense of righteousness leads to violence because conflicting claims to superiority, based on unverifiable appeals to God, cannot be adjudicated objectively.

Some critics of religion (in general) such as Christopher Hitchens and Richard Dawkins go farther and argue that religions do tremendous harm to society in three ways:[51][page needed][page needed]

- Religions sometimes use war, violence, and terrorism to promote their religious goals
- Religious leaders contribute to secular wars and terrorism by endorsing or supporting the violence
- Religious fervor is exploited by secular leaders to support war and terrorism

Regina Schwartz argues that all monotheistic religions are inherently violent because of an exclusivism that inevitably fosters violence against those that are considered outsiders. Lawrence Wechsler asserts that Schwartz isn't just arguing that Abrahamic religions have a violent legacy, but that the legacy is actually genocidal in nature.

Byron Bland asserts that one of the most prominent reasons for the "rise of the secular in Western thought" was the reaction against the religious violence of the 16th and 17th centuries. He asserts that "(t)he secular was a way of living with the religious differences that had produced so much horror. Under secularity, political entities have a warrant to make decisions independent from the need to enforce particular versions of religious orthodoxy. Indeed, they may run counter to certain strongly held beliefs if made in the interest of common welfare. Thus, one of the important goals of the secular is to limit violence."

Religion and the Law

There are laws and statutes that make reference to religion. This has led to claims from some scholars that religious freedom is literally impossible to uphold. Also, the Western legal principle of separation of church and state tends to engender a new, more inclusive civil religion.

Religion and Science

Religious knowledge, according to religious practitioners, may be gained from religious leaders, sacred texts (scriptures), and/or personal revelation. Some religions view such knowledge as unlimited in scope and suitable to answer any question; others see religious knowledge as playing a more restricted role, often as a complement to knowledge gained through physical observation. Some religious people maintain that religious knowledge obtained in this way is absolute and infallible (religious cosmology).

The scientific method gains knowledge by testing hypotheses to develop theories through elucidation of facts or evaluation by experiments and thus only answers cosmological questions about the physical universe. It develops theories of the world which best fit physically observed evidence. All scientific knowledge is subject to later refinement in the face of additional evidence. Scientific theories that have an overwhelming preponderance of favorable evidence are often treated as facts (such as the theories of gravity or evolution).

Christianity and Science

Many scientists have held strong religious beliefs (see List of Christian thinkers in science and List of Roman Catholic scientist-clerics) and have worked to harmonize science and religion. Isaac Newton, for example, believed that gravity caused the planets to revolve about the Sun, and credited God with the design. In the concluding General Scholium to the Philosophiae Naturalis Principia Mathematica, he wrote: "This most beautiful System of the Sun, Planets and Comets, could only proceed from the counsel and dominion of an intelligent and powerful being." Nevertheless, conflict has repeatedly arisen between religious organizations and individuals who propagated scientific theories that were deemed unacceptable by the organizations. The Roman Catholic Church, for example, has in the past reserved to itself the right to decide which scientific theories were acceptable and which were unacceptable. In the 17th century, Galileo was tried and forced to recant the heliocentric theory based on the church's stance that the Greek Hellenistic system of astronomy was the correct one.

Today, religious belief among scientists is less prevalent than it is in the general public. Surveys on the subject give varying results. The Pew Research Center found in 2009 that 33% of American scientists and 83% of the general public believe in God, another 18% of scientists and 12% of the public believe more generally in a higher power, and 41% of scientists and 4% of the public believe in neither. A mailed survey to members of the National Academy of Sciences found that 7% of respondents to believed in a personal God. Elaine Howard Ecklund found that about two-thirds of scientists at elite research universities believed in God and that nearly 50 percent of them were religious.

The philosophical theory of pragmatism (first propounded by William James) has been used to reconcile scientific with religious knowledge. Pragmatism holds that the truth of a set of beliefs is indicated by its usefulness in helping people cope with a particular context of life. Thus, the fact that scientific beliefs are useful in predicting observations in the physical world can indicate a certain truth for scientific theories and the fact that religious beliefs can be useful in helping people cope with difficult emotions or moral decisions can indicate a certain truth for those beliefs.

The Catholic Church has always concurred with Augustine of Hippo who explicitly opposed a literal interpretation of the Bible whenever the

Bible conflicted with science. The literal way to read the sacred texts became especially prevalent after the rise of the Protestant reformation, with its emphasis on the Bible as the only authoritative source concerning the ultimate reality. This view is often shunned by both religious leaders (who regard literally believing it as petty and look for greater meaning instead) and scientists who regard it as an impossibility.

Some Christians[who?] have disagreed with the validity of Keplerian astronomy, the theory of evolution, the scientific account of the creation of the universe and the origins of life. However, Stanley Jaki has suggested that the Christian worldview was a crucial in the emergence of modern science.[clarification needed] Historians are moving away from the view that Christianity was always in conflict with science-the so-called conflict thesis. Gary Ferngren in his historical volume about science and religion states: "While some historians had always regarded the conflict thesis as oversimplifying and distorting a complex relationship, in the late 20th century it underwent a more systematic reevaluation. The result is the growing recognition among historians of science that the relationship of religion and science has been much more positive than is sometimes thought. Although popular images of controversy continue to exemplify the supposed hostility of Christianity to new scientific theories, studies have shown that Christianity has often nurtured and encouraged scientific endeavour, while at other times the two have co-existed without either tension or attempts at harmonization. If Galileo and the Scopes trial come to mind as examples of conflict, they were the exceptions rather than the rule."

Other Religions and Science

In the Bahá'í Faith, the harmony of science and religion is a central tenet. The principle states that that truth is one, and therefore true science and true religion must be in harmony, thus rejecting the view that science and religion are in conflict. `Abdu'l-Bahá, the son of the founder of the religion, asserted that science and religion cannot be opposed because they are aspects of the same truth; he also affirmed that reasoning powers are required to understand the truths of religion and that religious teachings which are at variance with science should not be accepted; he explained that religion has to be reasonable since God endowed humankind with reason so that they can discover truth. Shoghi Effendi, the Guardian of the Bahá'í Faith, described science and religion as "the two most potent forces in human life."

Proponents of Hinduism claim that it is not afraid of scientific explorations, nor of the technological progress of mankind. According to them, there is a comprehensive scope and opportunity for Hinduism to mold itself according to the demands and aspirations of the modern world; it has the ability to align itself with both science and spiritualism. This religion uses some modern examples to explain its ancient theories and reinforce its own beliefs. For example, some Hindu thinkers have used the terminology of quantum physics to explain some basic concepts of Hinduism such as Maya or the illusory and impermanent nature of our existence.

Evolutionary Theory and Religion

At one time, evolutionists explained religion as something that conferred a biological advantages to its adherents. More recently, Richard Dawkins has explained it in terms of the evolution of self-replicating ideas, or memes as he calls them, distinct from any resulting biological advantages they might bestow. Susan Blackmore regards religions as particularly tenacious memes. Chris Hedges regards meme theory as a misleading imposition of genetics onto psychology. Analyzed as an aspect of culture arising from the nature of man and subject to the processes of evolution and natural selection religion has both adaptive and maladaptive characteristics.

BIBLIOGRAPHY

- Barzilai, Gad; Law and Religion; The International Library of Essays in Law and Society; Ashgate (2007),ISBN 978-0-7546-2494-3
- Beaver, Allan (2002). A Dictionary of Travel and Tourism Terminology. Wallingford: CAB International. p. 313. ISBN 0851995829. OCLC 301675778.
- Brodd, Jefferey (2003). World Religions. Winona, MN: Saint Mary's Press. ISBN 978-0-88489-725-5.
- Clift, Jean Dalby; Clift, Wallace (1996). The Archetype of Pilgrimage: Outer Action With Inner Meaning. The Paulist Press. ISBN 0-8091-3599-X. .
- Colin Wilson (1996). Atlas of Holy Places & Sacred Sites. DK Adult. p. 29. ISBN 978-0789410511
- Cooper, Chris; et al (2005). Tourism: Principles and Practice (3rd ed.). Harlow: Pearson Education. ISBN 027368406X. OCLC 466952897.
- Descartes, René; Meditations on First Philosophy; Bobbs-Merril (1960), ISBN 0-672-60191-5.
- Durant, Will (& Ariel (uncredited)); Caesar and Christ; MJF Books (1994), ISBN 1-56731-014-1
- Durant, Will (& Ariel (uncredited)); Our Oriental Heritage; MJF Books (1997), ISBN 1-56731-012-5.
- Durant, Will (& Ariel (uncredited)); The Age of Faith; Simon & Schuster (1980), ISBN 0-671-01200-2.
- Gonick, Larry; The Cartoon History of the Universe; Doubleday, vol. 1 (1978) ISBN 0-385-26520-4, vol. II (1994) ISBN#0-385-42093-5, W. W. Norton, vol. III (2002) ISBN 0-393-05184-6.
- Haisch, Bernard The God Theory: Universes, Zero-point Fields, and What's Behind It All — discussion of science vs. religion (Preface[dead link]), Red Wheel/Weiser, 2006, ISBN 1-57863-374-5
- Hunziker, W; Krapf, K (1942) (in German). Grundriß Der Allgemeinen Fremdenverkehrslehre. Zurich: Polygr. Verl. OCLC 180109383.

- Lennon, J. John; Foley, Malcolm (2000). Dark Tourism. London: Continuum. ISBN 0826450636. OCLC 44603703.
- Marija Gimbutas 1989. The Language of the Goddess. Thames and Hudsôn New York
- Marx, Karl; "Introduction to A Contribution to the Critique of Hegel's Philosophy of Right", Deutsch-Französische Jahrbücher, (1844).
- Quinion, Michael (26 November 2005). "Dark Tourism". World Wide Words. http://www.worldwidewords.org/turnsofphrase/tp-dar2.htm. Retrieved 9 April 2010.
- Saint Augustine; The Confessions of Saint Augustine (John K. Ryan translator); Image (1960), ISBN 0-385-02955-1.
- Saler, Benson; "Conceptualizing Religion: Immanent Anthropologists, Transcendent Natives, and Unbounded Categories" (1990), ISBN 1-57181-219-9
- Smith, Peter (2000). "Pilgrimage". A concise encyclopedia of the Bahá'í Faith. Oxford: Oneworld Publications. pp. 269. ISBN 1-85168-184-1.
- The Holy Bible, King James Version; New American Library (1974).
- The Koran; Penguin (2000), ISBN 0-14-044558-7.
- The Origin of Live & Death, African Creation Myths; Heinemann (1966).
- The Serotonin System and Spiritual Experiences - American Journal of Psychiatry 160:1965-1969, November 2003.
- The World Almanac (annual), World Almanac Books, ISBN 0-88687-964-7.
- Werner, Karel (1994). A Popular Dictionary of Hinduism. Curzon Press. ISBN 0700710493.
- Wurzburger, Rebecca; et al (2009). Creative Tourism: A Global Conversation: How to Provide Unique Creative Experiences for Travelers Worldwide: As Presented at the 2008 Santa Fe & UNESCO International Conference on Creative Tourism in Santa Fe, New Mexico, USA. Santa Fe: Sunstone Press. ISBN 9780865347243. OCLC 370387178.

Index